W9-BHN-050

Guide to the Recommended

COUNTRY INNS
of the West Coast

"The test of a good guidebook is whether the author's descriptions match your own experience. This guide passes that test with flying colors. Well designed, well written, and very informative."
—*Elaine Petrocelli*, Book Passage, *San Francisco, CA*

"Any inn-goer will find that this enticingly written book directs him to the finest in the West. It illustrates the tremendous variety of inns that are available in the West, and each write-up captures that individual spirit that innkeepers try to create."
—*Bobbi Zane, editor of* Yellow Brick Road *newsletter*

"Informal, personal descriptions by an enthusiastic writer from the region. Julianne Belote provides a good word picture of the inns included."
—*Toby Smith, editor and publisher of* California Inns *newsletter*

The "Guide to the Recommended Country Inns" Series

"The guidebooks in this new series of recommended country inns are sure winners. Personal visits have ensured accurate and scene-setting descriptions. These beckon the discriminating traveler to a variety of interesting lodgings."
—*Norman Strasma, publisher of* Inn Review *newsletter*

The "Guide to the Recommended Country Inns" series is designed for the discriminating traveler who seeks the best in unique accommodations away from home.

From hundreds of inns personally visited and evaluated by the author, only the finest are described here. The inclusion of an inn is purely a personal decision on the part of the author; no one can pay or be paid to be in a Globe Pequot inn guide.

Organized for easy reference, these guides point you to just the kind of accommodations you are looking for: Comprehensive indexes by category provide listings of inns for romantic getaways, inns for the sports-minded, inns that serve gourmet meals . . . and more. State maps help you pinpoint the location of each inn, and detailed driving directions tell you how to get there.

Use these guidebooks with confidence. Allow each author to share his or her selections with you and then discover for yourself the country inn experience.

Editions available:

Guide to the Recommended Country Inns of
New England • Mid-Atlantic States and Chesapeake Region
South • Midwest • Arizona, New Mexico, and Texas
Rocky Mountain Region • West Coast

Guide to the Recommended

COUNTRY INNS

of the West Coast

California • Oregon • Washington

by Julianne Belote
illustrated by Olive Metcalf

A Voyager Book

The Globe Pequot Press

Chester, Connecticut 06412

To Linda Roghaar, with thanks.

Excerpt from "The Sound of Music" on page 345 copyright © 1959 by Richard Rodgers & Oscar Hammerstein. Williamson Music Co., owner of publication and allied rights for the Western Hemisphere and Japan. International Copyright Secured. ALL RIGHTS RESERVED. Used by permission.

Text copyright © 1986 by Julianne Belote
Illustrations copyright © 1986 by The Globe Pequot Press

All rights reserved. No part of this book may be reproduced or transmitted in any form by any means, electronic or mechanical, including photocopying and recording, or by any information storage and retrieval system, except as may be expressly permitted by the 1976 Copyright Act or in writing from the publisher. Requests for permission should be addressed to The Globe Pequot Press, Old Chester Road, Chester, Connecticut 06412.

Library of Congress Cataloging-in-Publication Data

Belote, Julianne.
    Guide to the recommended country inns of the
West Coast.

    Includes index.
    1. Hotels, taverns, etc.—California—Directories.
2. Hotels, taverns, etc.—Oregon—Directories.
3. Hotels, taverns, etc.—Washington (State)—
Directories. I. Title.
TX907.B4 1986   647'.947901   86-14977
ISBN 0-87106-810-9

Manufactured in the United States of America
First Edition/Second Printing, March 1987

Contents

Indexes

How This Guide Is Arranged

The inns are arranged by states in the following order: California, Oregon, and Washington. California inns are subdivided into six areas: Southern California, The Central Coast, The San Francisco Bay Area, The North Coast, The Wine Country, and The Mother Lode and Sierras.

Before each state and area is a map and index to the inns in that section, listed alphabetically by town. At the back of the guide is a complete index to all the inns in the book listed alphabetically by name. Additional indexes list inns by category.

The Abbreviations

EP: European Plan. Room without meals.

AP: American Plan. Room with all meals.

MAP: Modified American Plan. Room with breakfast and dinner.

J: means a personal comment from Julianne.

The ☛ inserted here and there are *not* a rating. They are merely a way of pointing out something outstanding, unusual, or most memorable about an inn.

No inn was charged to be in this guide, nor were lodging or meals accepted in exchange for consideration. I visited all the inns included, as well as more than a hundred others that I did not choose. Obviously, things can change between my visit and the time you use the guide. But if you feel that I have steered you wrong, or if you have a comment, please write to Julianne Belote, The Globe Pequot Press, Old Chester Road, Box Q, Chester, Connecticut 06412.

Wayfaring at Country Inns: Caveats and Considerations

You may not need a passport or shots, but inns can be foreign territory if you've not tried them, and a few ground rules are in order.

Caveats

Rates: They can change almost as fast as the sheets. I list the high–low range for two people *at the time I visited.* Many innkeepers have unadvertised off-season and mid-week rates, but you sometimes have to ask.

Reservations/Deposits: These are almost always a necessity But even the most popular places have cancellations, and a last-minute telephone call or your name on a backup list can bring results. Policies vary, but you will likely be charged if you're a no-show or a last-minute cancellation.

Minimum Stay: A two- or three-night stay is commonly required over weekends and holidays. *Sometimes* you can negotiate this, if the traffic is slow.

Children/Pets: Most inns are not set up to deal with either. I specifically note it when the little nippers are welcome.

Credit Cards: Unless otherwise specified, most inns accept MasterCard and Visa.

Television/Air Conditioning/Telephone: Most inns do not have these facilities in the bedrooms, but I have noted when they do. You're supposed to be getting away from it all—remember?

Food: Small inns that serve meals usually have a limited menu. If you have a dietary request, inquire when you reserve.

Smoking: A majority of West Coast innkeepers prefer that their guests not smoke. I mention it when they are adamant.

Space: Pack lightly. The inn room with a place for long garment bags or a matched luggage set has eluded me.

Manners: At an inn, you're often a paying guest at someone's home. It is frowned upon to plop your bag down on Grandmother's prize quilt, monopolize the shared bathroom while you leisurely floss between your teeth, inhale all the sherry, or act silently superior at a common breakfast table.

Considerations

On the West Coast, at least, no one is certain what you mean when you talk about an inn. Inns snuggle uncertainly in a lodging land bordered by small hotels, motels, cabins, resorts, and homestays. We have only a few that serve meals beyond breakfast, and the emergence of urban inns rules out the strictly "country" definition. There are Old Guard innkeepers who insist that their profession is nothing less than the full-service nurturing of the wayfaring stranger and who scoff at the explosion of bed and breakfast establishments offering little more than a bed and a croissant but nevertheless calling themselves inns.

Let the innkeepers sort out the labels. My task is to acquaint you with a variety of hostelries up and down the West Coast that offer a level of individual décor not found at motels, an ambience cozier and more intimate than that found at a resort, innkeepers who treat you like their very special house guest, and homemade meals or knowledgeable pointers to the best food nearby.

These choices differ vastly from one another, from sleek urban digs to solitary island retreats. Each one has its own individual flavor. None is stamped out of a corporate room plan. There probably won't be a paper strip across the toilet or a chain lock for the door. You're likely to find a basket of fruit, a bouquet, a plate of freshly baked cookies, or a carafe of wine to greet you.

Not all of these lodgings will be your cup of tea. Even the best can disappoint, but keep a sour note in perspective. It does not signal the decline of civilization as we know it; it is the risk we take when we search for the noncommercial.

Unique lodgings are one of the last frontiers to explore. Dare a little! It can be exciting to check into a place where you don't know the floor plan and where someone may actually talk to you at breakfast!

At the best inns, when you bid an innkeeper goodbye, you leave feeling that you've made a friend whom you really must have to *your* place.

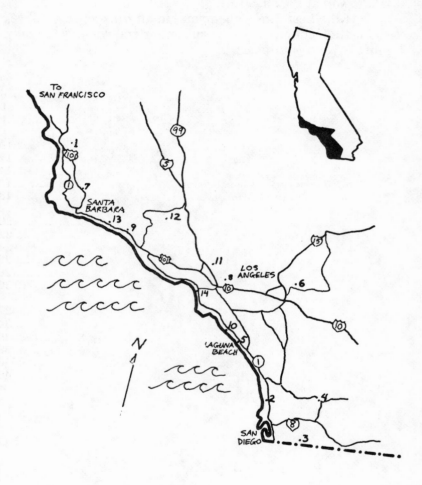

Southern California

Numbers on map refer to towns numbered below.

Olive Metcalf

Rose Victorian Inn
Arroyo Grande, California
93420

Innkeepers: Diana and Ross Cox
Address / Telephone: 789 Valley Road; (805) 481–5566.
Rooms: 8; 3 with private bath; 5 share 2 bathrooms.
Rates: $75 to $115, double occupancy; MAP. No smoking.
Open: All year, Thursday, Friday, Saturday, Sunday. Restaurant, wine bar.
Facilities and Local Attractions: Wedding, banquet facilities. Drive winding back roads to wineries. San Luis Obispo Mission, Mozart Festival in winter, Spring Fiesta.

When a four-story gingerbread Victorian house sits alone, surrounded by acres of flat farmland, you notice it. When it's painted four shades of pink—you can't miss it. The Rose Victorian is that rare California phenomenon, a country inn with breakfast and dinner included in the rate. It's a pleasant break in the long drive on Highway 101 between Los Angeles and San Francisco: a beautiful ☞ 1885 house surrounded by 200 rose bushes, with authentic period furniture, good beds, and a first-rate restaurant.

The intensely pink exterior tended to have me guessing

that the inside would be doilies and kitsch. Wrong. The rooms are tastefully decorated, blending some outstanding antique pieces with comfortable, traditional sofas and chairs. Bouquets of fresh roses, as well as good reading lights, are in every room.

At dinner we had two view choices: one to the green lawn with rose arbor and white gazebo (it's a wedding setting about as romantic as one could ask); the other to a large window looking into the kitchen where you can watch a talented young chef and her staff do their thing. We chose the kitchen view. (Tell me, Dr. Brothers, is this an indication of complacency, or merely hunger?)

Smug San Franciscans and Angelinos who think only *their* cities have sophisticated cooking have a surprise in store. Chef Shelley Cox was a pleasure to watch in full-speed–dinner-hour action . . . and the results were outstanding. My baked halibut was moist and dressed with zippy, fresh salsa and sliced avocado. The traveler's companion had fork-tender veal, sautéed with wine, fresh thyme, and finished with cream. A mostly California wine list, much of it from the surrounding Central Coast wineries, was very fairly priced.

A house specialty, peanut butter pie in a chocolate crumb crust, is so good, I regretted our decision to order one piece, two forks.

Breakfast is done elegantly. Inn guests gather around the dining room table for orange juice with champagne, sliced melons, hot orange muffins, and superior eggs Benedict, all served on delicate china.

How to get there: Two hundred miles north of Los Angeles, exit Highway 101 at Arroyo Grande. Turn left at stop sign (Fair Oaks). Go ¼ mile and turn left on Valley Road. Drive ¼ mile to the inn on your left.

☀

J: *A splendidly ornate piano that belonged to General John Fremont sits in one of the parlors.*

olive Metcalf

Rock Haus
Del Mar, California
92014

Innkeepers: Carol and Tom Hauser
Address / Telephone: 410 15th Street; (619) 481–3764.
Rooms: 10; 4 with private bath; 6 share 3 baths.
Rates: $75 to $125, double occupancy, including continental
breakfast. Cannot accept children or pets; no smoking.
Open: All year.
Facilities and Local Attractions: Short walk to Del Mar shops, res-
taurants, beach; near Del Mar Race Track, Torrey Pines Golf
Course/State Reserve

This is one of those absolutely captivating inns you visit
with enormous pleasure and contentment, then grumble on
the way home, "Why can't we make *our* house look like
that?"

You can, of course. Just start with an early California
bungalow that's a historical landmark and ☛ overlooks the
Pacific Ocean. Make sure it has a colorful past, as this one
has: stately home of a land company executive; a dining room
used for Catholic Mass by beach parishioners in 1911; gambling house in the roaring '20s; a boarding house, and hippie

pad. Then do the extensive renovation houses with "colorful pasts" always require, and you'll be close, but not there.

You'll still need a Carol Hauser to do the decorating, because she does have a touch. Today, her sprawling house on a hill looks just the way a 1910 summer house should look. There's wicker and rattan, floral cotton comforters, and fresh flowers everywhere. It all looks light, cheerful, and clean.

First-floor bedrooms are especially comfortable with private baths and 🖝 private entrances, and one has a fireplace. But upstairs you get the splendid ocean views.

We gave our room the tough Mother–Daughter Bunk-Together Test: Choose the smallest, least expensive room in the house to share, and see if somebody is snapping at somebody by morning. The Wren's Nest room was a total success—as serene to stay in as it is to look at. Its twin beds are dressed in crisp, pastel linens and big fluffy pillows; there's a *bright* reading light over each bed, and a wall of windows looking out at the ocean. Bathrooms are modern and so conveniently appointed that sharing was never a problem.

The broad, glassed-in sun porch is an inviting place to start your day with its clear view of the Pacific. Individual tables are set with teapots of fresh flowers, and newspapers, coffee, and tea wait on a sideboard. Carol or a helper brings in fresh fruit, juice, and just-made muffins. The staff enhances an already appealing breakfast atmosphere by scorning the easy jeans routine and wearing fresh, pretty outfits. It adds to a very pleasant breakfast. Just a block from the inn is a street of colorful restaurants, from small bistros and outdoor cafés to elegant eateries with ocean views.

How to get there: From Los Angeles on the San Diego Freeway, take Via de la Valle exit and head southwest along Jimmy Durante Boulevard to Del Mar Village. Turn left on Fifteenth Street to inn on the left at number 410. From San Diego, take Del Mar Heights exit off San Diego Freeway and go west to Camino Del Mar. Turn right, and at Fifteenth Street, turn right again.

Olive Metcalf

Brookside Farm
Dulzura, California
92017

Innkeepers: Judy and Edd Guishard
Address / Telephone: 1373 Marron Valley Road; (619) 468–3043.
Rooms: 6; 5 share 2 baths; carriage house with private bath.
Rates: $45 double occupancy, includes full breakfast. Weekend
  rates available with dinners. No children, pets, or cigars.
Open: All year.
Facilities and Local Attractions: Eat, sleep, sit by the stream. Hot
  tub under grape arbor, for the hyperactive.

Leading us into the old barn where the innkeepers plan
to build future guests rooms, Judy Guishard indicated a
large, unfinished room where local meetings are sometimes
held. "And this," she said, "is the Dulzura Convention Center."

Happily, both the Guishards possess a sense of humor
plus vision, and they have guests laughing with them over
the tribulations of renovation. But do look at their album of
"before-and-after" shots to appreciate the hard work it takes
to renovate a dilapidated building into the charming country
inn so many of us *think* we'd love to have. Even the real es-

6

tate broker was doubtful about selling them this 1928 farm-house, fearing it might ruin their friendship.

Judy and Edd's hard work has resulted in an unpretentious, rambling house wnere it's easy to feel utterly at home. A dining room and sunny living room have oversized Mexican bricks as flooring, covered with Oriental rugs. A comfortable sofa and chairs, taped music, books, and a fireplace are inviting. Guest rooms are simply done in a fresh country style using quilts Judy has made.

Dulzura is a mountain community about ten miles from the Mexican border and thirty miles southeast of San Diego. Things got pretty exciting once about fifty years ago when big-gun Adolph Spreckles considered running his railroad through the town. But after his engineers decided it was too mountainous, the town returned to its natural pace.

When you have an urge to "get away from it all" and do nothing, this is the place: four rolling acres to stroll, fresh country air, ☞ a tree-shaded patio, and the only sound a bubbling stream. Tell your troubles to Flower and Lydia, two lovable central-casting goats who'll never disagree with you.

But my kind of quiet contemplation goes better with food, so it was good to learn that your stomach is not stranded in Dulzura. Edd is a chef, and besides serving a full breakfast, he'll do ☞ dinners for guests on weekends by request. A spinach-stuffed boneless lamb roast or a succulently sauced loin of pork is typical, accompanied by a selection of Southern California's abundant fresh vegetables and fruit and, of course, wine. The rest of the house is country charm, but his new kitchen is strictly high-tech. There's first-rate equipment and space for the hands-on ☞ cooking-class weekends Edd likes to host. Given his talent and easy humor, it sounds like fun.

How to get there: From San Diego, take Highway 94 1½ miles past the Dulzura Café. Turn right on Marron Valley Road. Inn is on the left.

🍺

J: *Prices here aren't in the range of other inns with comparable pleasures simply because the world has not yet discovered Dulzura. Meanwhile, enjoy.*

olive Metcalf

Julian Gold Rush Hotel
Julian, California
92036

Innkeepers: Steve and Gig Ballinger
Address / Telephone: Box 856; (619) 765–0201.
Rooms: 17; 4 with private bath; 13 share 4 baths.
Rates: $38 to $78, double occupancy, including full breakfast. No
  pets. Children welcome weeknights.
Open: All year.
Facilities and Local Attractions: Walking, shopping, restaurants in
  historic Julian. Tour still-producing Eagle Mine. September
  Banjo and Fiddle Festival, fall Apple Festival, spring Wild-
  flower Festival. Anza-Borrego Desert State Park; ☛ unique
  day trips arranged by innkeepers.

Come to Julian for a scenic drive, the flavor of a gold
rush town, and for a stay in the ☛ oldest continuously
operating hotel in Southern California. You're 4,000 feet
high in this back country east of San Diego, and the ☛ air is
pure and clear. In the fall there's brisk weather that brings
changing colors and an abundant apple harvest.

The entire town is an historic California landmark, but
the Julian Gold Rush Hotel is the sole survivor of the fifteen
hotels it had in its heyday at the turn of the century. It was

known then as "Queen of the Back Country," a luxury hotel boasting two bathtubs and the "most modern mountain accommodations."

It was the remarkable achievement of a former slave, Albert Robinson, and his wife, Margaret, who built it in 1897. Albert planted the cedar and locust trees that encircle the hotel today. When the Butterfield Stage stopped here after its two-day journey from San Diego, Mrs. Robinson's cooking, especially her hot apple pie and bread, welcomed miners and travelers to the Southern Mother Lode.

The Ballingers are carrying on the Robinson tradition of hospitality and adding their personal country inn touches. They've decorated the lobby sitting room with big chairs, games and books, and an old Silvertone radio (masking a stereo) that will look familiar to anyone over the age of forty-five or fifty. Some evenings they play tapes of old-time radio shows.

The rooms all have a genuine ☛ American West feeling, simple and airy. If you arrive early enough in the afternoon, you're encouraged to peek into unoccupied rooms and choose the one that appeals to you most. Plaques on the doors bear the names of entries in the old guest register; U.S. Grant for one. Each room is decorated with authentic American antique pieces, without gimmicks or reproductions (except for a few light fixtures). A separate Honeymoon Cottage has pretty, ruffled bedcovers and pillows, a dressing room, and fireplace.

Guests are served a full, hearty breakfast on the patio in the summer: juice and fresh fruit, eggs Florentine, breads from Dudley's Bakery, and coffee and tea.

How to get there: From San Diego, take I-8 east to Highway 79. Turn north to Julian; about 1¾ hours from San Diego.

☒

J: *My advice is to eat every bite of breakfast and then embark on one of Steve's well-researched day trips. This country is rich in Indian and gold rush history. Rolling hills and streams are at one turn, mountains at another, and . . . no smog, no freeways.*

Olive Metcalf

The Carriage House
Laguna Beach, California
92651

Innkeepers: Tom, Dee, and Vern Taylor; Rick Lawrence
Address / Telephone: 1322 Catalina Street; (714) 494–8945.
Rooms: 6, all suites, with private bath, sitting room, and separate
  bedroom.
Rates: $70 to $95, double occupancy; $20 each additional person.
  No credit cards; no pets; no smoking.
Open: All year.
Facilities and Local Attractions: Two blocks from the ocean, steps
  down to beach; walk to Pottery Shack; visit Laguna's art gal-
  leries, shops, restaurants. Bus stop on corner.

Instead of one of the large modern hotels on the waterfront, this might be just the secluded, pretty spot you're looking for from which to enjoy Laguna Beach. Cecil B. De Mille
thought it was sweet enough to buy back in the '20s when
Laguna was Hollywood's Riviera. It's now one of the town's
designated historical landmarks, a charming old New Orleans–style house.

☛ Every room here is a suite with a sitting room and
separate bedroom. Several have two bedrooms and a fully
equipped kitchen. That kind of convenience and space is

scarce; in a beach town it's rare; and done with antique charm and in a lush setting, it's almost unheard of.

Each room is decorated uniquely with antiques and memorabilia. There's Mandalay with a tropical, oriental theme in shades of coral and pink and with an ocean view. Primrose Lane has an English country feeling in yellow and deep blue. Green Palms is elegantly cool with white wicker furniture against emerald green carpet, and a bay window opens onto the courtyard. Whichever suite you have, you'll be welcomed with a bottle of California wine and fresh fruit.

All the rooms surround the quiet brick courtyard filled with tropical plants. There's a tiered fountain, chairs, and plenty of room to relax. If you don't take breakfast in the dining room, it's delightful to eat here beneath the hanging moss of a carrotwood tree. In addition to juice, fresh fruit, and cereals, there's always something hot from the oven— such as a coffee cake or muffins.

It's an ☛ easy walk to the beach from here, but for exploring more of Laguna Beach you'll appreciate the convenient bus stop on the corner.

How to get there: From the Pacific Coast Highway going through Laguna Beach, take Cress Street up the hill away from the ocean. Driving south, Cress is the first stoplight past the Pottery Shack. Inn is two blocks up on the corner of Catalina Street, number 1322.

Olive Metcalf

Casa Laguna Inn
Laguna Beach, California
92651

Innkeepers: John Burson and John Johnson
Address / Telephone: 2510 South Coast Highway; (714) 494–2996.
Rooms: 20, all with private bath; includes 1- and 2-bedroom suites
  and The Cottage. TV.
Rates: $75 to $135, double occupancy; $10 for each additional per-
  son, $5 less for single. Includes breakfast. Two-night minimum
  on weekends; no smoking; no pets.
Open: All year.
Facilities and Local Attractions: Pool, patios and gardens with
  views of the Pacific; in-house library, TV. Walk to Victoria
  Beach; Laguna shops, galleries, restaurants.

Even local "Lagunatics" are reserving rooms at Casa
Laguna in order to see what's happened to their old landmark. It's always had a ☛ Southern California Spanish
glamour, but innkeepers Burson and Johnson have given it a
recent facelift, making it a more magical place than ever.
  The original Mission House and Cottage were built in
the 1930s as guest facilities for historic Villa Rockledge, the
Frank Miller (owner of the Riverside Mission Inn) estate
across the street. The Casitas, fourteen courtyard and bal-

cony bedroom suites, were added in the 1940s as the Laguna Beach art colony grew and more visitors began coming.

This is a romantic inn of meandering brick paths, courtyards, and fountains. Colorful tiles, rock walls, even a bell tower, provide a fantasy retreat. In the complex of balconies and decks, plants, and flowers, there are many private little spots to relax, away from the bustle of Laguna at the height of the tourist season. There's also a beautiful sitting room and a piano for guests to use.

Every room is decorated uniquely with a blend of antiques and contemporary furnishings, color TV, and refrigerator. Some rooms open onto the flower-filled Spanish patio and pool; some have superb views of the ocean. Suites have well-equipped kitchens and deluxe space, especially The Cottage.

But charming facilities don't make an inn; it takes the fine old innkeeping tradition of pampering guests to do that, and you're on safe ground here. "We have a home, and it happens to have twenty bedrooms," says Burson.

Taking care of that home and making guests comfortable is obviously Burson and Johnson's pleasure. From the extended continental breakfast buffet, to afternoon wine and cheese in the patio, with entertainment by a classical guitarist, they're doing the kind of personal innkeeping that makes a difference.

How to get there: On the east side of the Pacific Coast Highway, in the heart of Laguna Beach, number 2510. It's pink.

J: Sending an East Coast chum a color photograph of you in this patio some February—flowers, palms, pool, and blue Pacific in the background—would be cruelly insensitive. Do not do it.

Olive Metcalf

Eiler's Inn
Laguna Beach, California
92651

Innkeeper: Lucy Meierding
Address / Telephone: 741 South Coast Highway; (714) 494–3004.
Rooms: 12, all with private bath, including 1 suite.
Rates: $90 to $140, double occupancy; $10 for each additional person; $5 less for single; extended continental breakfast included.
Open: All year.
Facilities and Local Attractions: Swimming, sunning on Laguna Beach; restaurants, art galleries, shops.

You can lose your heart when you walk through the cozy entry lobby at Eiler's Inn into a central brick courtyard. It's a beguiling, airy scene of plants and flowers around a tiered fountain. Balcony rooms look down on round tables covered with blue-and-white print tablecloths. At one end is a brick counter where the breakfast buffet is set out: baskets of fresh fruit and hot breads, juices, cereals, and boiled eggs.

Laguna Beach may be the essence of Southern California beach towns, but Eiler's has a country French feeling. You'll notice it at once in the two inviting parlors on either side of the entry. One is a small library/den with books and a

TV. The other is a pretty sitting room with a small blue-and-white patterned wallpaper and a comfortable fat sofa and chairs. Afternoon wine and cheeses are served here or in the courtyard.

Some bedrooms are relatively small, but opening onto the courtyard or balcony above, as they do, gives them a pleasant openness. They're each furnished differently with antiques and especially colorful linens and comforters. You'll find fresh flowers, fruit, and candy in each room.

A suite upstairs has a fireplace. It's off ☞ a sun deck that is available to all guests. The ocean views are superb (☞ you're right on the beach), and you can enjoy both sunning and sunsets without so much as a grain of sand between your toes.

You couldn't find a more secluded, romantic setting in Laguna Beach on a Saturday night than the courtyard. Aperitifs and ☞ classical guitar music are the perfect additions to this Southern California inn.

How to get there: On the South Coast Highway in the center of Laguna Beach, the inn is at number 741 on the ocean side.

J: *I'm one who appreciates their complimentary tea and coffee available all day long, but the bottle of champagne you're presented at check-in is truly a sparkling extra.*

olive Metcalf

Bluebelle House
Lake Arrowhead, California
92352

Innkeepers: Rich and Lila Peiffer
Address / Telephone: 263 South State Highway 173 (mailing address: Box 2177); (714) 336–3292.
Rooms: 6; 2 with private bath; 4 share 2 bathrooms.
Rates: $55 to $70, including expanded continental breakfast. Seasonal weekday discounts; two-night minimum weekends. No pets; no smoking.
Open: All year.
Facilities and Local Attractions: Two-tenths of a mile from mountain village shops, restaurants, entertainment; Lake Arrowhead beach, fishing and excursion boats; private beaches available for swimming. Winter sports within thirty minutes.

Nestled in fir trees on the edge of a bustling mountain village, Bluebelle House has a Swiss-Alpine feeling. Fresh air and recreation on Lake Arrowhead are attractions in summer; in winter, skiing is less than thirty minutes away.

Rick and Lila Peiffer's innkeeping style is to 🖙 lavish hospitality and personal attention on their guests. The warmth of their welcome says unmistakably that they're sincerely glad to see you. And if you arrive after sundown, you'll be grateful for their well-lighted parking area.

After your drive up the mountain, relax with late-afternoon refreshments on a ☛ large deck with the smell of fresh pine all around, or indoors beside a warm fire on crisp winter days. This is a good time to look at the Peiffers' menu collection from village restaurants and their "Things to Do in Lake Arrowhead" scrapbook. Rick and Lila have helpful suggestions and will make any reservations you need.

Bluebelle House reflects the talents and interests of both its innkeepers. Rick is a skilled carpenter and has redesigned or improved every corner of the chalet. Lila specializes in silk floral arrangements that she has designed for each room. Objects they've collected from their European holidays are everywhere. Some are outstanding, like a ☛ cuckoo clock in the parlor, and others are cheerful bric-a-brac. There are posters, prints, art objects, lace, and crocheted items. What is cheerful to some taste may be kitsch to others, but Lila puts it all together fetchingly, and the housekeeping is impeccable.

While the four rooms on the main floor share two bathrooms, each room has a ☛ lighted makeup vanity (More inns should think of this!). Lila has decorated each room individually using patchwork quilts and ruffled spreads, chintz and lace curtains, pillows in velvet and eyelet, and romantic print wallpapers.

Breakfast appointments are as colorful as the décor: pretty china, linen, and crystal. Typical of the fare is fresh fruit and juice, bagels with cream cheese and homemade jam, hard-boiled eggs, and hot beverages.

How to get there: From Los Angeles, take Highway 91 past San Bernardino to Highway 173. Follow signs to Lake Arrowhead. At the Village, turn right at the only stoplight. Continue ²/₁₀ mile to the inn on the right.

Olive Metcalf

Union Hotel
Los Alamos, California
93440

Innkeeper: Kathleen Lee Johnson
Address / Telephone: 362 Bell Street (mailing address: Box 616); (805) 928–3838.
Rooms: 15; 3 with private bath; 12 with sink in room, shared bath.
Rates: $75 to $90, including full breakfast. Children discouraged.
Open: All year, Friday, Saturday, Sunday. Restaurant, saloon also available weekdays for private parties.
Facilities and Local Attractions: Swimming pool, Jacuzzi, pool table. Stories, music in saloon. Rides around Los Alamos in 1918 touring cars.

Make no mistake about it, when you visit the Union Hotel you're in for a happening, not a quiet mountain reverie. Owner Dick Langdon and innkeeper Kathy keep it an entertaining place, particularly for special events. A wedding celebration was in preparation the morning we visited. Bridesmaids ran up and down the stairway, and the dining room was being set up for the wedding buffet. Out in the yard, the grape arbor and gazebo looked gala decorated with ribbons and flowers.

Langdon and Kathy have a knack for turning every visit

into an occasion. Being open only three days a week keeps it fun. Beyond that, says Langdon, it becomes work.

The hotel is his home, hobby, and occupation. Knowing this, you might feel it possibly rude to laugh when you walk in, but he's obviously decorated with just that reaction in mind. In the lobby you'll see red-flowered wallpaper, stuffed life-size fabric figures, and a copper bathtub in front of the fireplace. It's an ☞ astonishing collection of wonderful antique objects, like 200-year-old Egyptian burial urns and funky furniture. Langdon claims it's all a re-creation of the original 1884 hotel.

Upstairs is a parlor for overnight guests with pool table and an extensive library. Each bedroom is restored and furnished with brass fixtures, pedestal sinks, and a variety of china wash bowls and pitchers and handmade quilts.

The saloon has a great Old West feeling. The doors came from a bordello, and the bar is about 150 years old. After 9 P.M., it's closed to everyone except hotel guests. Then ☞ everybody gathers for ghost stories, music, and popcorn.

☞ Family-style fare is featured in the large dining room. Platters of country-baked chicken and roast beef are the mainstays, along with soup, salad, corn bread, and honey butter.

The town of Los Alamos (it means "The Cottonwoods" in Spanish) is just a jog off Highway 101 and worth a stop for a look back at the West of the 1880s.

How to get there: From Highway 101, exit at Los Alamos. Follow the road into town. Inn is on the right.

J: *Kathy says the town's telephone system is not quite as efficient as Wells Fargo was at delivering messages. She hopes you'll keep trying when you call. Eventually, it works.*

Eastlake Inn
Los Angeles, California
90026

Innkeepers: Murray Burns and Planaria Price
Address / Telephone: 1442 Kellam Avenue; (213) 250–1620.
Rooms: 5, sharing 4 bathrooms.
Rates: $45 to $90, double occupancy. Special packages available.
No smoking.
Open: All year.
Facilities and Local Attractions: Minutes from central Los Angeles
business district; walk to Dodger Stadium, Music Center, Olvera Street, the Old Plaza, Echo Park Lake. Weekend adventures planned by innkeepers.

There is a Los Angeles lots of people don't know about: gracious old neighborhoods, houses that have survived since the 1800s, and tree-shaded streets where you actually *walk* places. Angelino Heights, the city's oldest suburb, is one of those areas making a comeback, and the Eastlake Inn sits on a hill in this ☞ first L.A. Historic Preservation zone.

It was built in 1887 as a duplex. Both innkeepers have years of historic preservation experience and have combined talents to restore the Victorian. From the spacious living and dining room, two stairways lead to the bedrooms upstairs. Two guest rooms are large, one with white wicker and a fireplace, and one with a romantic queen canopy bed and a pink velvet "fainting couch." Tom Thumb and Thumbelina are tiny, but cozy, rooms, fine for a solo traveler. All of them have antiques and curiosities of the period.

Amenities for the business traveler are thoughtful ones. Besides fresh flowers, fruit, and a robe in my room, I appreciated being asked how early I'd like my coffee and morning paper. When I said I'd be working at the inn a few hours before going out, Murray showed me to a small library with a desk. The sitting room would be just as quiet and pleasant for work, but you could easily be distracted with the stereopticon, jigsaw puzzles, old and new books, and the Victorian costumes from Planaria's collection.

After a day of business or touring, afternoon wine and cheese in this setting is a change that refreshes. Maybe you'll want to take in a night game at Dodger Stadium. No need to get out the car—just walk over.

Don't miss ☞ Carroll Street, just behind the inn. The contrast between its row of restored Victorian homes and the sight of modern downtown Los Angeles beyond is a pleasing one, especially at dusk when the lights are coming on.

How to get there: Drive north on the Hollywood Freeway; exit at Echo Park/Glendale Boulevard. Make hard right on Bellevue to first stop sign, left onto Edgeware, left at Carroll (to see the Victorian houses). Turn right on Douglas and go one block to Kellam. Turn left; inn is last house on left at 1442 Kellam.

J: *The* ☞ *special adventures the innkeepers have devised, from limousine tours of Los Angeles to horse trail rides to a Mexican restaurant, are an easy way to have a razzle-dazzle time in Lotus Land.*

Olive Metcalf

Salisbury House
Los Angeles, California
90018

Innkeepers: Kathleen and Bill Salisbury
Address / Telephone: 2273 West 20th Street; (213) 737–7817.
Rooms: 5, including an attic loft; 3 with private bath; 2 share large
bath with tub and shower.
Rates: $50 to $65, double occupancy; includes full breakfast.
Open: All year.
Facilities and Local Attractions: Close to downtown Los Angeles,
Convention Center; near freeways.

There's good news for travelers to downtown Los Angeles. Businesspeople who never considered an inn are likely to reappraise their usual lodgings if they sample the comforts of Salisbury House. Not many hotel suites provide the ambience of leaded-glass windows, beamed ceilings, wood paneling, and a sitting room filled with antique pieces and cushy sofas and chairs.

This spacious 1909 California Craftsman house is in Arlington Heights, a quiet, residential neighborhood regaining its former elegance. It's an oasis after a day of city bustle, yet it's 🐾 only minutes from the Convention Center and downtown businesses.

22

The five guest rooms are all individually decorated, one each in green, mauve, blue, rose, and the attic loft is paneled. They're comfortable rooms, with good beds and reading lights, as well as having pretty linens, lace curtains, and ceiling fans. The attic suite is 600 square feet of privacy and charm with an antique claw-foot tub, game table, king-sized bed, and pine walls and floors.

On the landing at the top of the stairway is a stocked wine rack with glasses, a desk, and a telephone—all for guests to use. During my visit, the desk also held a dish of homemade fudge. I wonder now how I've ever been able to make telephone calls without the comfort of a little chocolate.

In the morning, Kathleen opens sliding wood-paneled doors and reveals her blue and white dining room with the table set for breakfast. At the sight of sparkling crystal and silver, fresh flowers, and pastel linen napkins on white lace, you're likely to wonder why you ever put up with a plastic hotel coffee shop.

She varies the breakfast buffet (as she does the table settings), but at our visit it held a 🌶 bounty of mixed fresh fruits with praline cream, crêpes Normandy, sausage, corn pudding, and boiled eggs in pretty blue-and-white egg cups. At the table she poured orange juice and champagne.

How to get there: Take the Santa Monica Freeway (10) east to downtown. Go north on Western Avenue. Turn left onto West 20th Street; it's the first street. Inn is on your right at 2273 West 20th.

☼

J: *Early-morning jamoca almond coffee or herb tea and the newspapers is a pretty civilized way to start the day while you await breakfast. And you said you were dreading L.A.?*

olive Metcalf

San Ysidro Ranch
Montecito, California
93108

Innkeepers: Jim and Susie Lavenson
Address / Telephone: 900 San Ysidro Lane; (805) 969–5046.
Rooms: 39, all with private bath.
Rates: $99 for cottage rooms to $269 for cottages with private Jacuzzi; EP. Two-night minimum on weekends.
Open: All year. Breakfast, lunch, dinner, Sunday brunch, bar.
Facilities and Local Attractions: Horses, guided rides, swimming pool, tennis courts, golf. Music, dancing Wednesday through Sunday.

San Ysidro Ranch has been around since 1893, but its sense of humor remains young. In the lounge are two leather scrapbooks labeled "Meanwhile, Back at the Ranch." One contains love letters of praise from past guests. The other is "Ego Deflators," a collection of passionate gripes about everything from the prices and not finding a Bible among the books in one cottage, to complaints about the "stomach-churning humor" around the ranch. Apparently, not everyone appreciates cheery signs announcing "I am a Catalpa Tree," or "late check-outs will be charged an arm and a leg."
Amused or not, I think you'd have the curiosity of a tur-

nip if you didn't want to see the ☞ place where John and Jacqueline Kennedy honeymooned, Laurence Olivier and Vivien Leigh married, and where Winston Churchill and John Galsworthy relaxed and wrote.

☞ Privacy, in a setting of great natural beauty, was and still is the story of the ranch's appeal. The soft foothills of the Santa Ynez Mountains offer miles of riding trails with ☞ breathtaking views. You can disappear into one of the cottages and not see another soul for days, though the innkeepers claim if a guest doesn't come out for twenty-four hours, they do force-feeding.

There is no typical room in the buildings scattered around the lush grounds. Some are parlor suites with patio or deck; some are individual cottages nestled here and there. They're not all equally spiffy, it must be admitted. There's the odd piece of antique plumbing or worn upholstery, but luxury appointments aren't what has attracted people here for so long.

A kind of "we're all country gentlemen here" atmosphere is also part of the charm. Take the lounge, which has the only TV, and where guests get complimentary morning coffee and newspapers. It has an "Honor Bar." Mix your own and keep tabs. Very upper class, don't you think?

One other major lure is the outstanding food at the Plow and Angel restaurant. From al fresco breakfasts to candlelit continental dinners, its reputation attracts even diners who aren't ranch guests. A pleasant bar provides live music and dancing in the evening.

How to get there: From Highway 101, take San Ysidro Road exit in Montecito, 4 miles south of Santa Barbara. Follow signs to San Ysidro Ranch, 2 miles toward the mountains.

☒

J: *The loveliness of these evenings moves the heart; and of the mornings, shining, cool fragrant.*
—John Galsworthy, writing of San Ysidro Ranch

Olive Metcalf

Doryman's Inn
Newport Beach, California
92663

Innkeepers: Rick and Jeannie Lawrence
Address / Telephone: 2102 West Ocean Front; (714) 675–7300.
Rooms: 10, all with private bath, fireplace, TV.
Rates: $120 to $225, including extended continental breakfast.
Open: All year.
Facilities and Local Attractions: Directly across from Newport Pier;
    swimming, wind surfing, deep-sea fishing; largest pleasure
    craft harbor in the world; Newport restaurants, waterfront
    shops, cabarets. Bicycles and off-street parking available.

If you get up very early here, you'll see the commercial
Dory Fishing Fleet returning from the sea in their traditional
small boats with their catch. For nearly 100 years they've
supplied fresh fish for sale in the open-air market at McFadden Wharf, Newport Pier area. It's now one of California's
designated historical landmarks.

Such a humble basis for Newport's origins contrasts
sharply with the opulence of Doryman's Inn. The bed and
breakfast is on the second floor of a modest red brick building
that dates from the 1920s. The Rex restaurant occupies the
first floor (inn guests can order meals sent to their rooms),

but a private elevator whisks you to the inn's lobby upstairs.

Victorian is the motif and resoundingly elegant is the atmosphere. Rick and Jeannie spent five years and a couple of million dollars renovating and decorating the ten rooms. There's ample use of polished oak and brass for staircases and doors, hand-stenciled trim on ceiling borders, luxurious carpets, and etched-glass light globes.

The ☞ romantically decorated bedrooms are furnished with antiques and elaborate beds. Some are brass; others have carved headboards or canopied four-posters. There are matching floral draperies and quilted bedspreads, lace curtains, ruffled pillow shams, gilt-edged beveled mirrors, and plants. Each room has a gas fireplace turned on with the flick of a wall switch, and perhaps a porcelain animal sits on the hearth.

Should this setting sound too austere for your taste, I recommend you proceed to the bathroom where you'll find a taste of extravagant luxury. ☞ Tubs are sunken Italian marble—two with Jacuzzis—highlighted by sun streaming in from fern-filled skylights.

Guests can see each other in the parlor for breakfast, but it's not hard to see why many opt for enjoying it in the privacy of their rooms. Or you might prefer the blue-tiled roof deck with its unobstructed views of the pier and the Pacific. International coffees and teas are served along with fresh pastries, seasonal fresh fruits, brown eggs, and juice.

How to get there: From Highway 405 (San Diego Freeway), take Highway 55 to Newport Boulevard. Continue to 32nd Street, and turn right. Turn left on Balboa Boulevard; bear right at signs to Newport Pier. Inn is on right at 2102 West Ocean Front.

ᵍ

J: *The Newmans (Paul and Joanne to those of us who feel as though we know them) and Jerry Lewis were recent guests. Not at the same time, you understand.*

olive Metcalf

La Maida House
North Hollywood, California
91601

Innkeepers: Megan Timothy and Bruce Bisenz
Address / Telephone: 11159 La Maida Street; (818) 769–3857.
Rooms: 9; 4 in main house; 5 in bungalows, all with private bath.
Rates: $75 to $145, including continental breakfast and evening
    aperitif. No credit cards, no personal checks. No pets or chil-
    dren under 16; no smoking on premises.
Open: All year.
Facilities and Local Attractions: Convenient to Universal Studios,
    Beverly Hills, downtown Los Angeles, shopping, Holly-
    wood/Burbank Airport, restaurants. Access to pool.

No matter how splendid a stay you have at La Maida
House—and I don't see how you could avoid it—you're going
to leave feeling like an underachiever after meeting Megan
Timothy. She's turned a derelict 1920s Italianate mansion
into a ☛ luxury inn that rises above the valley bungalows
and exudes elegance, inside and out.

The formidable talents she brings to innkeeping start
with her design skills. The stunning décor in every room and
the ☛ ninety-seven original stained glass windows (and an
exquisite shower door) throughout the house are remarkable.

28

Then there are her professional-caliber cooking skills. Megan grows all the flowers and herbs and much of the fruit and vegetables she serves. Timothy standards are high, even for the continental breakfasts she serves her guests. "Every innkeeper should invest in a first-rate juice machine," she declares. Hers is one that can make juice out of everything but the *Los Angeles Times.* She makes it on the spot with fresh combinations every morning, and guests try to figure out what has been "juiced."

No other meals are served regularly, but everything is possible. Megan will prepare a picnic for the Hollywood Bowl, or an intimate dinner for two to four, served in a second-floor balcony overlooking the garden. She'll do an elegant dinner for eight around a glass-topped table in a solarium dining room, or a formal affair in the candle-lit, chandeliered dining room with seating for thirty-two at round tables covered with peach linen. This is a Limoges and crystal affair, you understand, not California pottery. The ☛ food, custom planned to your wishes, is as beautiful as the surroundings, and *everything* is made from scratch.

Every bedroom is a knockout and has all the comforts you might need: robes, bath toiletries, even crocheted lap throws made by Megan's mother. Some accommodations are in bungalows across the street, but they are every bit as comfortable as those in the mansion. From the entryway with its graceful staircase, to the handsome drawing room with grand piano, Carrara marble fireplace, and polished oak floors, this flower-filled house is a pleasure.

How to get there: From Hollywood Freeway, exit at Magnolia. Turn east to first light, and then turn right on Tujunga. At next light, turn left on Camarillo. Go three blocks to Bellflower and turn left. Continue one block to northeast corner of La Maida.

J: *It's no wonder the guest list includes movers and shakers; this is a ☛ class act in personalized Hollywood digs.*

olive Metcalf

Ojai Manor Hotel
Ojai, California
93023

Innkeeper: Mary Nelson
Address / Telephone: 210 East Matilija Street; (805) 646–0961.
Rooms: 6, sharing 3 bathrooms.
Rates: $65 to $75; special weekday rates. Continental breakfast, complimentary wine included.
Open: All year.
Facilities and Local Attractions: Walk to Ojai shops, galleries, restaurants. Golf, tennis close by. May music festivals, June Shakespeare Revels. Hiking, camping in surrounding mountains. Fishing, Lake Casitas.

Travelers on the California coast who dash between San Francisco and Los Angeles and fail to explore some of the more obscure places in between are missing copious treasures. The beautiful Ojai Valley is one of the jewels.

Imagine a small-town version of Santa Barbara's Spanish architecture, Carmel's artists and galleries, and San Francisco's smart shops. Bless it with Los Angeles weather (but with sparkling clean air), and you have the lovely little town of Ojai, population 6,325.

Comfortably settled into Mary Nelson's inn, you'll have

no need for a car to get anywhere in town. But you should take some of the 🖝 scenic drives around the area: up Dennison Grade for memorable vistas of the abundant valley; up Sulphur Mountain Road for spectacular views of the Pacific Ocean on one side, the Ojai Valley on the other.

Mary and her partner, artist Boyd Wright, have restored the oldest building in town as a fresh, inviting inn. In 1874, it was a school in the heart of this agricultural community. Now, the polished oak floors and the pale lavender-gray-white walls are an intriguing background for Boyd's 🖝 contemporary art pieces—many of them large and dramatic. Mary says there's an empty feeling when one is shipped off to an exhibition or sold. Meanwhile, guests enjoy a fascinating home gallery.

The colorful living room has a beautiful Oriental rug and an Art Deco–looking blue plush sofa and club chair by the fireplace. Adjoining it is a sunny dining room with a long table where Mary serves a generous continental breakfast. This day it was juice, fresh raspberries, and a variety of her freshly baked breads and muffins with preserves and cream cheese.

The six fresh bedrooms upstairs feature the 🖝 best-looking beds you'll find anywhere. It must be those oversize down pillows and fine linens! What a luxury for people who like to prop up in bed and read—and there are good lights on both sides of the bed, too.

How to get there: About one hour north of Santa Barbara on Highway 101, take Lake Casitas exit, Highway 150, east to Ojai—a beautiful drive. At Libby Park in town center, turn left one block to East Matilija.

🍸

J: *Be sure you walk to Bart's Corner, a unique outdoor meeting place, garden, and used-book store. Mary will direct you.*

olive Metcalf

The Cheshire Cat
Santa Barbara, California
93101

Innkeeper: Margo Cherne; Owner, Chris Dunston
Address / Telephone: 36 West Valerio Street; (805) 569–1610.
Rooms: 10, all with private bath.
Rates: $99 to $139, including generous continental breakfast. No
   credit cards. No children or pets; no smoking.
Open: All year.
Facilities and Local Attractions: Spa, patio, private telephones, bi-
   cycles. Walk to Santa Barbara restaurants, shops, theaters.

Chris Dunston knew exactly what she wanted to ac-
complish when she began restoring two elegant Victorian
houses: simply to create a ☞ showplace among Santa Barbara inns. By George, I think she's done it!

Her theme, beginning with the inn's name, is "Alice in
Wonderland." A set of porcelain figurines representing characters from the story sits on an antique desk in the living
room, and most of the rooms are named for the characters. If
all this sounds too cute for words, let me tell you it's gor-
geously done.

The finest Laura Ashley prints in fabric and wallpaper
are used throughout the house as the background for beauti-

ful English antique furniture. How can you resist an atmosphere of high ceilings and fresh flowers, where the glow of polished wood vies with the sparkle of beveled glass? How genteel.

Every room is a stunner with Ashley print bed linens and coordinated drapes and wall coverings. ☞ Color schemes have to be described as delicious: The Caterpillar Suite in rose, moss green, and stone; Mad Hatter in plum and cream; Alice's Suite in ivory and pink, which has a private patio overlooking an oak tree, gardens, and mountains.

A flower-filled brick patio with a white gazebo is between the two houses. White chairs and round tables are dressed for breakfast in pink cloths. Add blue and white Wedgwood china and you have a scene as engaging as a stage setting. A beautiful continental breakfast is set out around a palm tree in the center of the courtyard: fresh fruits, fresh croissants, homemade jams and granola, yogurt, tea, and just-ground coffee.

Take a look at the professionally equipped kitchen. It was designed for more ambitious things than mere continental breakfasts. ☞ Week-long gourmet cooking classes are planned with notable chefs from across the country invited to teach inn guests. Ask about them when you call.

How to get there: From Highway 101 going through Santa Barbara, take Valerio Street toward the mountairs. Inn is on your left at number 36.

olive Metcalf

The Glenborough Inn
Santa Barbara, California
93101

Innkeepers: Jo Ann Bell and Pat Hardy
Address / Telephone: 1327 Bath Street; (805) 966–0589.
Rooms: 4 in the main house sharing 2 baths; 4 in the cottage with
    private bath.
Rates: $55 to $115, with full breakfast; singles $5 less, $10 per extra
    person. No smoking in main house; no children or pets.
Open: All year.
Facilities and Local Attractions: Hot tub, gardens. Walk to Santa
    Barbara's museums, shops, restaurants, galleries. Close to
    beach, harbor, mountains.

A couple of real inn "pros" own and operate The Glen-
borough Inn. They know all the right moves to give an inn
flavor, and what's more, they share their techniques in a
book they've written and in classes on innkeeping they give.
If you're thinking of becoming one of the thousands of people
each year who open an inn, they have a ☛ bonanza of information about everything from how to balance the budget to
how to avoid inn burnout.

Their inn consists of two charming houses in a pleasant
neighborhood: the Main House, a two-story 1906 home, and

the early 1880s Cottage across the street. You can tell from the warmth of your welcome that these innkeepers aren't suffering from burnout. They obviously enjoy giving guests ☞ the kind of personal attention that defines an inn's style.

The four bedrooms in the Main House are cozy and very Victorian. Curtains of old lace, embroidered pillows, velvet coverlets, and quilts enhance the antique furniture. I'm crazy about sun porches, so I was smitten with the smallest room of all, the Garden, with old-fashioned wicker and a view of backyard flowers.

If privacy and easy access are important, you'll like the four rooms in the Cottage. Each has a separate entrance and bath, and two are suites with a sitting room and fireplace. Plants and flowers inside and out live up to Santa Barbara's reputation for lushness. Indulge yourself with breakfast in bed when it arrives in a picnic basket, or take it alfresco in the secluded backyard garden.

Ah, those ☞ breakfasts of Pat's. She does everything from scratch, salt-free, with low-fat and low-cholesterol ingredients fresh from the garden or local markets. One of her menus is Spanish: juice, Huevos Rancheros, Ban Huelos (crispy flour tortilla sprinkled with cinnamon sugar), and sliced grapefruit lightly touched with brown sugar beside fresh berries. She has many such specialties, all scrumptious.

Everyone who feels like socializing is encouraged to gather in the cheerfully cluttered Main House parlor for evening wine and hors d'oeuvres. Pat and Jo Ann know all the best restaurants in a city full of them, and they'll direct you to one that's bound to please. After dinner, stroll back to the inn for ☞ a very private hot tub under the stars. Don't forget to put out the "occupied" sign.

How to get there: From Highway 101, exit at Carrillo Street. Go east toward the mountains to Bath Street. Turn left onto Bath Street; inn is three-and-one-half blocks ahead at number 1327.

olive Metcalf

The Old Yacht Club Inn
and
The Hitchcock House
Santa Barbara, California
93103

Innkeepers: Lucille Caruso, Nancy Donaldson, Sandy Hunt, Gay
    Swenson
Address / Telephone: 431 Corona Del Mar; (805) 962–1277.
Rooms: 5 sharing 2 baths, sink in each room in Old Yacht Club; 4,
    each with private bath, in Hitchcock House.
Rates: $50 to $75 at Old Yacht Club; $80 to $105 at Hitchcock
    House. All rates double occupancy; extra person $15. Includes
    full breakfast. No children or pets. Smoking discouraged.
Open: All year. Dinner by reservation, usually weekends.
Facilities and Local Attractions: Bicycles provided. Walk half a
    block to beach. Swimming, fishing, sailing, tennis, golf close by.

After the first clubhouse of Santa Barbara's Yacht Club
was swept out to sea during a terrible storm in the 1920s, this
house served as the headquarters. The name seemed a perfect choice when it became Santa Barbara's first bed and
breakfast inn. It does sit a mere ☞ half a block from the waterfront, but there's nothing nautical about it.

36

It's a 1912 Craftsman-style house, which means it has the period charm of a wide, covered front porch, and balconies and dormers that provide charming, light-filled rooms. Two of the upstairs bedrooms at the Old Yacht Club have built-in window seats—surely one of the most appealing details a room can have. They're decorated with an old-fashioned, personal touch and accented with fresh flowers and decanters of sherry.

Hitchcock House is just next door, a good choice for privacy. Its four large rooms have the advantages of sitting areas plus private baths *and* private entrances. These are especially personal rooms, since each of the four innkeepers decorated a room to reflect her heritage. The Italian Room, for instance, has the trunks that came with the immigrants from Europe, family photographs, and other treasures.

Downstairs at the Old Yacht Club, guests of both houses are welcome to enjoy the warm atmosphere of antiques and Oriental rugs and to join in sherry or tea by the fire. An exceptional breakfast is served here in the dining room or delivered in a basket to your door at Hitchcock House: freshly gound coffee, juice, fresh fruit, home-baked breads, and interesting omelets (maybe spinach or zucchini).

Check the dinner schedule with the innkeepers when booking your room. Most weekends (and for special events) Nancy Donaldson does a five course candle-lit dinner, by reservation, that could be the highlight of your visit. She's a professional member of the American Wine and Food Institute and loves to cook. Homemade fettuccine, Artichokes Athena, Halibut Florentine, and Chocolate Decadence are some of her specialties.

How to get there: Driving north on Highway 101 to Santa Barbara, exit (left lane) on Cabrillo. Turn left, continue past Sheraton Hotel; turn right on Corona Del Mar Drive and turn right to inn, number 431. Coming south, take second State Street exit, turn right. Turn left on Cabrillo; just before Sheraton Hotel, turn left on Corona Del Mar.

Olive Metcalf

The Parsonage
Santa Barbara, California
93101

Innkeeper: Hilde Michelmore
Address / Telephone: 1600 Olive Street; (805) 962–9336.
Rooms: 5; 4 with private bath; 1 with half-bath in room and shared
shower.
Rates: $65 to $105 for suite; includes full breakfast. Two-night
minimum on weekends. Visa card only. No children under 14;
no pets. Smoking discouraged.
Open: All year.
Facilities and Local Attractions: Sun deck. Walk to Mission Santa
Barbara, shopping, theater, restaurants.

    If ever the talk about splitting California into northern
and southern states is seriously considered, you can bet that
the custody battle over Santa Barbara will be ferocious. Both
sides would fight to keep this lush, distinctly Mediterranean
city.
    From The Parsonage, one of Santa Barbara's many nota-
ble Victorian houses, you can explore a host of the city's attractions on foot. The inn is nestled between the mountains
and the downtown area in a quiet residential neighborhood.
This splendid Queen Anne was built in 1892 as a parsonage

for the Trinity Episcopal Church. It's now home and business to Hilde Michelmore, who has restored and decorated it with her impressive collection of antiques and rugs.

The minister's library is the only bedroom on the first floor. It's now the Rosebud Room in pinks and mauves and furnished with antiques. You might appreciate having immediate access to an attractive living room with a fireplace and oversize sofa. A large iron baker's rack filled with books and plants decorates one wall, and there's a small TV. I wonder what the long-ago cleric would think of the ☞ unusual lilac-and-green Chinese rug that now decorates his Victorian sitting room. It's memorable!

At the top of the redwood staircase are four uniquely decorated rooms. There's the Peacock Room, with exotic blues and greens in comforter and Oriental rug; the Lavender and Lace Room; and Las Flores, with a bay window looking out at the ocean. The Honeymoon Suite runs the entire length of the house. It comprises a bedroom, a solarium (old-fashioned sun porch), and an enormous bathroom with a handsome pedestal sink and footed tub. It has a king-size canopied bed and an antique armoire. The ☞ views from here of mountains, ocean, and city are quite spectacular.

A formal dining room with a graceful bay window, or a sunny deck with more outstanding views are equally pleasant spots for breakfast. Hilde serves a large one, with favorites like scrambled eggs, quiche, or French toast.

How to get there: Driving south on Highway 101, exit at Mission Street east toward The Mission. Cross Laguna Street, turn right to Olive Street, and continue to the inn at number 1600. Driving north on 101, exit at Laguna Street; cross town to Arrellaga Street, and turn right on Olive Street.

The Tiffany Inn
Santa Barbara, California
93101

Innkeepers: Carol and Larry MacDonald
Address / Telephone: 1323 De La Vina Street; (805) 963–2283.
Rooms: 5, 3 with private bath.
Rates: $65 to $95 double occupancy, includes continental breakfast
   and evening refreshments. Reduced rates in winter season;
   two-night minimum on weekends. Smoking outside only; no
   pets.
Open: All year.
Facilities and Local Attractions: Walking distance to many restau-
   rants, shops; close to The Mission, Stearn's Wharf. Hike
   mountains, walk beach, visit museums, galleries, theaters.
   Tour local wineries.

Some inns are just so outlandishly pretty, it hardly mat-
ters if they serve a good breakfast, are conveniently located,
or indulge your need to be pampered with some degree of
style. The Tiffany Inn scores high on all counts, but the truth
is, it's just such a beautiful, ☛ enchantingly decorated
house, the rest is all lagniappe.
   This stately 1898 Victorian that Carol and Larry have restored so lovingly and authentically is a picture-perfect set-

ting for the ☞ collection of fine furniture and antiques that they've acquired over the years. The ambience begins with the genuine articles—glowing dark wood, colonial diamond-paned bay windows, a century-old wood staircase, and a bathroom with all the original fixtures.

What Carol MacDonald has done is make the antique background stunning by lavishly decorating with the finest colorful fabrics, artfully arranging her splendid furniture, and then maintaining it all immaculately.

I couldn't choose a favorite among the upstairs bedrooms. They each have a romantic feeling and delicious appointments: rockers placed to look out at mountains or garden, lace curtains at French windows, elegant bed linens, and a wood-burning fireplace in several.

The impeccable garden is as Victorian in atmosphere as is the house. It's a lovely place to relax, or you might enjoy the wicker chaise on the old-fashioned lattice-covered porch.

I would love to see the house when the MacDonalds and son David decorate it for Christmas. They offer a low holiday rate then to encourage guests to come and stay while doing their Christmas shopping in Santa Barbara—where there's some of the greatest shopping anywhere. The idea sounds appealing to me. Shop all day, have dinner at one of Santa Barbara's outstanding restaurants, and return to the richly decorated inn for wine or a grog in the elegant parlor around the fire. Retire for the night to your beautiful cozy room and dream of no-limit Visa Land. Next morning, after fresh fruit, croissants, and coffee, you'll be ready to hit the shops again.

How to get there: From Highway 101 through Santa Barbara, exit at Mission Street. Drive east to De La Vina Street and turn right. Inn is on the right at number 1323.

olive Metcalf

Venice Beach House
Venice, California
90291

Innkeeper: Karen Zimmer
Address / Telephone: 15 Thirtieth Avenue; (213) 823–1966.
Rooms: 8; 4 with private bath, 4 sharing 1 large bathroom.
Rates: $50 to $125, includes continental breakfast. No pets, no
  smoking. Children over 10 welcome.
Open: All year.
Facilities and Local Attractions: Walk to swimming beach, Venice
  Pier. Close to Los Angeles Airport, restaurants, shops.

Abbot Kinney bought this stretch of California coast at
the turn of the century with a slightly wacky but grandiose
vision of re-creating Venice, Italy: canals, elegant hotels,
boardwalks, piers, and cultural events—and he did it. "Kinney's Folly" was a success for more than thirty years before it
fell out of fashion.

This gray-shingled beach house was built a half-block
from the beach in 1911, the heyday of Venice, by Warren
Wilson, a wealthy newspaper publisher. Two of his eight
daughters married Kinney sons, and the house was filled
with family for many years. It's that kind of house still—big
and friendly.

Now that the '60s hippie encampment is past, Venice is having a revival of popularity. The beach is clean for swimming, property values have skyrocketed, and the boardwalk is lively with shops, tourists, and roller skaters.

Once you're over the age of sixteen, it's probably best to dip into the exotic scenes of Los Angeles beach life from a base that is utterly sane, even conventional. This house is a quiet, tasteful retreat that will welcome you back when you've had enough "colorful sights."

The living room is restful in shades of rose and mauve with a beautiful antique Oriental rug in those shades, comfortable furniture, and a fireplace. Bedrooms are romantically decorated with fabric over padded walls, and there are fine bathrooms. One has a deep, tiled shower with dueling shower heads at either side of the shower, one is a Jacuzzi tub for two, and another has two gilded, claw-foot tubs.

A sheltered veranda or the cheerful sun room adjoining the living room are the breakfast spots. Fruits, cereals, hot breads, tea, and coffee are set out to help yourself. You sit at small, round tables covered with flowered skirts. Outside the bay window are pink hibiscus and a bit of ocean view.

How to get there: From San Diego Freeway (405), go west on Washington, one street past Pacific to Speedway. Turn right, and go one block to 29th Street. Turn right; park immediately at gray board fence.

J: *Among the performers on the boardwalk this summer were a one-man blues band, the "Texas Chainsaw Juggler," and a man who swallows dipsticks. Just your everyday, homespun entertainment—Venice style.*

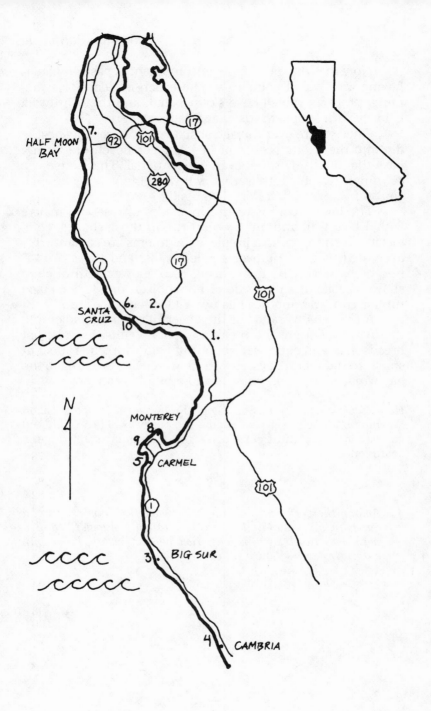

HALF MOON BAY

7.

92

101

17

280

17

101

1

SANTA CRUZ

6. 2.

10

1.

N

MONTEREY

8

9

5 CARMEL

101

1

3. BIG SUR

4. CAMBRIA

California: The Central Coast

Numbers on map refer to towns numbered below.

The Bayview Hotel
Aptos, California
95003

Innkeepers: Nancy and David Martin
Address / Telephone: 8041 Soquel Drive; (408) 688–1927.
Rooms: 16; 8 with private bath, 8 sharing 2 baths.
Rates: $50 to $60 with continental breakfast.
Open: All year. Dinner, summer lunches, full bar.
Facilities and Local Attractions: Unique Aptos shops. Three quarters of a mile to beach, swimming, barbecue facilities. Entertainment in bar evenings.

Were you aware that the very cutting edge of culinary chic (momentarily) is Creole food? Food commentators are shouting about the country's infatuation with New Orleans–style cuisine, and here it is at The Bayview Hotel, a few miles off the freeway in little old Aptos. It is an impressive old building hiding behind a cluster of shrubbery and a giant magnolia tree, but you would miss it if you didn't make a point of taking the side trip. Other buildings and trees now obscure the bay view, but the kitchen has ☞ Cajun cooking clearly in sight.

They have it all—Turtle Soup and Chicken Gumbo, Barbecued Shrimp, Cajun Smothered Pork Chops, ☞ Blackened Red Snapper, and Red Beans and Rice. Don't even *think* of passing up dessert; your tongue will need cooling by one of those Southern ice-cream spectaculars—Flaming Bananas Foster or Cherries Jubilee.

The Bayview's Creole menu is oddly appropriate. At one time, a sign at the Aptos rail station next door said "San Francisco 87 miles; New Orleans 2,478 miles." The connection was the hotel's first proprietor, Joseph Arano, who was French and had lived in New Orleans before coming West to build the Bayview in 1870. In an old photograph of Arano sporting a drooping mustache and sitting on the front veranda around 1890, he bears an uncanny resemblance to the present owner, David Martin.

The hotel became a gathering place for a mixture of social classes unlikely to occur anywhere but in small western towns. Millionaire entrepreneurs socialized with lumbermen and railroad workers, and the guest list included names from high society and politics to Lillian Russell and actor John Drew.

The Martins have been restoring the sleeping rooms with many of the original furnishings. Arano's carved and hand-painted bedroom set is in the same room where he placed it in 1878. Bathrooms and carpets are comfortable additions, and white wicker accents add a nostalgic touch.

A continental breakfast is delivered to your room. Lunch and dinner are served on two glassed-in verandas or on a shaded patio. Friendly owners, good food, and a lively bar still bring as diverse a crowd as ever. Nightly entertainment might be country rock, a single guitar, or an Irish band.

How to get there: From Highway 1, take Aptos exit to Soquel Drive. Follow to inn on your right.

☀

J: *If you don't yet know about Creole food, you're missing an American phenomenon. Laugh heartburn in the face and go for it.*

Fairview Manor
Ben Lomond, California
95005

Innkeepers: Heidi and Dan Sullivan
Address / Telephone: 245 Fairview Avenue; (408) 336–3355.
Rooms: 5; 3 with private bath.
Rates: $65 to $89, double or single. Breakfast and complimentary wine included.
Open: All year.
Facilities and Local Attractions: Fishing the San Lorenzo River; walk to Ben Lomond restaurants, shops; Henry Cowell Park; Roaring Camp Narrow-Gauge Railroad rides from Felton; 20-minute bus ride to Santa Cruz Boardwalk.

If you ever want to hide out for awhile but can't go far from San Francisco, you might head for Ben Lomond. Once at this remote little town in the Santa Cruz Mountains, follow a country road to a tree-shaded driveway and a sign saying Fairview Manor.

The house you see is deceptive—just a well-maintained 1920s vintage attractive country house. But open the front door and you look straight through a large living room/dining room to a deck, and beyond that to a green forest of redwoods, madrone, and live oak trees. Walk through those trees down a short path and you're on the San Lorenzo River. Here's your hideaway.

It's the idyllic kind of shaded, sandy river bank with smooth round rocks and see-through water that some of us could spend whole days playing on. Others are much more interested in the ☞ steelhead and salmon fishing in season.

The house sits on two-and-a-half acres of total privacy, but it's just a short walk to central Ben Lomond, where there are restaurants and antique shops. Landscaped grounds around the house have winding paths, ponds with guppies, and shady areas to sit in. The whole ☞ feeling here is of an earlier, quieter time.

Inside are five simple but immaculate guest rooms. The wood-paneled living room is cheerful, with a rich green carpet and a comfortable sofa and armchairs. Magazines, books, and a fireplace make a warm, inviting atmosphere for relaxing or enjoying the complimentary afternoon wine and snacks.

Heidi and Dan have taken over running the inn from Dan's parents.They've made a few tasty additions—blintzes, custards, and quiches—to the breakfast menu of fruits and juices, nut breads, and other home-baked goods. It's all served at a long dining table sitting in front of a big window looking out at the trees, or out on the deck.

How to get there: From San Jose on Highway 17, turn right on Highway 9 north to Ben Lomond. Turn right on Main Street at the Bank of America, left at Central, and right on Fairview. Inn is on the left.

ᶲ

J: *You'll feel completely remote here, but it's all of two hours from San Francisco.*

Olive Metcalf

Deetjen's Big Sur Inn
Big Sur, California
93920

Innkeeper: Bettie Walters; Restaurant Manager, Kaye Andrews
Address / Telephone: Highway 1; (408) 667–2377.
Rooms: 20; 14 share adjoining baths, others share 2 bathrooms.
Rates: $25 to $75, EP. No credit cards; cash or traveler's checks
   preferred. One bedroom, one dining room smoke free. No pets;
   children welcome.
Open: All year. Breakfast, dinner daily. Wine/beer bar.
Facilities and Local Attractions: Walk high meadowlands, beaches,
   redwood canyons. Several restaurants, shops along six-mile
   section of Highway 1.

   "When I have to begin *explaining* Big Sur Inn to people,
I know it's probably not for them," says restaurant manager
Kaye Andrews. In other words, if you like the manicured luxury of The Lodge at Pebble Beach, Big Sur Inn is probably
not your style. But for many people, Deetjen's Big Sur Inn
reflects the character of the area better than any other place.
   You can't compete with the ☞ heart-stopping beauty of
the Big Sur coast stretching eighty miles from Carmel to San
Simeon, and the inn does not try. It is a rustic lodge with an
add-on tumble of cottages that simply blend into the moun-

tains and trees. Helmuth Deetjen, a Norwegian immigrant, built the homestead in the '20s. Today, the inn is owned by his estate and leased to a nonprofit corporation owned by local residents.

The 🖝 atmosphere is California casual, a nonpolyester, natural-fabric feeling, with a few traces of hippie life remaining. You're as likely to meet a San Francisco stock broker as you are a breakfast companion who'll discuss the meaning of Zen. Accommodations are unabashedly simple, still very much the way Grandpa Deetjen built them—bathrooms are shared, and heating is provided by fireplace, wood-burning stove, or heaters. Recent improvements are new beds, down comforters, and new rag rugs.

Fresh food, thoughtfully prepared, is the premise behind a menu that ranges from old counter-culture favorites like crisp vegetable stir-fry with brown rice, to duckling with fresh peach sauce, or pasta with fresh basil. A good wine list is frequently revised. A comfortable, family feeling among the staff extends over to guests, and the atmosphere is enhanced by hearth fires always burning, candles lit, and classical music playing. Breakfasts are popular here, too.

Ask the innkeeper for directions to Pfeiffer Beach. A hidden one-lane road leads to a 🖝 very private, special beach. And don't miss having a drink or lunch down the road at 🖝 Nepenthe. Originally an adobe and redwood house that Orson Welles bought for Rita Hayworth, and at one time a refuge for Henry Miller, it's become a California equivalent of the Via Veneto: Eventually *everyone* makes the scene on the terrace perched 800 feet above a dramatic surf.

How to get there: The inn is on the east side of Highway 1.

J: *If that fine word* funky *did not exist, it would have to be invented for Deetjen's Big Sur Inn.*

Clive Metcalf

Ventana Inn
Big Sur, California
93920

Innkeeper: Randy Smith
Address / Telephone: Big Sur; (408) 667–2331 or (408) 624–4812.
Rooms: 40, all with private bath; most with fireplace; cable TV.
Rates: $125 to $525, double occupancy; includes continental
    breakfast, afternoon wine and cheese buffet.
Open: All year. Restaurant serves lunch, dinner; cocktail lounge.
Facilities and Local Attractions: Hot tubs, saunas, swimming pool.
    Hike, picnic; the Ventana general store.

The Big Sur Coast has always welcomed the offbeat, and
even this sybaritic paradise was designed as a "different"
kind of place: no tennis, no golf, no conventions, no Muzak,
no disco delights.

What it does offer is a window (*ventana* means "window" in Spanish) toward both the Santa Lucia Mountains
and the Pacific Ocean from a redwood and cedar lodge on a
magnificent slope. This is the ☞ ultimate hideaway, a tasteful, expensive world of its own harmonizing with the wilderness surrounding it. For activity there is a handsome
swimming pool, luxurious Japanese hot tubs, and walking on
grassy slopes, through the woods, or on the beach. From

52

every point your eyes go to the ☛ spectacular Big Sur coast, where boulders send white foam spraying into the air.

Some rooms in the cottages clustered around the lodge look down into a canyon of trees; others face the ocean. Their ☛ uncluttered blend of natural fabric and design makes each room seem to be the best one. Every detail—folk baskets holding kindling, window seats, quilts handmade in Nova Scotia, private terraces—has been carefully conceived.

A gravel path leads to the restaurant, with the opportunity of seeing native wildflowers and an occasional deer or bobcat on the way. The food is colorful California cuisine: fresh fish, veal, chicken, creative pastas, and a good wine list. The place to be at lunch is the ☛ expansive terrace with a fifty-mile view of the coast. Dinner inside is a candlelight and pink linen affair. If you've walked the hills enough, indulge in a chocolate torte the *Washington Post* called "celestial."

At breakfast, a continental buffet, accompanied by baroque music, is spread in the lodge lobby by the rock fireplace: platters of melons, papayas, strawberries—whatever is fresh—pastries and breads baked in the Ventana kitchen, honey and preserves, yogurt and homemade granola. An afternoon wine and cheese buffet has an incredible array of domestic and imported cheeses.

The Store by the restaurant (books, baskets, mountain clothing, handmade knives, bird whistles) is as intriguing as its staff—all of whom seemed to be bilingual and have fascinating histories.

How to get there: On State Highway 1, Ventana is 311 miles (about a six-and-a-half-hour drive) north of Los Angeles. The inn's sign is on the right. From San Francisco, the inn is 152 miles, 28 miles south of Carmel.

J: *I've heard that the best substitute for a rich father is a rich father-in-law. Short of that, a few days at Ventana will do.*

olive Metcalf

The J. Patrick House
Cambria, California
93428

Innkeeper: Molly Lynch
Address / Telephone: 2990 Burton Drive; (805) 927–3812.
Rooms: 7, all with private bath. Room and bath facilities for wheel-
chairs.
Rates: $80, including tax and breakfast. No smoking; no pets. Chil-
dren over 16 welcome.
Open: All year.
Facilities and Local Attractions: Close to Cambria shops, restau-
rants. Visit nearby Hearst Castle, fifteen vineyards. Pick your
own fruit at Orchard Farms.

It wasn't too long ago that this warm early American–style inn wasn't here, only the log house in front where
Molly Lynch lives. Guests gather there in her living room for
wine and cheese in the early evening. With its blue rug and
red wingback chairs flanking the fireplace, it's especially inviting on those damp, cool days that come winter and summer along the Central Coast.

Passion vine is growing up an arbor that connects the
main house to a fine new, two-story cedar building with
seven bedrooms. I liked the feeling of the guest house the

moment I walked in, partly because of the wonderful aroma. The cedar gives it a light fresh look, besides smelling good. All the bedrooms are spacious and have great tile baths. Another pleasant sitting room is on the first floor.

The early American décor is not the fussy, uncomfortable kind. It's apealing but uncluttered, with cushioned window seats framed by pretty curtains, some beautiful hand-crocheted bed coverings, and a few special pieces. A huge California-willow rocker and headboard in one room are wonderful. (A smaller version of the rocker is in the living room.) They're the work of a local craftsman, says Molly.

Across the back of the house is a sunny breakfast room that looks out on the garden. Molly's idea of continental breakfast is first-rate: coffee from freshly ground beans, freshly squeezed juice, cinnamon rolls or another baked treat just made, as well as granola, yogurt, and fresh fruit to layer and mix as you choose.

Running an inn is a business, but it's an intensely personal one for this innkeeper. It bears her father's name, and every room is named for a county in southern Ireland: Tipperary, Kerry, Kilkenny, and the like. Says Molly, "My whole point is that people are comfortable and that they feel they've been treated well. After that, this business is all fluff."

How to get there: North on Highway 1, exit at signs to Cambria; follow Main Street into town. At Burton Drive (Chevron Station on left), turn left; follow about ¾ mile. Just before reaching the inn, Burton takes a hard right turn. Inn is on left at number 2990.

J: *There's not a shred of truth to the rumor that you have to be Irish to get a reservation here.*

Clive Metcalf

Pickford House
Cambria, California
93428

Innkeeper: Darryl Gorman
Address / Telephone: 2555 McLeod Avenue; (805) 927–8619.
Rooms: 8, all with private bath.
Rates: $65 to $90, double occupancy; includes full breakfast. Prefer children over 12.
Open: All year. Dinner, wine/beer bar nightly.
Facilities and Local Attractions: Close to Cambria restaurants, shops, beach. Short drive to Hearst Castle.

William Randolph Hearst, the newspaper mogul, owned 275,000 acres of these beautiful hillsides when he built his dream mansion, San Simeon. Darryl Gorman came up with an appropriate theme for the inn he built in its shadow—silent-movie stars. It also happens to have ☞ panoramic views and a first-rate restaurant, but the movie stuff is always fun.

Up at his famous castle, Hearst and his significant other, Marion Davies, were hosts during the '30s and '40s to everyone who was anyone—royalty, rascals, and flocks of movie stars.

"The Ranch," as Hearst called it, is a phenomenal attraction to the Central Coast. But Cambria itself is a delightful town to explore, with its beaches, Victorian architecture, and unique shops and galleries.

The comfortable ☞ rooms at Pickford House are named for some of the stars who visited San Simeon and are decorated with a feeling for their image. Pickford Room is for Mary, of course, very feminine and beautiful, with Victorian furnishings, a fireplace, and a rich rose rug.

Down the hall, the Fairbanks Room is done in masculine dark green and Art Deco furniture. For the Barrymore suite, there's an extravagantly dramatic black satin bedspread. Other rooms are named for Gish, Valentino, Talmadge, and Lloyd. Some have fireplaces, and three have views of the valley and mountains.

In the restaurant on the main floor called Harlow's, wine and beer are served at an 1816 bar shipped from New York. A picture of the sensational Jean hangs over the bar, and another is on the menu. Sautéed veal scallops, rack of lamb marinated in red wine and roasted, and pork chops with mustard, in cream and tomato sauce, are specialties. Fresh California ingredients are always featured, as in their popular appetizers: whole boiled artichokes, and fresh mushrooms sautéed with garlic and herbs.

Breakfast is a full-fledged meal. In addition to coffee, tea, fresh juices, and fruit, something hot and hearty is always served, like cheese omelets, or Danish pancakes topped with powdered sugar and jam. It should see you through a San Simeon tour with vigor.

How to get there: Driving north or south on Highway 1, exit at signs for Cambria and follow the main street toward town. At Eaton Road, turn toward the ocean. Take a short jog left onto Wood and left again on McLeod Way. The inn is on the left at number 2555.

clive Metcalf

The Cobblestone Inn
Carmel-by-the-Sea, California
93921

Innkeeper: Dan Murphy
Address / Telephone: Junipero Street between 7th and 8th (mailing address: Box 3185); (408) 625–5222; (1-800) AAA–INNS.
Rooms: 24, each with private bath; fireplace, color TV, small refrigerator in most rooms.
Rates: $85 to $170, double occupancy; $10 each additional person. Included are breakfast buffet, afternoon hors d'oeuvres, wine. No smoking inside.
Open: All year.
Facilities and Local Attractions: Short walk to Carmel Beach, shops, restaurants, art galleries. Picnics: Drive to Point Lobos State Reserve, Pebble Beach, Big Sur. Tennis, golf facilities within short drive.

The Cobblestone is one of five inns owned by the same management. Having visited all their inns, I'm ready to suggest that this group write a text on the art of personalized innkeeping. Each of their inns, from the Cobblestone here in Carmel, to the Petite Auberge in San Francisco, is a classic example of exquisite decorating, first-class comforts, and exceptionally high standards of service and personal attention.

The on-duty innkeeper keeps it all working—in this case, Dan Murphy. He oversees all the basics thoroughly, like impeccable housekeeping and a friendly staff, but it's those ☞ deftly done little extras that are so winning: flowers, fruit, and a handwritten card in your room welcoming you by name; champagne, if he knows it's a special occasion; a morning newspaper outside your door, and your shined shoes or golf clubs, too, if you put them out the night before.

Bedrooms have a French country feeling, with pretty wallpapers, fresh quilts and pillows, and handsome antiques. It's a pleasure to relax in a room with a comfortable sitting area, good reading lights, and a ☞ cobblestone fireplace.

When you cross the courtyard to the living room lounge, you'll discover still another area where the Cobblestone shines. The ☞ lavish breakfast buffet is beautifully presented and is the essence of fresh California eating. There are fresh juices and colorful platters of fresh fruit, homemade hot muffins and breads, a daily-changing hot baked egg dish, homemade granola, yogurt, cider, hot chocolate, teas, and coffee.

From 5:00 to 7:00 P.M. guests are invited to gather by the big stone fireplace and enjoy complimentary tea, sherry, wine, and a variety of hors d'oeuvres. The tempting platters of fine cheeses alone make it mandatory that you *walk* to dinner. Dan is happy to make dinner suggestions and reservations for you. When you return, your bed will be turned down, and a fresh rose and a piece of candy will be on the pillow.

Given this kind of comfort and attention, it's not surprising that a weekend reservation is needed almost three months in advance. Weekdays and winter are easier.

How to get there: Exit State Highway 1 on Ocean Avenue. Proceed down Ocean to Junipero; turn left. The inn is two blocks farther on the right, at the corner of 8th Street.

Olive Metcalf

The Happy Landing
Carmel-by-the-Sea, California
93921

Innkeepers: Dick Stewart, Bob Alberson, Janet and Ken Weston
Address / Telephone: Monte Verde Street between 5th and 6th
    (mailing address: Box 2619); (408) 624–7917.
Rooms: 9, all with private bath, including 2 suites; 3 have fireplaces;
    1 nonsmoking room.
Rates: $60 to $105; children over 12 welcome. Small pets accommo-
    dated by prior arrangement.
Open: All year.
Facilities and Local Attractions: Wedding facilities. Short walk to
    Carmel Beach, unique shops, art galleries, restaurants.

    I'm not the first to describe the architecture of this inn
as pink Hansel and Gretel. It has a picturesque, fairy tale
cottage-in-the-woods look, and Carmel is exactly the right
setting. To be perfectly accurate, however, it's really not a
cottage, but rather a cluster of accommodations all connected by rambling flagstone paths.
    Each room opens onto a ☛ colorful central courtyard
with a gazebo and a small pond. As I arrived, a young couple
were making arrangements to have their wedding there. The
poor kids didn't realize that a veteran mother-of-the-bride

was standing right there ready to approve their choice . . . if only they'd asked. This was late November, but the abundant plants, flowers, and bright hanging baskets of fuchsias were dazzling. Ah, California.

The rooms are delightfully decorated with antiques and a romantic flair. Their steep roofs are especially inviting. The high cathedral ceilings make even the smallest room seem light and open. A TV and a decanter of sherry in every room are pleasant to come back to after a day of shopping at Carmel's unusual stores or walking the beach.

A warm, attractive common room is also available for guests to use. You might enjoy afternoon coffee or a steaming cup of English tea here by the fireplace.

Breakfast is delivered to guest rooms on silver trays, but given the pleasant courtyard, many people elect to take theirs outside. Janets says a hot, baked item is always fresh every morning in addition to juice and fresh fruit. This fall day it was warm gingerbread with a lemon sauce.

The four innkeepers are professionals, but better still, they have the ☛ knack of making each guest feel special and comfortable. You can't beat the personal touch.

How to get there: From State Highway 1 at Carmel, turn off at Ocean Avenue. Continue to center of town; turn right at Monte Verde Street. Inn is two blocks on the right.

Mission Ranch
Carmel-by-the-Sea, California
93923

Innkeeper: Ole Christensen
Address / Telephone: 26270 Dolores; (408) 624–6436.
Rooms: 6 in The Farmhouse, all with private bath; a variety of other accommodations available, including cottages, The Bunkhouse (sleeps 3 couples or a family), and motel units.
Rates: $55 to $67.25 for The Farmhouse, including generous continental breakfast; $74.25 to $80 for cottages, without breakfast (prices include tax). The Bunkhouse, with kitchen, $80; motel units $40 to $50 (tax not included) without breakfast. Children welcome.
Open: All year. Restaurant (dinners only), piano bar, cocktail lounge.
Facilities and Local Attractions: Nature trails; eight tennis courts, tennis clinics offered. Safe swimming at Carmel River Beach; short walk to beach, Carmel Mission. Drive to Point Lobos, Big Sur. Party Barn available for parties, dancing.

A friend waxing nostalgic about his college days (thirty-five years ago) remembered when he and his friends would drive down to Carmel from San Francisco to dine and dance at the Mission Ranch. It's downright reassuring to see that places which gave us happy memories are still around and looking good.

The Mission Ranch is charming a new generation with its historic buildings, ☛ hundred-year-old cypresses, and its outlook on the rugged beauty of Point Lobos. The restaurant still serves hearty dinners, and the ☛ piano bar—how's *that* for nostalgia?—still gives repressed saloon singers an atmosphere for crooning.

One change at the Ranch is that the family homestead is now a bed and breakfast inn. The Farmhouse, built a century ago, was home to the Martins, a family of Scottish immigrants who came to California in 1856 and bought large acreage encircling an old Spanish mission.

The two-story, white frame house, sitting under several enormous cypress trees, is now sound-proofed and newly decorated in a homey, not high-fashion style. The large rooms are furnished very simply with odd pieces from the 1920s and 1930s. Bathrooms are large too, with showers added, and complimentary toiletries.

A spacious parlor has Victorian sofas flanking a wood-burning fireplace, and a TV and telephone are in the room. A long buffet is where a generous continental breakfast is set up in the morning: fruit, juices, breads, cold cereals, coffee, and teas.

This is an atmosphere different from the usual Carmel lodgings—an authentic ranch, not a manicured resort. And it's a mere few blocks from the chichi streets of art galleries and stylish shops . . . twenty acres to roam and enjoy, with long vistas of fields and water. Bring the children.

How to get there: At Carmel, exit State Highway 1 on Rio Road west, toward the ocean. Immediately past the mission, turn left on Lasuen Drive; follow around to the Ranch on your left.

J: The ☛ mission just up the road is officially "San Carlos Borromeo de Carmelo," a romantic gem in the mission chain, with a Moorish tower and tranquil gardens. It's the resting place of Father Junipero Serra, who founded nine missions and died there in 1784.

Olive Metcalf

Normandy Inn
Carmel-by-the-Sea, California
93921

Innkeeper: Ann Hansen
Address / Telephone: Ocean Avenue (mailing address: Box 1706);
(408) 624–3825.
Rooms: 45, all with private bath; some with kitchens and fireplaces;
suites and cottages accommodating 2 to 8 persons.
Rates: $64 single to $135 for 3-bedroom cottage; includes continental breakfast. No credit cards; no pets.
Open: All year.
Facilities and Local Attractions: Heated swimming pool. Heart of Carmel location; walk to beach, shops, restaurants, art galleries.

The Normandy Inn is a French Provincial complex of white stucco and dark-timbered buildings right on Ocean Avenue. This is the main street of Carmel and proceeds from the inn straight down to the beach to the spot that's so frequently photographed.

The inn was built in 1937 by architect Robert Stanton, but units have been added through the years. Virginia Stanton, a former party editor of *House Beautiful,* was involved with the design and décor. The newer accommodations have large picture windows and more luxurious appointments, like extra-long beds and Wamsutta linens. But you may, like me, find the older ones more charming. Many have corner fireplaces decorated with painted tiles, multi-paned windows, and cozy shuttered alcoves.

There is such a range of accommodations here, you should be able to reserve precisely the facilities you want—a fireplace, a TV, kitchen, a separate living room, or a cottage with a private patio.

The units are clustered around beautiful gardens banked high with flowers. Pots of brilliant blooms and hanging baskets are everywhere, and a winding flagstone path (a necessary ingredient for romantic gardens) takes you through the area. Some rooms open to the kidney-shaped swimming pool.

Your complimentary breakfast is served in a cheerful country dining room. Mrs. Stanton's collection of Quimper plates from France and large flower arrangements add color and interest. The morning newspapers will be there as you help yourself from the buffet of juices, fresh fruits, coffee, teas, and hot muffins or breads.

How to get there: Exit Highway 1 on Ocean Avenue. Proceed to the center of Carmel; inn is on your left.

J: *Winter visitors to Carmel have some distinct advantages. Not the least of them is that on winter weekdays, you can often find appealing lodgings on the spur of the moment. Advance reservations still needed for weekends.*

Olive Metcalf

The Sandpiper Inn
Carmel-by-the-Sea, California
93923

Innkeepers: Irene and Graeme Mackenzie
Address / Telephone: 2408 Bay View Avenue; (408) 624–6433.
Rooms: 15, all with private bath; 2 cottages.
Rates: $70 to $105, double occupancy; 2-day minimum on weekends. Includes continental breakfast, afternoon sherry.
Open: All year.
Facilities and Local Attractions: Ten-speed bicycles for rent, in-house library, color TV in lounge. Golf, tennis club privileges by arrangement. Perfect location for walking Carmel Beach.

"We're different from those B&Bs," Graeme Mackenzie says emphatically. "No miniature rooms here; no cold croissant and call it breakfast; no rules and regulations saying you must do this or you can't do that. *We're an inn!*"

The declaration is delivered in an unreconstructed Scottish burr, and with a smile, but the message is clear: ☞ The Mackenzies are professional innkeepers, and not to be confused with those other birds. Graeme has a wealth of experience in Europe, Hong Kong, Bermuda, and Dallas, where he became president of a hotel company.

Mackenzie's blue eyes are scornful as he relates the unbelievable behavior of some hosts who call themselves inn-keepers. "Why, I know of one place that demands you take off your shoes in the house! Is that any way to treat a guest?"

Since returning to the Monterey Peninsula in 1975 and acquiring The Sandpiper Inn, Graeme and Irene have remodeled and redecorated the fifteen guest rooms and cottages. Now they all have private baths, queen- and king-size beds (Graeme recalls his unhappy encounters with small beds in other inns), and quilted bedspreads. They're furnished with country English and French antiques, and he's particularly proud of some recently acquired antique headboards. Freshly picked nosegays add to an impeccable, tranquil atmosphere, with no TV or telephone to intrude.

Some rooms have wood-burning fireplaces, and others are situated to take full advantage of the inn's ☞ sweeping views across Carmel Bay and out to the Pacific. The house is set only 70 yards from the beach in a quiet, private neighborhood. Just a quirk of luck—it was an inn before the strict zoning laws went into effect—accounts for its being there. The result is that ☞ you feel like a house guest at someone's exclusive seaside home.

That's precisely the mood Irene and Graeme promote. They invite you to help yourself to glasses, ice, coffee or tea in the kitchen; ride one of their ten-speed bikes down the cypress-dotted streets along Carmel's beach; enjoy the warm English-feeling library, or relax by the fireside in the gracious living room ("lounge," to the Mackenzies) with sherry at 5:00 P.M.

How to get there: Take Ocean Avenue through Carmel to Scenic Avenue; turn left and proceed along the beach to the end. Just past the stop sign in the middle of the road, turn left at Martin. Inn is one block on the right at the corner of Bay View.

J: *The Scottish motto hanging above the door reads* Ceund Mile Failte—*"A Hundred Thousand Welcomes."*

Olive Metcalf

The Stonehouse Inn
Carmel-by-the-Sea, California
93921

Innkeeper: Virginia Carey
Address / Telephone: Eighth below Monte Verde (mailing address: Box 2517); (408) 624–4569.
Rooms: 6, sharing three baths.
Rates: $75 to $100. No credit cards. No smoking.
Open: All year.
Facilities and Local Attractions: Walk to Carmel Beach. Unique shops and art galleries two blocks away. Explore Point Lobos State Park two miles south. Seventeen Mile Drive at Pebble Beach.

Writers have always been attracted to the Monterey Peninsula. It's an atmosphere that seems conducive to creativity—dramatic surfs, the misty cool weather, towering pines and evergreen oaks, and the famous Monterey cypresses with their twisted, gnarled shapes. It's inspiring even if you're only writing post cards.

The original owner of The Stonehouse, Mrs. "Nana" Foster, often invited notable artists and writers to stay in her Carmel home. Sinclair Lewis, Jack London, Lotta Crabtree, and George Stewart were among her guests. It seems to still reflect the old, quieter Carmel, when it first became an artist colony.

This is just the kind of sprawling, old-fashioned vacation house many of us would choose—if a staff came with it. It's large and luxurious, with a completely stone exterior, hand-shaped by local Indians when it was built in 1906. It's surrounded by wonderful gardens and a big, broad, partially glassed-in front porch, with pots of flowers and comfortable chairs and sofas.

There's a warm, colorful living room with a large stone fireplace. Fine furniture and white wicker with bright cushions are all put together so tastefully with vivid rugs, plants, flowers, books, and *things,* you tend to think it just happened. On consideration, you realize it's been done artfully, that it's invitingly clean and fresh, and that innkeeper Virginia Carey is a pro.

Two bedrooms on the main floor and four upstairs have board and batten walls painted white that are typical of early Carmel houses. They're beautifully decorated in soft colors (peach, ivory, mossy green, pale blue), with quilts and antiques. Each room is reminiscent of the artist or writer for whom it was named. The Jack London has dramatic, gabled ceilings, a bed and a day bed set in brass, with a ceiling fan and a glorious ocean view. The Lola Montez has a four-poster bed, a gabled ceiling, and a view of the garden.

You eat well here, too. Breakfast is the only meal served, but it's a full and proper one. There are always several juices, at least two fresh fruits, at least two homemade breads or muffins, and homemade granola. Then Virginia serves a hot entrée that changes daily, and plenty of fresh coffee and tea.

How to get there: Exit State Highway 1 on Ocean Avenue; continue into town to Monte Verde. Turn left two blocks to 8th Street; turn right. The inn is in the center of the block.

☀

J: *When you gather around the fireplace for wine and hors d'oeuvres, you're likely to meet people who have been returning to The Stonehouse for years.*

olive Metcalf

Vagabond House Inn
Carmel-by-the-Sea, California
93921

Innkeeper: Bruce Indorato
Address / Telephone: Fourth and Dolores (mailing address: Box 2747); (408) 624–7738.
Rooms: 10, all with private bath; most have fireplace, kitchen, or small refrigerator. TV; no telephones.
Rates: $65 to $105; lower winter rates.
Open: All year.
Facilities and Local Attractions: Walk to Carmel shops, art galleries, restaurants, beach. Short drives to Pebble Beach golf courses, Big Sur, Point Lobos.

It's hard to believe that this romantic inn ever had a military connection, but it did. It was built during World War II to provide lodging when nearby Fort Ord was bursting at the seams.

A more poetic part of its history is that the poet Don Blanding lived here in the '40s, but no one seems to know if the house was named for his poem *Vagabond House*, or if he named his poem for the house.

The shake-roofed, oak-shaded Vagabond has heart-robbing qualities that have won it a loyal following through the years. One of its steadiest fans was a seventeen-year-old who began working here as a gardener and has remained to become the innkeeper—Bruce Indorato.

The Vagabond's brick, half-timbered look is English Tudor, perfectly appropriate for the picture-book village of Carmel. A ☞ flagstone courtyard dominated by old and very large oak trees is the focal point for each of the rooms. It's a lush scene of camellias, rhododendrons, hanging plants, ferns, and flowers.

The bright, airy, and ☞ especially spacious rooms are constructed of knotty pine, brick, and barn board. Decorating themes range from nautical to early American to Victorian. Each room is supplied with its own coffeepot, freshly ground coffee, and a decanter of cream sherry.

Continental breakfast is served buffet style in the large common room off the patio. It's most pleasant to fix a tray from the selection of juices, fruits, muffins and rolls, boiled eggs, and cheeses, and then take the newspaper and repair to the courtyard. What better place to plan a day than under a hanging pot of brilliant fuchsias?

The management here at Vagabond House also owns ☞ Lincoln Green, a cluster of four spacious English country-style cottages. They're in a quiet, residential neighborhood near the ocean and the Carmel River. Each beautifully decorated unit has a living room with fireplace, separate bedroom, and kitchen. There is no food service here, but guests are invited to come up to Vagabond House for breakfast, if they wish.

How to get there: From State Highway 1, take Ocean Avenue turn-off to downtown Carmel. At Dolores Street, turn right to 4th Street. The inn is on the right.

olive Metcalf

New Davenport
Bed and Breakfast Inn
Davenport, California
95017

Innkeepers: Marcia and Bruce McDougal
Address / Telephone: 31 Davenport Avenue; (408) 425–1818 or
  426–4122.
Rooms: 12, all with private bath.
Rates: $50 to $85, single or double occupancy, with $10 charge for
  each additional guest. Continental breakfast with champagne
  included. Children over 12 welcome, but pets not allowed. No
  smoking.
Open: All year. Lunch and dinner.
Facilities and Local Attractions: Folk art, textiles, pottery, other
  crafts in the Cash Store. Beach walking, whale watching; near
  state parks, Santa Cruz, University of California campus. Cabrillo Music Festival each summer.

You can talk to native Californians who have never
heard of Davenport—and that's just fine with most of the citizens of this town. But there it is, halfway between San Francisco and Carmel, smack dab on one of the most spectacular
coastlines anywhere.

The McDougals saw it as the perfect site for their pottery gallery (Bruce once taught pottery) and decided to build a new Davenport Cash Store. The original Cash Store occupied the same corner for many years during the first half of the century when Davenport was a thriving town with a cement plant, hotels, and businesses. When Marcia and Bruce rebuilt, they added delightful accommodations and a restaurant.

The Cash Store is a gathering place for local artisans. It sells their ☛ wares in pottery, textiles, wood, and glass. The original jewelry, especially, took my eye.

Some of these arts and crafts articles also decorate the eight bedrooms above the store. Each one has a cheerful mixture of antiques, ethnic treasures, and local arts. The pleasant rooms all open onto the balcony that wraps around the building.

Beside the Cash Store is the oldest remaining original building in Davenport. The McDougals have renovated it to provide a warm sitting room and four bedrooms. These rooms are smaller than the new ones over the store, but they're fresh and pretty, with quilts and an old-fashioned appeal. The ☛ quiet garden patio here is another attraction. In the sitting room are books, a comfortable sofa and chairs, coffee makings, and an ocean view. Breakfast for all guests is served here, including ☛ champagne, fresh juice, coffee, teas, and homemade pastry.

In the restaurant your eyes go from one interesting display to another: costumes from Yugoslavia, Mexican rugs, African masks, and handcrafts from around the world. The menu seems to offer as wide a variety of dishes as the décor is varied—and the bakery is outstanding. My luncheon choice of shredded, cooked chicken on a fresh tortilla topped with spicy salsa, cilantro, avocado, and lettuce was a winner.

After lunch, walk across the highway and down a short path to savor the discovery of ☛ a secluded stretch of sandy beach. It could be awfully pleasant to take a blanket and a book, maybe some provisions from the restaurant, and spend a few hours here listening to the surf.

How to get there: On California Highway 1, nine miles north of Santa Cruz.

Clive Metcalf

San Benito House
Half Moon Bay, California
94019

Innkeeper: Carol Mickelsen
Address / Telephone: 356 Main Street; (415) 726–3425.
Rooms: 12; 9 with private bath, 3 share divided bath.
Rates: $49 to $108, including continental breakfast. Guests receive
    10% off in restaurant.
Open: All year. Lunch, dinner, Sunday buffet; full bar.
Facilities and Local Attractions: Sun deck, sauna, croquet. Com-
    plete conference facilities. Thirty minutes from San Francisco
    airport and Silicon Valley.

Here is a refreshing coastal wonder—an inn that takes
dead aim on European-style flavor and delivers it minus the
pretensions or obscene prices that often are part of the story.
(Simple country charm doesn't come cheap, you know.)
Carol Mickelsen is the owner and inspiration behind trans-
forming the old Mosconi Hotel into a hostelry in the European tradition. And she offers travelers more than
picturesque ambience.
☛ Food—gloriously innovative, fresh, and colorful—is
her forte. She has seriously studied cooking and trained with
famed French chefs Jacques Pépin and Roger Verge at

Cannes. Now she has promoted herself out of the kitchen most of the time, but directs four female chefs through the no-short-cuts facets of California cuisine, classic country French, and Northern Italian. On the October day I stopped, they were preparing fresh ravioli with an unusual spicy pumpkin filling for lunch.

Meat and fish are impeccably fresh and often grilled on mesquite. And the vegetables are something to write home about. Most of them come from Carol's large garden: delicate lettuce, green beans, baby carrots, and fresh herbs. Two memorable cakes are among an array of dessert specialties: a lemon almond, and a dense chocolate called Queen of California.

Dinners are served in a dining room with brass chandeliers, blue cotton tablecloths, bright peach napkins, and a profusion of fresh bouquets. All around is an ☛ exceptional collection of original paintings by early 1900s coastal artists, particularly Galen Wolf and Greer Morton.

French doors lead onto a large ☛ redwood deck overlooking the English Garden. Here's the place to have lunch on a summer day, or to gather around the massive fire pit at night when the fire is lit to sip cognac and stargaze.

The stairway to the upstairs begins at an elaborate mirrored hallpiece and continues under an ornate cornice. Carol found many of the decorative accessories on trips to Europe. The stained-glass partitions she bought are a unique touch in the bathrooms.

Bedrooms on the garden side are the most elaborately decorated with antique light fixtures, brass beds, and walls painted in vivid colors, some with stenciled details. It's pleasant having coffee makings up here, and a small deck off the end of the hallway.

How to get there: From San Francisco, take Highway 280 south to Half Moon Bay. Turn west at Highway 92 to Main Street; turn left. Inn is on the right at the corner of Mill Street. From the south, Highway I passes through Half Moon Bay.

The Jabberwock
Monterey, California
93940

Innkeepers: Jim and Barbara Allen
Address / Telephone: 598 Laine Street; (408) 372–4777.
Rooms: 7; 3 with private bath, 4 sharing 2 baths.
Rates: $75 to $135, including full breakfast and evening aperitifs
and hors d'oeuvres. No credit cards. No children; no pets.
Open: All year.
Facilities and Local Attractions: Airport pickups by arrangement.
Walk to Cannery Row, Monterey Bay Aquarium, restaurants.
Short drive to Carmel, Pebble Beach.

Have you ever breakfasted on Snarkleberry Flump-tious? How about Burndt Flambjous? You'll recognize the inspiration of ☞ Lewis Carroll nonsense as the theme of The Jabberwock, with originally named breakfast dishes, décor, and room names. There's also a Burbling Room (a telephone nook), and The Tum Tum Tree (a refrigerator stocked with complimentary soft drinks).

Now I'm the first to admit that a little whimsy oozes like chocolate on a hot day—and can be just as sticky, but the innkeepers use this bit of fancy with a winning sense of fun. It seems only to enhance the charm of a well-run, solidly comfortable inn. As a kid, Jim Allen loved the poem "Jabber-wocky" from *Through the Looking Glass* (he says it was the only one he ever learned), and he and Barbara thought it was the perfect name for their inn.

The towered and turreted 1911 house sits on a hill in a neighborhood four blocks above Cannery Row. A glassed-in veranda wraps around two sides of the building and over-looks their ☛ colorful English garden and beyond to Monterey Bay. A chalkboard on the wall lists each room name, and beside it, the first names of the occupants. Barbara says she wants everyone to be on a first-name basis when a five o'clock bell summons guests to the veranda for aperitifs and hors d'oeuvres.

Every room is engagingly decorated with elegant antique beds, beautiful linens, and down pillows and comforters. Robes and every toiletry you might have forgotten are thoughtfully provided. The third floor has an arrangement two couples will enjoy—two bedrooms, The Mimsy and The Wabe, share a bath and a private sitting room that has views all the way to Santa Cruz.

When you breakfast by the fireside in the dining room, the name of the day's special dish is etched in reverse on a glass sign. You have to hold it up to a mirror to read it. Notice the clock on the mantle, too. It's backwards!

Steady yourself, and have a brillig day. Retire with one of the house volumes of Lewis Carroll, and the homemade cookies and milk Barbara sets out.

How to get there: Exit State Highway 1 at Munras Avenue. Take an immediate left at Soledad Drive; then turn right at Pacific Street. Continue as name changes to Lighthouse. Turn left at Hoffman; proceed two blocks to Laine Street. Inn is on the left corner, number 598.

☒

J: ☛ *The Allens will prepurchase your Aquarium tickets so you can go when you please and not stand in line.*

Olive Metcalf

Old Monterey Inn
Monterey, California
93940

Innkeepers: Ann and Gene Swett
Address / Telephone: 500 Martin Avenue; (408) 375–8284.
Rooms: 10, all with private bath; most have fireplaces.
Rates: $110 to $165, generous continental breakfast included. No
    credit cards. No children; no pets; no cigars.
Open: All year.
Facilities and Local Attractions: Short walk to historic district of
    Monterey, Fisherman's Wharf, shops, restaurants. Short
    drives to Carmel, Pebble Beach, Point Lobos State Reserve, Big
    Sur coastline.

    Let's discuss lodgings for particular people. Does the
word *rustic* give you a headache? When the phrase "Victorian charm" is mentioned, do you have an acute attack of
nausea? Do you feel that anything built after World War II is
faintly tacky? Have I got an inn for you!
    The Old Monterey Inn is an elegant architectural gem
built in 1929 and until recently has always been a private residence. It's a half-timbered, Tudor-style house sitting on an
oak-studded hillside in a quiet residential neighborhood.
More than ☞ an acre of astonishingly beautiful gardens sur-

round it and give each room a view of begonias, fuchsias, hydrangeas, and wooded banks of ferns and rhododendrons.

Ann and Gene Swett are the proprietors of this paradise, the family home where they raised their six children. Their hospitality and these beautifully appointed rooms are all the most discriminating guest could want. Choose any room and you can't go wrong, but The Library *did* capture my heart. It's walls are book-lined, and there's a stone fireplace and a private sun deck overlooking the garden.

Seven of the ten rooms have wood-burning fireplaces. All of them have luxuries like goosedown comforters, the gleaming wood of period furniture, family antiques, and bathroom items you might have forgotten. Other personal touches include a refrigerator stocked with complimentary juices and soft drinks, and the loan of ☛ an outfitted picnic basket for a day's outing. The Swetts include a list of the best delis, the most interesting picnic sites, and directions for getting there.

Another fireplace is in the elegant step-down dining room where breakfast is served. You can have breakfast sent to your room, but it's awfully grand to sit around the long oak table with your hosts and meet the other lucky people who are here. Fresh fruit compotes and the inn's special popovers and homemade jams are featured.

In the evening, a fire burns in the living room and the Swetts join their guests for wine and cheese. It's another lovely room, with Oriental rugs and fine furniture. The ultimate standard of good taste runs throughout the house, that of ☛ comfort and quality, without pretention.

How to get there: Take Munras Avenue exit from Highway 1; make an immediate left on Soledad Drive, then right on Pacific. Continue 6/10 of a mile to Martin Street on the left. Inn is on your right at number 500.

☒

J: *If checking into an inn is buying a bit of magic for your life, get ready to be enchanted.*

Olive Metcalf

The Centrella
Pacific Grove, California
93950

Innkeeper: Dr. Joseph Megna
Address / Telephone: 612 Central Avenue (mailing address: Box 884); (408) 372–3372.
Rooms: 20, including suites and cottages for 2 and 4. Private bath in all but 2.
Rates: $65 to $175, including continental breakfast, wine and hors d'ouevres. No pets; children under 12 in cottages only. Handicap accessible room. Two-night minimum on weekends.
Open: All year.
Facilities and Local Attractions: Bay side walking-bicycle path. Walk to Cannery Row, Monterey Bay Acquarium. Nearby 17-mile drive, Carmel, restaurants, shops.

Time your journey down Highway 1 to arrive at The Centrella in time for the social hour, 5:30 to 6:30 P.M. Its inviting living/dining area offers just what a weary traveler needs: decanters of wine and sherry and a ☞ substantial cocktail buffet: rye bread sliced thin, pâté, cheese spreads, hard cheese, crackers, guacamole and tortilla chips, marinated artichoke hearts, and dieter's delight—crudités.

It's difficult, but use some moderation at this repast, or

you'll tend to tune out the good information that Dr. Megna and his staff have about the excellent choice of restaurants you can walk to in the area or that are just a short drive away. It's tempting to just relax by the fire in this pleasant room and read. There are books and magazines about, good reading lights, even an in-progress stitchery project set up with an invitation to contribute a few stitches.

Unlike so many inns of this vintage, The Centrella was never a private home. Built in 1889, it was described by the Monterey newspaper as "The largest, most commodious and pleasantly located private boarding house in 'The Grove.'" It's now listed in the *National Register of Historic Places* and has survived restoration beautifully, earning several design awards.

Guest rooms are decorated and appointed for comfort, but old touches remain. I liked the big claw-footed bathtub, the high ceilings, and the quilt in my room. But the good firm bed, a telephone, and an ice machine down the hall were appreciated, too.

 Cottages in the back garden are a good arrangement for family vacations. One that sleeps four has an attractive sitting area, fireplace, TV, small refrigerator, and wet bar.

Breakfast in the dining room is an easy introduction to a day of touring. A morning paper is at the door of your room, and the continental breakfast buffet has all you require. A friendly staff going in and out of the adjoining kitchen might even pop your Danish into the oven for a few minutes, if you ask.

How to get there: From Highway 1, take Del Monte/Pacific Grove exit. Continue on as street name changes to Lighthouse, then to Central. Inn is on the right.

J: *I had an early-morning walk along the Bay Shore—just me, the scuba divers, and the seals.*

Olive Metcalf

The Gosby House
Pacific Grove, California
93950

Innkeeper: Sarah Long
Address / Telephone: 643 Lighthouse Avenue; (408) 375–1287.
Rooms: 23, 2 sharing a bath; 16 in main house, 7 with private entrances.
Rates: $70 to $105, full breakfast, afternoon wines and hors d'oeuvres included. Smoking and children in newer rooms only.
Open: All year.
Facilities and Local Attractions: Bicycling and walking paths along shoreline; Victorian architecture in Pacific Grove; watch seals, otters, and migrating whales. Close to golfing, tennis; deep-sea sport fishing, charter boats, tours available.

The Gosby House is a  showcase Victorian, vintage 1887, the kind you turn around to look at again as you drive by. Though it was built as a private residence, it's not a newcomer to the proliferation of elegant inns in this area. It's been providing accommodations to Monterey Peninsula visitors for nearly one hundred years.

The inn's current brochure includes the Oscar Wilde quotation, "I have the simplest of taste. I am satisfied with only the best." Oscar would not be disappointed were he to magically check into Gosby House. He'd be captivated right at the front door with the brimming pots of bright flowers clustered on the steps, and with the ☛ rich, colorful interior. And he'd appreciate the quiet, private places to relax throughout the house and along the brick garden paths.

You've seen dark, serious Victoriana? This is cheerful, ☛ playful Victoriana. (One does hope Herself would have been amused.) In the elegant parlor are polished woods, fine antiques, and comfortable English and French furniture around the fireplace. There's also a carrousel horse, old teddy bears, a set of *Winnie the Pooh* volumes in the bookcase, and a grand glass-door cabinet filled with antique dolls. Guests gather here for afternoon tea or sherry, fresh fruits, and hors d'oeuvres.

In the handsome dining room, a large buffet is covered in the morning with an array of fresh fruits, cereals, hot breads, a hot dish like a frittata or quiche, and granola and yogurt—for yogurt parfaits.

The charm doesn't fall off when you go upstairs. Bedrooms are a special delight in a house of this style. With turrets and dormers you get window seats to be decorated with fat cushions in bright prints, and cozy slanted ceilings with delicately colored wallpapers. Fluffy comforters, good reading lights, and a handwritten card welcoming you by name are nice touches.

Oscar surely would have appreciated the teddy bear waiting on the bed.

How to get there: From San Francisco, take Highway 1 south past Monterey; exit at Highway 68 west to Pacific Grove. In town, follow Forest Avenue to Lighthouse Avenue; turn left, and go three blocks to the inn.

J: *A wistful comment written by one guest in the register reads: "I wish home was just like this!"*

Olive Metcalf

The Green Gables Inn
Pacific Grove, California
93950

Innkeeper: Linda Kravel
Address / Telephone: 104 Fifth Street; (408) 375–2095.
Rooms: 10; 6 with private bath, 4 sharing 2 full baths; includes 1
    suite and separate Carriage House accommodations.
Rates: $75 to $130, breakfast included.
Open: All year.
Facilities and Local Attractions: Shoreline paths for bicycling and
    jogging; public beach, scuba diving, simming, picnicking;
    short walk to Cannery Row, Monterey Bay Aquarium; close to
    golf and tennis.

Green Gables is a romantic gem of a Queen Anne–style
mansion with a fairy-tale look about it, half-timbered and gabled, sitting above the shoreline of Monterey Bay.

Looking at the dormers and peaks of the roof line, you
just know that the ☞ upstairs ceilings will be entertaining—and they are. One cozy accommodation tucked under
the eaves is The Garret Room, an enchanting hideaway with
dark beams against bright-flowered wallpaper. The Chapel
Room is larger, also with a steep slanting ceiling, and tiny
diamond-paned windows. The Gable Room, once a children's

84

playroom, has a sitting area, a loft, and superb views. Adjoining the Balcony Room is a glassed-in porch fitted with tall camp chairs to enjoy the Bay view.

In the adjacent Carriage House accommodations, every room has a fireplace and bath, but the most romantic rooms are those in the main house. A suite off the living room is quite grand, with a fireplace, sitting room, and a large private bath. All the rooms are furnished with antique pieces, and beautiful fabrics cover the quilts and pillows. Fresh flowers and fruit, those gracious extras, are in every room.

The large living room and dining room are elegant, yet completely inviting. An ornate ceiling with delicate plaster designs painted in blue and apricot is impressive. Low tables and chairs are in bay-window alcoves facing the bay. ☛ A unique fireplace framed by stained-glass panels is flanked on either side with matching, dark blue sofas. Flowered draperies are at the tall windows, polished wood gleams, and ☛ tasteful accessories are everywhere. You'll feel terribly civilized having a nip of sherry and an hors d'oeuvre here in the afternoon.

Linda and the staff serve breakfast in a style appropriate to the surroundings—sitting down in the dining room. Juices and a wide offering of fresh fruits are followed by muffins, cereals, granola, and a substantial hot dish, perhaps a frittata or quiche.

How to get there: From San Francisco, take Highway 1 past Monterey and exit at Highway 68 west to Pacific Grove. Once in town, continue on Forest Avenue to the beach. Turn right on Ocean View to Fifth Street.

J: *Green Gables proves you can have Victorian charm, without a trace of cloying quaintness.*

Olive Metcalf

The House of
Seven Gables Inn
Pacific Grove, California
93950

Innkeepers: The Flatley Family (Susan, John, Nora, Ed, and Fred)
Address / Telephone: 555 Ocean View Boulevard; (408) 372–4341.
Rooms: 14, all with private bath.
Rates: $85 to $125, with generous continental breakfast included.
    Two-day minimum on weekends. Children over 12 welcome.
    No pets; no smoking.
Open: All year.
Facilities and Local Attractions: Four patios for sunning; shoreline
    paths for bicycling, walking; short walk to Cannery Row,
    beaches. Close to all attractions of Monterey Peninsula.

It was surprising to walk into this big, showy Victorian and find, not the Victoriana I expected, but an ☞ extraordinary collection of French antiques. The Flatley family has collected so much that visitors who have been coming to the inn for years still find things they hadn't noticed before.

Guests here can enjoy the best of both times. While the house and the antique collection are old, the quality of the linens, bedding, and the plumbing is fresh and new. This is an especially well-maintained inn.

The house was completed in 1886 and still has the same unobstructed view of Monterey Bay it had then. At the end of the century, Lucie Chase, a well-to-do widow and civic leader, added sun porches and gables, giving the house its amazing configuration.

Every room has excellent beds, good reading lights, a private bath, and elegant appointments. Most have beautiful views and a sitting area. Some of the newer bungalows behind the house are every bit as grand. No rustic country style here.

This is a fine house for relaxing, and the Flatleys think of every comfort. Tea is served in the afternoon on the sun porch or outdoors on the patio. There's always something homemade—shortbread, mini-muffins, and often Nora's homemade fudge. A TV is on the sun porch, and an antique (working) telephone booth is in the hallway. Chilled champagne is kept on hand, just in case there's a sudden need.

Breakfast is an elegant sit-down affair. Beautiful blue-and-white china is used on white linen at the dining room table. Silver platters of every available fresh fruit are always served along with fine teas and coffee, and a variety of homemade breads and cakes, or Nora's apple cobbler.

How to get there: From San Francisco, take Highway 1 to Pacific Grove–Del Monte exit. Follow Del Monte as it becomes Lighthouse, into Pacific Grove. Go right one block to Ocean View Boulevard; then turn left to Fountain Avenue and the inn.

J: *With a name like The House of Seven Gables, I felt there must surely be a Hawthorne Room—and there is—but the theme isn't labored. In all those nooks and crannies, alcoves and bays, I couldn't possibly have avoided naming at least a little closet "Hester," or perhaps putting a simple scarlet "A" on a door.*

Olive Metcalf

The Martine Inn
Pacific Grove, California
93950

Innkeepers: Marion and Don Martine
Address / Telephone: 255 Ocean View Boulevard; (408) 373–3388.
Rooms: 19, each with private bath.
Rates: $85 to $165, breakfast included. No children under 16;
    smoking only in rooms with fireplace.
Open: All year.
Facilities and Local Attractions: Conference facilities. Ocean-front
    views, paths for bicycling, walking; short walk to Cannery Row,
    California Repertory Theatre, Monterey Bay Aquarium, restau-
    rants; close to tennis, golf.

Don't lose heart when you pull into the parking area of
this big pink palace and see how far above you the house is.
As befitting a palace, you merely step to the handy house telephone, tell them you've arrived, and help will come.

The mansion looms ☞ high on the cliffs of Oceanview
Boulevard overlooking the shore of Monterey Bay. It was
built in 1899 and purchased by the Parke-Davis Pharmaceu-
ticals family. Looking at the distinctly Mediterranean style it
is today, it's hard to imagine that it was originally a true Victorian with cupola and dormers, all changed over the years.

Mr. Parke was especially fond of exotic woods and employed one craftsman to create ☞ Siamese teak gates, Honduras mahogany trim in the living and dining rooms, and a Spanish cedar staircase.

A huge parlor with one wall of windows looking to the ocean is the setting for afternoon wine and hors d'oeuvres, as well as for an extravagant breakfast. Lace-covered tables by the windows are set with juices and fruit. Then guests help themselves from a buffet in the formal dining room. The Martines' special collection of ☞ Old Sheffield and Victorian silver is used to display and serve the rest of the menu, perhaps omelets, pancakes, or eggs Benedict.

As you might suppose in a house this large, the bedrooms are spacious, almost regal. Many have a fireplace, and all are furnished in Victorian style with authentic antiques. Telephones are available on request. A pleasant sitting room is also upstairs with a spectacular ocean view.

A courtyard, protected by the carriage house and a 14-foot wall, is at the back of the house. With a pond and an elaborate Oriental fountain, the courtyard makes a lovely setting for a wedding. The Martines chose it for their wedding.

One of the joys of staying in a grand house is all the special places in it to enjoy. Besides upstairs and downstairs sitting rooms, there's also a spa, a game room, and a marvelous library. It looks just the way a Victorian library ought to look—beautiful wood paneling, shelves of books and magazines, a fireplace, Oriental rugs, and oversized dark furniture.

How to get there: From Highway 1, exit on Highway 68 west to Pacific Grove. Once in town, continue on Forest Avenue to the beach. Turn right and continue to inn on the right, between 5th and 3rd streets.

Olive Metcalf

The Old St. Angela Inn
Pacific Grove, California
93950

Innkeeper: Alan Forrest, with Carmen, Rachel, and Donna
Address / Telephone: 321 Central Avenue; (408) 372–3246.
Rooms: 8; 5 with private bath, including 2 suites that accommodate
4.
Rates: $75 to $125, double occupancy, with champagne breakfast,
afternoon wine and hors d'oeuvres. $20 each additional person.
No smoking.
Open: All year.
Facilities and Local Attractions: Area tour packages; conference fa-
cilities; Jacuzzi hot tub. One block to ocean beaches, parks;
short walk to Monerey Bay Aquarium on Cannery Row, restau-
rants.

The Old St. Angela is a refreshing change in the midst
of so many Victorian inns. It was designed by a Boston architect, so it's not surprising to find true Cape Cod details. It
was built in 1910 and was the first Roman Catholic church in
Pacific Grove, then a rectory, later a convent.

When Alan Forrest began the restoration he used an
Americana theme, with mellow pine antiques and country
wallpaper. The living room has a large country-stone fire-

place, antique game table, beveled windows in Dutch doors, and comfortable furniture in warm, earthy colors. Among the handsome accents are duck prints, decoys, and a collection of Currier and Ives prints.

An enviable library of fine books with many ☞ first-edition Steinbecks is a pleasure to browse through. The afternoon light in this attractive room, a glass of sherry, music, and a crackling fire add up to the perfect place to dispel the winter of your discontent.

The bedrooms have a well-decorated country ambience—upscale country, that is, with tile bathrooms, fine linens, and down comforters. The Newport Room has a nautical feeling with a smart navy and brick color scheme. Ocean views from everywhere in the house are pleasing, but the best of all is from the Bay View Room. And you can't beat fresh flowers and fruit to give a room appeal.

Rooms in the ☞ Carriage House are especially well equipped to handle small conferences. A VCR system in place is another convenience.

Outside attractions are a white, latticed gazebo for dreaming under, and a hot tub that soaks eight friendly people.

Breakfast in a solarium of glass, redwood, and tile is a memorable part of your visit. Champagne precedes fresh fruits, eggs, and pastries. Occasionally the host surprises guests with his own "famous" blueberry pancakes.

How to get there: From San Francisco, take Highway 1 south; exit at Del Monte/Pacific Grove. Follow Del Monte Street. The name changes to Lighthouse, then to Central. Inn is on the left at 321 Central.

Roserox Country Inn by-the-Sea
Pacific Grove, California
93950

Innkeepers: The Browncroft Family
Address / Telephone: 557 Ocean View Boulevard; (408) 373–7673 or 373–ROSE.
Rooms: 8, all sharing 4 baths.
Rates: $85 to $155, full breakfast included. No children under 13; no smoking.
Open: All year.
Facilities and Local Attractions: Walk to Cannery Row, Monterey Aquarium. Close to all Monterey Bay events: Monterey Jazz, Bach, Steinbeck Festivals in summer; rodeo, golf tournaments, antique shows.

If it weren't for the need to acquaint you with the sumptuous accommodations and thoughtful attention that awaits you at Roserox, I could regale you with tales of Julia B. Platt, the dynamic maiden lady who built the mansion. She was either "hell on wheels" or a "grand old gal," depending on whose views you read.

Miss Platt was a scientist—a zoologist—and never hesitated to admit that she had more intelligence than most of the other citizens of Pacific Grove. With an assertiveness that was almost scandalous for her times, she tried single-handedly to make the strait-laced turn-of-the-century town more progressive. Despite her unorthodox views on religion, her sex ("gentle"), her age (seventy-four), and her lack of tact, she was elected mayor in the 1930s.

Her picture hangs in the sitting room of the house she named Roserox. Your hosts can tell you more about the formidable lady, if you wish, as you sip a glass of wine and enjoy the fire. As you relax here, you might want to have a game of Monopoly, with the unusual option of playing with Italian, Greek, or Australian money.

You're bound to be extraordinarily comfortable here. The views are superb, and ☛ every appointment in the guest rooms is of top quality. Antique beds, some brass and black enamel, some decorated in mother-of-pearl, are outfitted with down comforters, piles of pillows, and designer linens. A basket of fresh fruit and a bottle of California wine are welcoming gifts to Roserox. Fresh flowers are another thoughtful touch, as is the imported English soap—so nice as you soak in a ☛ six-foot-long jade-green clawfooted tub in a bathroom with a spectacular ocean view.

Before you venture out for dinner, there's a "happy hour" in the parlor with wine, beer, Irish coffee, and hors d'oeuvres. When you return, your bed will be turned down and a basket of taffy kisses waiting to end the day sweetly. If the night is cool, your toes will touch a hot water bottle as you slide between the sheets.

The Browncrofts know about good food, having years of experience in the restaurant and bakery business. The breakfast served in the sunny, tiled Morning Room is definitely hearty. The day I visited it was juices, fruits, cereals, salmon croquettes, a variety of muffins, breads, and jams, and coffee and teas.

How to get there: From Highway 1 south, exit on Highway 68 to Pacific Grove. Stay in right lane; continue on Forest Avenue to the ocean (Ocean View Boulevard). Turn right; go one block to Grand Avenue. Inn is on the right.

olive Metcalf

The Babbling Brook Inn
Santa Cruz, California
95060

Innkeeper: Gayle Brosee
Address / Telephone: 1025 Laurel Street; (408) 427–2437.
Rooms: 12, all with private bath.
Rates: $60 to $95, continental breakfast included. Corporate and
seasonal discounts. No children under 12.
Open: All year.
Facilities and Local Attractions: Walk to Municipal Wharf, beach,
boardwalk, specialty shops. Picnics, hot-air ballooning, wine
tasting at local wineries arranged.

Babbling Brook Inn couldn't be named better. It's built
right over the sight and sounds of Laurel Creek, a bubbling
natural brook which cascades at this point into a pond. 🖝
Lush landscaping is around the pond and follows the creek
through winding garden pathways and patios, complete with
a covered footbridge and a gazebo.

The Ohlone Indians lived on the cliffs surrounding Laurel Creek and fished where the waterfall is now. A touring
acting couple built a log cabin on the site in 1909, and some
silent motion pictures were filmed here. Later owners in-

cluded the flamboyant Countess (so she claimed) Florenzo de Chandler, who added the upstairs and balcony.

Gayle Brosee acquired the property after touring Europe and coming home inspired by the country inns she had visited there. When she opened The Babbling Brook Inn in 1981, she really started a trend in Santa Cruz; it was the *first* bed and breakfast establishment in the area.

A "European-type feeling, with California convenience" is what she strives to offer, and that's just what you'll find. Many of us claim a desire for a simple country-style atmosphere, but we *do* like our conveniences. You'll lack nothing for comfort here—from private baths and telephones, to shampoo, ironing boards, and hidden-away TVs.

The rooms are decorated in a country-French ambience with antiques, French wallpaper, and pine. Most are named for painters, and the colors—delft blues, rich burgundies, and beiges—were chosen to complement the individual artist. Almost every room has a fireplace or wood-burning stove, and a private deck. It seemed to me that every room was designed to provide maximum privacy and lovely views of the trees.

Wine and sherry are served in the attractive reception room in the afternoons, and in the morning, a continental breakfast buffet. The inn staff does its own baking, and the selection of muffins, strudels, fruits, and juices is beautifully arranged and presented. An opportunity for more indulging is the cappuccino and dessert bar offered in the evening.

How to get there: From Highway 17, take the Half Moon Bay exit and continue to Mission Street. Bear right; continue about ¼ mile, and turn left on Laurel. Inn is on your right.

☼

J: *Gayle and manager Loren Wilken are especially knowledgeable about the area—wineries, restaurants, picnic spots. Just ask, and they'll help you see it all.*

Clive Metcalf

Chateau Victorian
Santa Cruz, California
95060

Innkeeper: Franz Benjamin
Address / Telephone: 118 First Street; (408) 458–9458.
Rooms: 7, all with private bath; 5 with fireplaces.
Rates: $70 to $100, with expanded continental breakfast, afternoon
    wine and cheese. No pets or children; no smoking.
Open: All year.
Facilities and Local Attractions: Walk to beach, boardwalk, restau-
    rants, shops.

It is amazing what people will do in the name of improving a house. Chateau Victorian was constructed around the
turn of the century, a perfectly typical and lovable Victorian
house. Then came the 1950s with architectural philistines
who decided that graceful lines were old-fashioned and un-
functional. With righteous fervor, bay windows and dormers
were removed; thus, a charming period house became a typical '50s tract house, with a "picture" window.
    Hooray for the arrival of Franz Benjamin and friends!
They set about turning the lamentable hybrid back into a
cozy Victorian home with modern comforts to serve as an
inn. Back came a graceful bay window, and ☞ fine tile baths

96

for each bedroom were added. Franz landscaped a sheltered patio garden and renovated a cottage that opens onto it.

Then Franz individually decorated (with plenty of advice and help, he says) each room in beautiful colors to suit the era of the house—mauves, burgundies, and blues. He's chosen fine fabrics for bedcovers, draperies, pillows, and appealing window seats. The expected antique furniture pieces were added, including some particularly handsome armoires, and fresh flowers are everywhere. Now we're talking about a pretty house!

The house sits high enough on a hill to offer splendid ocean views from most of the rooms. It's location makes it an easy walk to restaurants, shops, and Santa Cruz's claim to fame, the last of the real boardwalks.

Breakfast, with the morning papers, is an expanded continental, meaning there's plenty of variety. Fine coffee and teas, juices and fruits, cream cheese, and croissants or other pastries are served from the dining-room buffet. You can eat there or enjoy a sunny morning in the patio.

How to get there: Driving south on Highway 1, exit on Bay. At West Cliff, turn left, then right on Beach to Main. Turn left at Main, and at First Street, turn right. Inn is on left at number 118.

🌞

J: *This boardwalk has a major attraction: the ☞ oldest surviving roller coaster in California—tested by my daughter many times and rated a four-star screamer in all the books.*

Olive Metcalf

Cliff Crest
Santa Cruz, California
95060

Innkeeper: Cheryl McEnery
Address / Telephone: 407 Cliff Street; (408) 427–2609.
Rooms: 5, all with private bath.
Rates: $65 to $90, expanded continental breakfast included. No smoking.
Open: All year, closed Christmas.
Facilities and Local Attractions: Boardwalk attractions of Santa Cruz; Monterey Bay.

What a pleasure to stay in this well-maintained Queen Anne Victorian. If you don't "ooh" and "ah-h" the minute you walk in, you're just not a fan of Victorian style. Everything sparkles, from the beveled glass front door, to the sitting room that opens onto a ☞ glassed-in bay solarium that looks out on the garden and patio.

This was the home of William Jeter. You do remember, don't you, that he established Henry Cowell Redwoods State Park, was interested in ecology, and was lieutenant governor of California in 1890? Of course you do. Jeter also had the good luck to have as a personal friend John McLaren, the designer of Golden Park in San Francisco. McLaren planned the beautiful grounds around this mansion.

Each of the bedrooms looks freshly decorated and offers special attractions. The smallest, the cozy Pineapple Room, is on the main floor and has pineapples carved on the four-poster double bed. The Rose Room is the largest and has an extra-long clawfoot bathtub and a 🖝 sitting area with a view of Monterey Bay. All the bathrooms are a particular pleasure with their thick towels and terry cloth robes, shampoo, and lotions.

The sitting room is deliciously pretty: white wicker furniture against soft blue–gray woodwork and blue rugs. A white latticed archway opens to the solarium with two round lace-covered tables and chairs. Across the top of the large bay window is a stained-glass border, and under the sills is an inside window box spilling over with grape ivy. Can you imagine a cozier setting for breakfast?

Coffee is ready at 8:00 A.M. in a silver urn by a tray holding delicate china cups and the morning paper. At nine you're served fresh juice and fruit with a yogurt topping, hot-out-of-the-oven muffins, and soft-cooked eggs in egg cups. In the afternoon, wine and cheese magically arrive, accompanied by classical music. And later in the evening, you're invited to help yourself to brandy while you enjoy this tranquil house.

How to get there: From Highway 17, exit on Ocean Street. Follow to San Lorenzo Boulevard; turn right. Go to stop light, and turn left on Riverside Drive. Go over bridge, turn right on Third Street; go up the hill to Cliff Street and turn left. Inn is on the left.

ℤ

J: *I concur with the feelings of a previous guest: "The ambience at Cliff Crest is warmth, charm, timeless. I feel the anxiety melting away."*

Olive Metcalf

The Darling House
Santa Cruz, California
95060

Innkeepers: Karen and Darrell Darling
Address / Telephone: 314 West Cliff Drive; (408) 458–1958.
Rooms: 8, sharing 5½ baths; marble lavatories in rooms.
Rates: $50 to $115, continental breakfast included. No smoking.
Open: All year.
Facilities and Local Attractions: Walk to secluded beach, sailing;
    good place to see wintering monarch butterflies; Santa Cruz
    Boardwalk.

If you guess from its name that this inn is a gabled Victorian, you would be way off-track. It's ☛ a 1910 Mission Revival masterpiece sitting on the cliffs high above Monterey Bay. The owners and innkeepers, Karen and Darrell Darling, are simply calling it by their own name—although their children did have some doubts about the idea.

The house was designed by William Weeks, probably the most active architect on the Central Coast during the first decade of the century. He was known particularly for designing public buildings, but his talent and versatility can also be seen in the private homes he designed. Karen calls Darling House a "Colorado Spanish" design, since Weeks and his clients the William Iliffs (cofounders of Denver University Graduate School) were both from Colorado, but Mission Revival is the true name of the popular style. The most striking features are the portico with its series of arches, the terra cotta tile roof, and beveled, leaded glass windows.

The imposing inn gives guests an opportunity to experience living in a period piece that is almost completely in its original state. Plumbing fixtures, for instance, are seventy-five years old and still working beautifully. Tiffany lamps and Art Deco (before its time) features are just as they were designed.

Bedrooms are large, and most have ocean views. One with an especially sweeping view has a big chair and a telescope ready for serious marine watching. Antique furnishings and beautiful details of inlaid woods on pillars, beams, and floors are fascinating to examine.

Breakfast is the only meal available, but Karen makes it special. She serves it family style in the oak dining room or on the ocean-side veranda: espresso, nut breads, croissants, granola, and fresh fruits. Whatever the menu, everything you eat is fresh or made from scratch.

The Darlings have home-grown walnuts for sale, also sixty-five tea blends, and six coffees. Darrell is a minister, but he also imports coffee and tea for his local coffee shop.

How to get there: From Highway 17, take Highway 1 north. Exit left on Bay Street, and turn right on West Cliff Drive. Inn is on the right.

❧

J: *A stroll down West Cliff Drive will bring you to a secluded beach. This stretch of the coast is a good place for tide-pooling, and for seeing the dizzying magic of wintering monarch butterflies.*

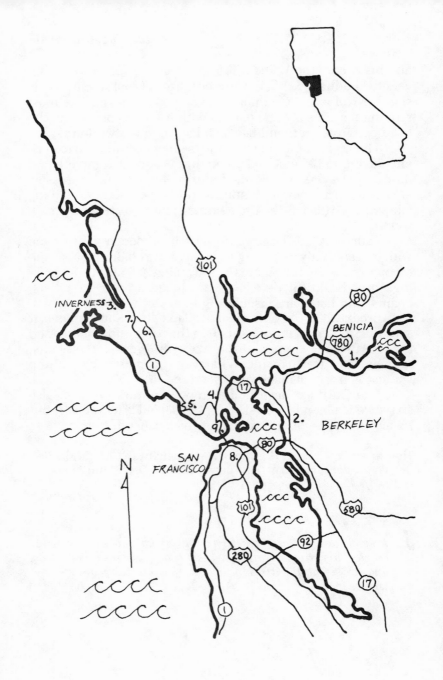

INVERNESS

BENICIA

BERKELEY

SAN
FRANCISCO

N

California: The San Francisco Bay Area

Numbers on map refer to towns numbered below.

olive Metcalf

The Union Hotel
Benicia, California
94510

Innkeeper: John Ebert
Address/Telephone: 410 First Street; (707) 746–0100.
Rooms: 12, with 2 suites; all have private bath, Jacuzzi tub, telephone, color TV, air conditioning.
Rates: $60 to $105, continental breakfast included. Special weekend package and corporate rate.
Open: All year. Breakfast, lunch, bar every day. Sunday brunch. Dinner weekends only, except by arrangement.
Facilities and Local Attractions: Visit old capitol. Open artisans' studios in glass blowing, pottery, sculpture; antique hunting. Marina, fishing, bird watching, picnicking. Guitar music in bar weekends.

Water, water, everywhere. Benicia is nestled on the north shore of the Carquinez Straits where the Sacramento and San Joaquin rivers flow into San Francisco Bay. When history and prosperity passed it by, this nineteenth-century town was largely forgotten. Once the capital of California, it boasts the ☞ oldest standing capitol in the state.

The stately three-story Union Hotel was restored in 1980, but even before guest rooms were ready, its ☞ authentically American food and regional dishes began attacting people to Benicia. The owners consulted food writer Marion Cunningham (author of the new *Fanny Farmer*) to design a menu, and the results have gathered raves around the state.

The kitchen staff is proud that all produce is hand selected and that everything from potato chips to sausage is homemade. Deceptively simple old favorites like pan-fried chicken, cream biscuits, and cottage fries are done outstandingly well. But so is the fresh fish, a duck and spinach salad, and pasta. You get the idea . . . this is excellent cooking.

The second and third floors have been entirely rebuilt to make the twelve bedrooms. Each is large and airy, named for a different theme—Mrs. Miniver, Mei Ling, Summer Skies—has period furnishings, and uses large armoires for closets. The best views are from the Massachusetts Bay Room and from Louis Le Mad, where you look out at the Carquinez Straits and bridge. And the bathrooms are splendid. They're big and tiled, with some of the Jacuzzi tubs large enough for entertaining.

No, you're not roughing it at the Union Hotel. But I've always thought that was overrated, haven't you?

How to get there: From San Francisco, take Highway 80 north to Vallejo. Take Benicia turnoff; exit Second Street, turn left. Proceed to Military; turn right and go to first stoplight, which is First Street. Turn left and drive through town to the hotel on the right.

⧖

J: *Innkeeper John Ebert says, "Benicia is one of the last non-touristy semi-undiscovered little towns left." I say, catch it while it's still free from the dreaded disease "Boutique-itis."*

olive Metcalf

Gramma's Bed & Breakfast Inn
Berkeley, California
94705

Innkeeper: Kathy Kuhner
Address/Telephone: 2740 Telegraph Avenue; (415) 549–2145.
Rooms: 19, each with private bath.
Rates: $61 to $88, double occupancy. Breakfast included. No children under 6.
Open: All year.
Facilities and Local Attractions: Walk to University of California Explore Berkeley shops, museums.

I love Gramma's because it takes many people's preconceptions about Berkeley and knocks them for a loop. The beautiful Tudor mansion with a sweet name (and no campy implications) has an ☞ atmosphere that surprises many visitors to this city of intellect and rebellion: Wholesome leaning to elegant is the feeling. It's the perfect antidote for outdated ideas of what goes on in Berkeley.

Go up a flower-lined walk and into a sunny living room where fat chintz-covered sofas and chairs invite you to "sit a spell." There's a pretty ☞ flower-tiled fireplace, and newspapers, magazines, and fresh flowers everywhere.

Beyond the light-filled dining room is a deck (Gramma would call it a back porch) and a cool grassy lawn. Tables and chairs are out here, along with pots of petunias, pansies, marigolds, white alyssum, and blue lobelia. It's a popular place for weddings and entertaining.

A portrait of Gramma—the real one, to whom the inn is dedicated—is on the landing on the way upstairs. Guest rooms are decorated in different colors but all in a country style. The antique furniture and handmade quilts are cozy. Some rooms have private decks, fireplaces, sitting areas, and access to the garden. The very nicest rooms are in the rear of the garden. They have fireplaces and windows on two sides.

The dining room has round tables with ruffled skirts to the floor and bright top cloths. One side of the room is all windows and offers a pleasant view of the garden. Dinner is not available here, but up and down Telegraph Avenue are some of Berkeley's best restaurants.

The breakfast served, as you might expect, is nourishing and substantial. (Would Gramma have served any other kind?) Juices and fresh fruit, muffins, scrambled eggs, and ☞ wonderful granola—the very thing to give you the energy to walk over to the university and raise Cain all day.

How to get there: From Highway 80 (the Eastshore) through Berkeley, take the Ashby Avenue exit; turn left at Telegraph Avenue. The inn is three blocks on your left at number 2740.

☖

J: *All that civility and charm . . . pretty radical stuff!*

olive Metcalf

Blackthorne Inn
Inverness, California
94937

Innkeepers: Susan Wigert and Bill Hemphill
Address/Telephone: 266 Vallejo Avenue (mailing address: Box 712); (415) 663–8621.
Rooms: 5, 3 with private bath. Not convenient for children.
Rates: $75 to $95, with extended continental breakfast.
Open: All year.
Facilities and Local Attractions: Decks for sunning, hot tub. Point Reyes National Seashore, nature walks, wildflowers, bird watching.

"This is really an adult treehouse," says Susan Wigert. This ☞ fascinating redwood, cedar, and fir structure began with a small cabin built in the 1930s. Now it rises through the treetops to four levels, joined by a 40-foot spiral staircase. Flanked with decks and balconies, approached by walkways and bridges, the building is crowned with the ☞ octagonal Eagle's Nest Room. Your first adventure after arriving will be exploring the ways around it.

The inn was designed by Bill Wigert, Susan's husband,

and she and her brother Bill run
some of the wood from trees on the
construction quite a salvage operation.
from San Francisco piers, boulders from se
the walk-in fireplace, and huge doors rescued
San Francisco Southern Pacific building.

The main level has a large, airy living room w
lights, comfortable furniture, and a stone fireplace.
sounds of Handel (or was it Vivaldi?) came from a stereo th
afternoon I arrived, cats snoozed, and the wine tray was
ready. All good signs.

Adjoining the living room is a glass-enclosed solarium
where a California-style continental breakfast is served:
juice, fresh fruit, quiche, pastries, yogurt, and granola. This
is the only meal served at the inn, but guests often walk or
drive into the village to buy picnic munchies to lunch on
back at the house while enjoying the decks.

Dinner choices in this coastal area used to be slim pick-
ings, but these days in the villages there are cafés, a French
restaurant, two Czechoslovakian ones, a bakery that makes a
great pizza, and at the Olema Inn, a daily changing menu of
fresh fish and local food prepared expertly. The innkeepers
are happy to help you choose and make reservations.

Guest rooms are attractive and cozy, some with pitched
ceilings and arched windows, some with small decks. A
2,500-square-foot sun deck surrounds the main level of the
house—with a ☛ fireman's pole to slide down, if you're
nimble. Another deck on the hillside has hot and cold tubs,
and on the roof is a private sun deck for the Eagle's Nest.

This is a unique spot, for the young at heart.

How to get there: From San Francisco, take Highway 101 through
Olema toward Inverness. Turn left at the Inverness Park Grocery
onto Vallejo Avenue, two miles south of Inverness. The inn is on
your right.

☙

J: *Innkeeper Susan Wigert says she recently traveled in Mexico
and on the East Coast and came home to Blackthorne con-
vinced that she lives in paradise.*

olive Metcalf

Mountain Home Inn
Mill Valley, California
94941

Innkeepers: Cathy Larson, Gerald Falley, Judy Curtin
Address/Telephone: 810 Panoramic Highway; (415) 381–9000.
Rooms: 10, all with private bath and deck; suite with wheelchair access.
Rates: $95 to $175, with extended continental breakfast.
Open: All year. Lunch, dinner, Sunday brunch. Wine bar.
Facilities and Local Attractions: Walk to Muir Woods, hike up Mt. Tamalpais, great eating.

This inn has it all: knock-your-socks-off views of the Bay and Marin hills, fascinating architectural design, luxury rooms, a lauded restaurant, and a professional staff just dying to pamper you. Even the twisting drive up to its mountain perch is beautiful.

Longtime Marin residents remember the inn on the slope of Mt. Tamalpais through many incarnations. It was built in 1912 by a Swiss couple supposedly homesick for an Alpine view. Most recently it was a German beer-and-sandwich place serving dusty hikers. What a difference a few mil' makes.

A blond hardwood interior softly announces "California chic," with cathedral ceilings and ☛ pillars of redwood still covered with bark. Muted colors—beiges, apricots—are punctuated with unusual hickory furniture pieces.

Guest rooms are sleek and serene, each with its own deck to enjoy the sweeping view. Appointments include grand tubs (some with Jacuzzis), complimentary toiletries, thick robes, and towels. Guests have a private dining room/lounge with fireplace and outside deck. If you've stayed the night, enjoy the daily papers and a buffet breakfast here, or in your room: hot and cold beverages, fresh fruits, pastries, and the ubiquitous California breakfast statement—yogurt and granola.

At the heart of the inn is the beautiful bar and intimate dining room, with deck overlooking the dazzling view. The no-smoking rule in the dining rooms speaks to the ☛ serious way they regard food. Menus change twice a month to reflect the availability of seasonal fresh fish and produce. A mesquite grill and the trendy ingredients are here—status greens like radicchio, baby vegetables cooked *al dente,* and pastas—but with this kitchen's own artful stamp on them. The day I visited, two offerings were grilled swordfish with sun-dried tomato butter and stewed mushrooms, and a whole chicken breast stuffed with feta cheese and thyme. ☛ Homemade ice cream made with fresh berries is a specialty, and so is the bittersweet chocolate cake.

How to get there: From San Francisco, cross the Golden Gate Bridge, and take Mill Valley/Stinson Beach exit to Highway 1 junction. Turn left at light; follow signs to Mt. Tamalpais State Park. Road becomes Panoramic Highway; follow 8 miles to the top. Inn is on the right.

olive Metcalf

The Pelican Inn
Muir Beach, California
94965

Innkeeper: Charles Felix
Address/Telephone: Muir Beach; (415) 383–6000.
Rooms: 6, all with private bath.
Rates: $95, with full English breakfast.
Open: All year. Lunch, dinner, full bar. Closed Mondays, except to
  inn guests.
Facilities and Local Attractions: Piano entertainment Wednesday
  through Sunday, 6:00 P.M. to 10:00 P.M. Point Reyes National
  Seashore, beachcombing, bird watching.

Would Schweppes have succeeded without Commander
Whitehead? Could the Pelican Inn thrive without Charles
Felix? Talking to this fourth-generation publican (inn-
keeper), it's hard to separate the delights of his inn from the
British charm of the innkeeper.

Just twenty minutes from the Golden Gate Bridge, his
replica of a sixteenth-century English country inn has
white stucco and is crisscrossed with dark beams. It seems a
proper spot, considering that it was here on the Marin Coast
that Sir Francis Drake beached his *Pelican* (renamed the

Golden Hind) some 400 years ago and claimed California for Queen Elizabeth I and her descendants forever.

You enter a ☞ cozy English pub with low beams, dart board, and a good stock of brews. Almost everything here came from the inn Felix previously owned in Surrey. The four-centuries-old paneled bar is packed on weekends with San Franciscans and guests who enjoy pub fare like Scotch eggs and shepherd pies. A piano player Thursday through Sunday makes it a lively spot.

An adjoining dining room has a huge fireplace and sturdy, dark tables and chairs. The dinner menu appropriately offers roast beef, Yorkshire pudding, and mixed English grill among its choices. Breakfast also is served here, in the enclosed patio, or in your room. Breakfast is big and English: juice, eggs, bacon, bangers, tomatoes, homemade bread, and marmalade.

The bedrooms upstairs are wonderfully English. Beds have a brocade-draped half-canopy called a "tester." The device was once used not for décor, but to keep small rodents who might be frolicking in the thatched roof overhead from falling on your face while you slept. Other ☞ "mod cons" (modern conveniences) are a stone with a hole hanging over each bed to ensure no rickets in case of pregnancy. Felix, who claims a trust in every known superstition, successfully keeps witches and evil spirits away with buried bones under the hearth and holly over the doors.

Felix may be a San Francisco advertising man, but he takes the profession of publican seriously and laments mere B&Bs' calling themselves inns. The Pelican is in the traditional mold, where ☞ the innkeeper is a public servant and feels it his duty to see that you are lodged, fed, and looked after properly.

How to get there: From San Francisco, take Highway 101 to the Stinson Beach/Mill Valley exit. Follow Highway 1 through Mill Valley to Muir Beach.

⧗

J: *I'm a pushover for an innkeeper who calls out as you're leaving for a walk on the beach, "Better take a woolie with you, do!"*

Olive Metcalf

The Olema Inn
Olema, California
94950

Innkeeper: Donn Downing
Address/Telephone: Sir Francis Drake Boulevard (mailing address:
  Box 10); (415) 663–8441.
Rooms: 3 rooms, 1 with private bath.
Rates: $60 to $70, includes breakfast. Children welcome.
Open: All year. Lunch, dinner, Sunday brunch. Bar.
Facilities and Local Attractions: Art gallery in library/bar room.
  Point Reyes National Seashore, hiking, bird watching, whale
  watching, horseback riding, swimming at beaches. String
  music during weekend dinners.

Judging strictly from the outside, you might not guess
what an appealing refuge this century-old inn offers. Spare,
almost stark in appearance, it stands slightly above the surrounding land. Jack London and John Steinbeck are among
the names of those who were once frequent guests.

Inside you'll find a restored, inviting parlor room/lobby.
Or maybe you would call it a library/art gallery, with its 🖝
changing exhibition from the Olema Inn Gallery. Either way,
it also has an attractive bar and three dining rooms beyond,

with high ceilings and handsome French doors. We sat in the garden room that looks out to a patio with tables and umbrellas, and to a rock garden bordered with California poppies waving in the sea breeze. The airy atmosphere of clean white walls, tall windows, and white linen seems perfect for the excellent fresh food.

My broiled striped bass with a lime-cilantro butter must have been caught that morning. And all green salads are *not* the same. This one was special: every leaf perfect and dressed with tarragon vinegar, oil, and fresh herbs from the garden. Other specialties from the innovative menu are Drakes Bay Oysters baked with lemon-garlic topping and a tagliarini entrée prepared with chicken, rocket (that's a chic green), garlic, and jalapenos! The traveler's companion drank three glasses of water and half a bottle of wine with *that* one, but insisted it was marvelous.

Upstairs are three spic-and-span guest rooms. Some of you might find them a little plain, but I thought they were a pleasant change of pace from Victorian settings. They have country-style furnishings, iron and brass beds, pretty quilts, and fresh curtains at the windows. These rooms share a common room where breakfast is served.

The location is wonderful—about an hour's drive from the Golden Gate Bridge, at the gateway to one of America's most beautiful national parks, Point Reyes National Seashore. A very pleasant place.

How to get there: From San Francisco, take Highway 101 across the Golden Gate Bridge to Highway 1 cutoff; follow to Olema.

🍷

J: *When I find a coastal town like Olema, it seems only natural to want it to have just two kinds of people: (1) the residents and (2) me.*

Holly Tree Inn
Point Reyes Station, California
94956

Innkeepers: Tom and Diane Balogh
Address/Telephone: 3 Silverhills Road (mailing address: Box 642);
(415) 663–1554.
Rooms: 4, all with private bath.
Rates: $64.80 to $74.60, including tax and full breakfast. Children
welcome.
Open: All year.
Facilities and Local Attractions: One mile from Point Reyes National Seashore. Area offers horseback riding, hiking, fishing,
boating, bird watching, mushrooming, nature walks. Unique
shops, fine restaurants. Horses boarded.

There is something especially pleasing about fine
houses built before World War II: They're modern enough
for comfort, yet old enough to have a spacious elegance few
of us enjoy at home. Holly Tree Inn has those qualities, and
sits on ☛ nineteen lush acres of lawns and gardens. It was
built in 1939 by a Swede with a British wife, who probably
accounts for the arbor of holly trees, the English laurels,
lilacs, privet, and the herb garden.

The house is decorated in understated British taste that suits it perfectly: Laura Ashley prints, plump upholstered chairs and sofas, antiques, fresh flowers, and whimsy. A row of tiny wooden buildings ranges across both fireplace mantels in the dining and living rooms. A guest sipping a sherry in the big sofa might look at it for some time before realizing it is Point Reyes in miniature—made by innkeeper Tom Balogh.

Bedrooms are each different and delightfully English. The smallest, Mary's Garden Room, is done in a red-and-green-sprigged Ashley print and opens onto a patio and perennial flower garden. The larger rooms are equally tasteful and have beautiful views.

Diane's enthusiasm for decorating this great house extends even to a newly tiled bathroom sink. She pointed out the pretty gray-green color of the grouting. "Did you know grout comes in almost any color you want? It doesn't have to be white!"

Christmas at Holly Tree Inn is special. Polished wood gleams in the glow of both blazing fireplaces, and there are decorations galore. Santa made an unexpected appearance once by way of a working electric dumbwaiter beside the fireplace, usually used for bringing up logs.

Mid-January is ☛ whale-watch time on cool, misty Point Reyes Peninsula. The Baloghs arrange for a naturalist to speak about the phenomenon to guests, followed by a short drive out to the coast to watch the migration.

A fine breakfast is served in the dining room—juice, fresh fruit, bran muffins or croissants, homemade poppyseed bread, several cheeses, and then something special, like individual asparagus soufflés. For other meals, there is a wide choice of good restaurants in the area.

How to get there: From San Francisco, exit Highway 101 north at Sir Francis Drake Boulevard. Follow signs to Olema, and turn right onto Highway 1. At sign for Inverness, turn left onto Sir Francis Drake Boulevard; take first left onto Bear Valley Road (unmarked); then take first right onto Silverhills Road (unmarked). Look for Holly Tree Inn sign.

Olive Metcalf

Alamo Square Inn
San Francisco, California
94117

Innkeepers: Wayne Corn and Klaus May
Address/Telephone: 719 Scott Street; (415) 922–2055.
Rooms: 5, including a suite; 1 bath.
Rates: $65 double to $175 for suite arrangement. Full breakfast included.
Open: All year.
Facilities and Local Attractions: Historic Alamo Square District for walking, viewing Victorian architecture; 10 blocks west of San Francisco Civic Center; close to Golden Gate Park.

The beautiful harp sitting in one of the parlors of this Victorian home seems to be made for its setting. But it's not merely a decorative accent; it's often played at weddings and sometimes during afternoon wine and hors d'oeuvres gatherings here. It's just one of the grace notes added to another old San Francisco mansion lovingly restored and now maintained as an inn.

You see why prospective brides frequently choose the inn as the scene of both their wedding ceremony and reception; it's a 🖝 romantic house. There are two parlors fur-

118

nished in a blend of Victorian and Oriental styles, a grand staircase, and a large formal dining room.

Innkeepers Wayne and Klaus have been restoring the 1895 mansion for almost ten years, but Wayne says it is still a house in transition. Their future plans call for a private bath for each of the guest rooms. Presently underway is an ambitious outdoor project that will add decks and an even larger garden area.

Guest rooms are comfortably decorated with antique touches, and some have sweeping views of the city. A suite that can be one or two bedrooms with a pleasant sitting area is especially spacious. A TV is available on request.

Klaus is a professional chef and takes pride in his breakfast productions. It's a hearty, sit-down meal in the dining room, but it can also be delivered to your room or served in the garden. Gorgeous fresh raspberries were the stars of the fruit selection when I visited. Then there was juice, cheese omelets, and the chef's specialty, ☛ homemade Danish and other breakfast pastries. (He makes special hors d'oeuvres too.)

Both Wayne and Klaus know San Francisco well. They're ready to help guests with information about what's happening in town, the best play, or the newest restaurant.

How to get there: From Highway 80 going north to the Golden Gate Bridge, take Fell Street west about seven blocks. Turn right at Scott Street to number 719, on the left.

Olive Metcalf

The Archbishops Mansion
San Francisco, California
94117

Innkeepers: Jonathan Shannon and Jeffrey Ross
Address/Telephone: 1000 Fulton Street; (415) 563–7872.
Rooms: 15, all with private bath; all but 2 have fireplaces.
Rates: $95 to $360, continental breakfast included. Two-night minimum on weekends.
Open: All year.
Facilities and Local Attractions: Dinners catered by arrangement. Near San Francisco Opera House, Davies Symphony Hall, Galleria Design Center, Moscone Convention Center.

Let us not pussyfoot about the kind of establishment this is: *opulent, romantic, dramatic,* and *grand* will do for starters. Messrs. Shannon and Ross call themselves innkeepers, but the lodgings and service they offer give the term a new dimension.

This ☛ impressive mansion in the Alamo Square District was built in 1904 as the private residence of the archbishop of San Francisco and his entourage. It survived the 1906 earthquake and became headquarters for a citywide effort to rebuild San Francisco. Pope Pius XII stayed here in

120

the mid-1930s while he was still a cardinal. It was purchased six years ago by Ross, a trained architect, and Shannon, a fashion designer, and they've combined their considerable talents to restore it.

You enter a great hall with an elegant parlor on one side and ahead a ☞ magnificent staircase. The style is French Empire, rather than Victorian. In fact, the intricate ceiling details, splendid rugs, furniture, antiques, and lush draperies could convince you that it was a European palace.

Each of the luxurious bedrooms upstairs is named for an opera. The Rosenkavalier Suite has gracefully curved construction, even in the thresholds and bookcases. In one corner of its bathroom is ☞ a silver-gray velvet settee on a base of silver swans that was once Ethel Barrymore's. The opera's libretto hangs from a nearby cord—providing suitable bathroom reading.

Other rooms are Carmen, with appropriate Spanish touches, Così fan Tutte, and Madama Butterfly, all with ☞ exceptional antiques and exquisitely embroidered linens. Don Giovanni has an intricately carved bed that is just one of the prizes in a house full of treasures. Some of the bathrooms are like good-sized rooms, with fireplaces, Oriental rugs, chandeliers, and tall stands for keeping the champagne cold while you soak in a hot tub. Surely, *you* don't tub without champagne at the ready?

Guests gather for wine in the afternoon in a downstairs parlor. Breakfast is served in the enormous dining room or delivered to your room in a French picnic basket. Several ☞ salons are available for small conferences or where the hosts cater dinners or cocktail parties by prior arrangement. The surroundings are palatial but warm, with all the personal attention you could desire.

How to get there: From Van Ness, take Fulton Street west to Alamo Square. Inn is on the right, number 1000.

☧

J: *Jonathan Shannon says: "Innkeeping is a theatrical event; it's nice to provide guests with an environment they don't have at home."*

Olive Metcalf

The Bed and Breakfast Inn
San Francisco, California
94123

Innkeepers: Marily and Robert Kavanaugh
Address/Telephone: 4 Charlton Court; (415) 921–9784.
Rooms: 5 rooms with private bath; 4 rooms with shared baths; 1 penthouse.
Rates: $63 to $174, including light breakfast.
Open: All year.
Facilities and Local Attractions: Located on one of the most fashionable shopping streets in San Francisco; restaurants, shops, Victorian architecture. Bus line to downtown.

You say you want intimate ambience . . . Cotswolds-cozy atmosphere . . . in San Francisco? It awaits you, with elegance, down a narrow cul-de-sac off Union Street.

Occasional guests have been heard to utter the word *alley*—probably some down-to-earth midwestern types—but the preferred location description here is "mews," or possibly "courtyard." Whatever you call it, it *is* adorable. Red geraniums in window boxes stand out against the blue and white exterior of the inn, which is really three restored Victorian houses. 🖝 You'll be greeted like an old friend. Sit down on the white wicker settee and have a glass of sherry.

The breakfast room just off the entrance can entertain a china lover for hours. Much of Marily's 🖝 collection of Spode, Copeland, and Wedgwood, among others, is displayed along with a vast number of teapots. Even better, it's all used on pretty linen settings for morning and afternoon tea. You can breakfast on a different china setting every day in a garden patio, or be served in your room. You'll get the *Chronicle* and freshly ground coffee or English teas, fruit, and hot "good things" like croissants or sticky buns.

Rooms are decorated with 🖝 extraordinary flair using family heirlooms from England. They all have the bright, fresh look of just having been redone. Dainty Laura Ashley print is in a delicate room called Celebration; grass cloth and rattan furniture in Mandalay. Other rooms are Covent Garden, Green Park, and Kensington Garden, which opens to a flower-filled deck behind the inn. The Mayfair is a private flat with living room, kitchen, latticed balcony, and spiral staircase to the bedroom loft.

A small library room downstairs is a cozy retreat with a TV, games, and books. You're invited to brew yourself a cup of tea, if you like. Very 🖝 personal service is the pride of everyone around here.

Within a two-block circle around the inn are dozens of interesting restaurants. Perry's is one that's always fun—one of San Francisco's most famous bars, specializing in interpersonal relations and great hamburgers.

How to get there: From Van Ness Street, take Union Street west. Between Laguna and Buchanan streets, turn left into Charlton Court.

🍸

J: "Masterpiece Theatre" *buffs will love the "upstairs" treatment you get here. If the* Titanic *hadn't failed her, Lady Marjory would have been right at home.*

Hermitage House
San Francisco, California
94115

Innkeeper: Jane Selzer; owner, Marian Binkly
Address/Telephone: 2224 Sacramento Street; (415) 921–5515.
Rooms: 10, some with studio couches; private and shared baths, depending on arrangement of room or suite.
Rates: $80 to $105, double occupancy, extended continental breakfast included. Long stays given special rates.
Open: All year.
Facilities and Local Attractions: Good public transportation to downtown; near Presbyterian Hospital. Beautiful neighborhood for walking. Restaurants close by.

This seventeen-room Greek Revival house, built between 1900 and 1903, displays some of the most ☛ stunning use of redwood you'll ever see in a private home. The present owners did a lot of scrubbing, rubbing, and oiling to restore the original beauty, and the results are a masterpiece. From the entryway, with is beautiful carved redwood detail in pillars, beams, and stairway scrolls to the superbly carved mantels, it is a unique interior.

Seven working fireplaces are in the home, including one

in the large living room. Wine is served here in the evenings, a tastefully decorated room with comfortable furniture and fresh flowers. Just off it is an alcove room that was once used as a chapel. It's a particularly pretty spot for weddings.

Despite the old-time formality of a grand house, the atmosphere is ☛ comfortable and unpretentious. The morning routine, for instance, accommodates the most finicky early-morning riser. A generous and beautifully arranged breakfast buffet is provided in the dining room. You can help yourself and eat here, or take it to a less formal room with your morning paper. But if *no one* can time an egg just the way you like it, or make oatmeal exactly the consistency you like, just make yourself at home in the large family kitchen and fix your own.

Bedroom facilities are adaptable too. One downstairs room has an outside entrance. Some of the larger upstairs rooms have sinks, fireplaces, and baths that connect with another bedroom, making it convenient for a family. The rooms are beautifully decorated and have added thoughtful touches like fresh flowers, radios, private outside lines, and alarm clocks. ☛ The Judge's Study on the third floor under the eaves is especially inviting and cozy with paneling, shelves of books, and ☛ a marvelous view of the city.

An out-of-towner will love walking this most San Francisco of neighborhoods. It is only minutes from Nob Hill and some of the city's most glamourous restaurants. A garden, a sheltered deck, and off-street parking are other conveniences.

How to get there: From Van Ness Avenue, turn west on Sacramento Street to the inn on your right.

☗

J: *If you know a morning grouch who's coming to San Francisco, steer him to this understanding inn.*

olive Metcalf

The Mansion Hotel
San Francisco, California
94115

Innkeeper: Robert Pritikin
Address/Telephone: 2220 Sacramento Street; (415) 929–9444.
Rooms: 19, all with queen-sized bed and private bath.
Rates: $89 to $200 double occupancy; $74 to $150 single. Breakfast
　　included.
Open: All year. Dinner.
Facilities and Local Attractions: Concerts, billiards, Bufano Sculp-
　　ture gardens. A neighborhood of splendid San Francisco
　　homes; cable car four blocks away; tennis courts nearby.

　　In the words of Monty Python, ☛ and now for something completely different: a twin-turreted Queen Anne Victorian that has nightly musical séances; real British masters
like Turner and Reynolds on the walls; pigs, rendered in all
media, throughout the house; rooms of fine antiques, funky
junk, and cages of doves; a neighborhood polling place whose
costumed staff offers voters beverages and pâtés from silver
platters . . . it's all The Mansion!

　　Ad man Robert Pritikin has been called eccentric and
whimsical, but he also may be the most original innkeeper in
the city. His inn is a little quirky, but it's lavishly decorated

and great fun. Parlor, billiard room, and kitchen are splendid. Even more elegant is the crystal-chandeliered restaurant opening onto a garden of flowers and ☞ Bufano sculptures. This magnificent marble and bronze collection constitutes the definitive display of the artist's works.

It's the ☞ pigs, in a porcelain, painting, and sculpture, that tell you a sense of humor is loose here. The perfectly reasonable explanation for the swine element in the midst of Victoriana is that they're to pacify Claudia, the Mansion ghost. She kept pigs in this house where she lived and died, and according to demonologists, her "extremely heavy" (but not negative) presence is still in the mansion.

Claudia appears nighly in the music room in her empty Victorian wheelchair and invisibly plays selections requested by the guests. Sometimes the concert closes with ragtime or a Sousa march, assisted by the audience members, who have been supplied with cowbells, maracas, and tambourines. ☞ Weekend concerts feature innkeeper Pritikin on the Concert Saw and other class acts.

Up the grand staircase are guest rooms in turn-of-the-century-style décor with modern plumbing and other contemporary comforts. Some have balconies and marble fireplaces; each has a private speaker which plays classical music when you wish.

A capable chef prepares continental dinners, served in the candlelit dining room looking out at the sculpture garden. Breakfast is served in your room or in the country kitchen: juice, fresh fruit, muffins or croissants, plus cooked eggs. Coffee is always ready in the kitchen for guests to help themselves.

How to get there: Entering the city from the east or south, follow signs to the Golden Gate Bridge until you come to the Van Ness exit. If you are entering over the Golden Gate Bridge, follow signs to downtown and Lombard Street. Go east on Lombard to Van Ness and turn right. From Van Ness Avenue, turn west on Sacramento to the Inn on your right.

ℤ

J: *This is a classy place to fulfill the need of people who visit San Francisco searching for something offbeat.*

Olive Metcalf

Petite Auberge
San Francisco, California
94108

Innkeeper: Karen Ochsner Johnson
Address/Telephone: 863 Bush Street; (415) 928–6000.
Rooms: 26, including 1 suite; all with private bath, 18 with fireplace.
Rates: $90 to $180, with generous continental breakfast. Parking $10 per day.
Open: All year.
Facilities and Local Attractions: Walking distance to San Francisco's theater district, shopping, Nob Hill, Union Square, fine restaurants, cable-car connections.

Hard to believe, but in the very heart of downtown San Francisco is an inn with all the 🖝 ambience of a French country inn. Not rustic-country, mind you, but classy-country. Step into the blue canopied entrance from busy Bush Street and you enter a warmly inviting lobby of large, brick-colored tiles that look old (but probably aren't), Oriental rugs, fresh flowers, and a carrousel horse that for some reason looks French.

But everything looks French with bright Pierre Deux

fabric designs on lampshades, picture mats, and French Provincial furniture. (Robin, at the desk, told me that the Pierre Deux company, by the way, was begun by two men both named Pierre; thus the "deux.") White porcelain ducks sporting ribbons around the neck, and grapevine wreaths entwined with ribbons give the impression of perennial springtime, French style.

Upstairs, even the smallest rooms are impeccably decorated with every possible convenience. Handsome armoires hide TVs. ☛ Good reading lights are on either side of the beds, which have beautiful linens and lacy pillow shams. On an antique writing desk is a hand-written welcome for the expected guests.

One of the medium-size rooms has space for a creamy tiled fireplace, rose loveseat, blue wingback chair, and a window seat. Bathroom fixtures have elegant porcelain handles, and special toiletries and thick towels await.

What makes this an inn instead of an elegant, small hotel? ☛ Hands-on taking care of you, that's what. Do you want to be picked up at the airport, have your car parked, or have your shoes shined? Do you need someone to handle those tiresome details of dinner reservations and theater tickets? Would you like to lay on a smart dinner party but abhor the crassness of a public restaurant?

Relax, mon ami. All can be arranged. During the 1984 Democratic convention Time-Life was one group that entertained in the intimate comfort of Petite Auberge. Downstairs from the lobby is a comfortable lounge, dining room, and courtyard garden. Breakfast is served here mornings; tea, wine, and nibbles in the afternoons. The inn offers an extended continental breakfast, with fresh fruit, juices, cereals, homemade breads and pastries, and an ever-changing main dish.

How to get there: From Union Square, go left (west) on Sutter Street to Taylor; turn right, go to Bush; turn right. Inn is on the right at number 863.

ᛏ

J: *I've always loved the pastoral life. It's good to see it thriving here on Bush Street.*

olive Metcalf

The Spreckels Mansion
San Francisco, California
94117

Innkeeper: Donna Fallon
Address/Telephone: 737 Buena Vista West; (415) 861–3008.
Rooms: 10, all but 2 with private bath.
Rates: $88 to $260, breakfast included. Two-night minimum on weekends. Children and cigars discouraged.
Open: All year.
Facilities and Local Attractions: Small conferences, catered dinners can be accommodated. Beside Buena Vista Park; neighborhood of beautiful homes; walk to Haight Street, shops and restaurants; fifteen minutes from Union Square.

The Spreckels Mansion is one of the city's fine "country inns." When it was built in 1887 for a nephew of Adolph Spreckels, the famous sugar baron, it really was a country estate, probably an hour's carriage drive from downtown San Francisco. Sitting high on Buena Vista Hill, the inn has the advantage of beautiful views and the privacy of an ☛ interesting neighborhood. Jack London and Ambrose Bierce once lived here. More recently, the top-floor ballroom was a recording studio for a rock band, and the guest house next door was owned by a rock musician, Graham Nash.

A two-bedroom suite now covers the entire third floor of the mansion. It has a marble fireplace and kitchen and is understandably expensive. But the pleasures of this grand house are in the smaller rooms, too. Five guest rooms in the mansion and five in the guest house are each an achievement in ☞ comfortable elegance. There's no getting away from the fact that they *are* grand, but nothing about the décor is stiff or off-putting. Most have fireplaces and views of either Buena Vista Park or Golden Gate Park and the ocean.

A broad central hallway, Oriental rugs on parquet floors, chandeliers, stained glass, and fresh flowers reward every guest. To sit in the handsomely decorated library/parlor, with its dramatic wallpaper and myriad bookshelves, is to enjoy a kind of old-world experience most of us find only at special inns like this. Sipping wine by the fireplace in these surrounding is bound to make you feel rather elegant. So will the continental breakfast and morning paper delivered to your room on a silver tray.

High standards of taste, talent, and lots of money have brought the mansion back to architectural prominence, but it's the ☞ tender loving care lavished on guests that ultimately makes it an exceptional inn. If you want a dinner catered, reservations made, or touring suggestions, help is on the spot. Innkeeper Donna will tell you about some local restaurants that are among the best in the city.

How to get there: From Van Ness, take Fell Street west to Masonic, and turn left. At Fredrick, jog left to Buena Vista. Follow to inn on your right.

☒

J: *The world does not exist to satisfy your every whim, but they don't know that at The Spreckels Mansion. Lucky you.*

olive Metcalf

Victorian Inn on the Park
San Francisco, California
94117

Innkeepers: Lisa and William Benau
Address/Telephone: 301 Lyon Street; (415) 931–1830.
Rooms: 12, all with private bath.
Rates: $75 double occupancy to $200 for suite for 4. Continental
    breakfast included; not convenient for children. Two-night
    minimum on weekends. No smoking.
Open: All year.
Facilities and Local Attractions: The Panhandle and Golden Gate
    Park for walking and bicycling; De Young Museum, California
    Academy of Sciences, Japanese Tea Garden.

When Queen Victoria celebrated her Diamond Jubilee
in 1897, the Victorian Inn on the Park was built by a local
lumberman for his son Thomas Clunie. The Clunie House
reflected the family business with its intricately paneled
entry and parquet floors lavishly inlaid with oak, mahogany,
and redwood. The history of the ornate house progresses
from first owner Clunie, who became a state senator and
United States congressman, to a recent cult group who held
rebirthing rites in a hot tub in the basement!

Since the Benaus rescued it, they have restored and decorated the house as an inn with faithful attention to turn-of-the-century details. Lisa and her mother chose the antique pieces. There are fascinating old photographs on the walls and a red velvet upholstered Queen Anne sofa and chair in the parlor. They've found, or had designed, some of the most ☞ flamboyant fringed lampshades I've ever seen ... and they look wonderful in rooms this size.

Six guest rooms are upstairs, another four in what was once the ballroom on the top floor, and two more bedrooms in the basement. The largest room has a fireplace and a good view of the Panhandle, but the most unusual is the ☞ Persian Suite, with exotic fabric covering a multitude of pillows and draping a sitting area tucked under a dormer window. All the rooms have pretty comforters and down pillows.

My favorite room is the ☞ library downstairs. It's rather dark, with lots of wood and books, and very cozy. The Benaus will pour the sherry.

Breakfast, served in your room or in the dining room, consists of fresh fruit, juice, croissants, homemade breads, and the morning *Chronicle*. The Benaus will give you good ideas for dinner choices nearby, or they'll arrange small catered dinners at the inn.

How to get there: From Highway 101 north, take Fell Street toward Golden Gate Park. Inn is on the right at Lyon Street.

☒

J: *One of the world's zaniest races, the annual San Francisco Bay to Breakers, goes right by the inn's front door. Each May for seventy-five years, world-class runners race from San Francisco Bay, up the murderous Hayes Street hill, and out Fell to Ocean Beach. The event has grown to be the city's best party, with 100,000 runners, many in outrageous costumes. You could have a front-row seat here to see all the sights—and they're astounding.*

olive Metcalf

The Washington Square Inn
San Francisco, California
94133

Innkeeper; Judy Scott
Address/Telephone: 1660 Stockton Street; (415) 981–4220.
Rooms: 15; 10 with private bath, 4 shared, 1 half-bath.
Rates: $60 to $145, including continental breakfast. Children welcome. Telephones; TV available on request at no charge.
Open: All year.
Facilities and Local Attractions: Great walking area of San Francisco: restaurants, shops, markets. Close to cable car line; one block from Telegraph Hill; easy walk to Ghirardelli Square, the Cannery, financial district.

The inn faces Washington Square, in the heart of North Beach, to my eye the 🖛 most colorful neighborhood in the city. Saints Peter and Paul Church dominates one side of the square; on the other sides are wonderful restaurants (the Washington Square Bar and Grill is the mecca for politicians and literary types), shops, and markets displaying fresh pasta, salamis, and produce. In the park a covey of shining black bangs clutching brown bags (a Chinese kindergarten class) settles down on the grass for a picnic lunch. Several old men practice *tai chi* exercises, oblivious to the bustle on all sides. Over all is the aroma of freshly ground coffee.

You can see much of this scene from the comfort of the inn's lobby/sitting room. There is a handsomely carved fireplace, comfortable provincial furniture on a blue rug, magazines, and books. A big basket of fresh fruit looks as if you're actually supposed to take a piece. Continental breakfast with freshly squeezed juice is served here or in your room. Since this is North Beach, with some of the best restaurants and bakeries anywhere, the croissants and pastries will be the best. Afternoon tea is served here, too, with tiny sandwiches and shortbread.

The inn is as ☞ convenient for business travelers who want a personal atmosphere as it is for families who want bedroom-sitting room combinations with sofa beds that sleep four. From hiring you a stenographer, to packing a picnic lunch, to arranging baby-sitting or tours, the staff are ready to help. High-anxiety types may find that the most considerate personal service is an innkeeper who will find at 10:00 P.M. that aspirin or Alka Seltzer you forgot to pack.

The rooms are pure pleasure. San Francisco designer Nan Rosenblatt decorated them with English and French antiques and a good eye for comfort. She has chosen bright French floral fabrics for quilted comforters and matching canopies. Some rooms look out on a small courtyard, and those in front overlook the square and a bit of city skyline.

The colors, aromas, and sights of North Beach are the very essence of San Francisco. And you can ☞ walk to most of the city's attractions from this location.

How to get there: From Van Ness, take Union Street east; turn left on Stockton. The inn is on your right.

Olive Metcalf

Casa Madrona Hotel
Sausalito, California
94965

Innkeeper: John Mays
Address/Telephone: 801 Bridgeway; (415) 332–0502.
Rooms: 29 rooms, all but 2 with private baths.
Rates: $60 to $140 for rooms; cottages, $140 to $160; 3-room suite,
$275. Continental breakfast included.
Open: All year. Lunch, dinner, beer and wine bar.
Facilities and Local Attractions: Sausalito's shops and galleries,
ferryboat rides across the bay, fine dining.

John Mays knows how to create an atmosphere. He's
turned this luxurious, old mansion perched on a hill above
Sausalito into ☞ one of the most romantic inns you'll find.
Of course, he has a lot going for him with a town almost too
winning for words and spectacular views of the yacht harbor.
Casa Madrona is one hundred years old. Time had taken
its toll on the former residence, hotel, bordello, and boarding
house when John Mays rescued it in 1978. It nearly slid off
the hill during the rains of '82, but renovations already
begun saved it from gliding away.
Since then he's added an elegant tumble of cottages

that cascade down the hill to Sausalito's main street. Each one is different, with dormers, gables, peaked roofs, and hidden decks. Amazingly, the whole gray-green jumble lives perfectly with the old mansion.

You've seen "individually decorated" rooms before, but these beat all. Mays gave each one of his new hillside cottages over to a different Bay Area decorator. The range of their individual styles resulted in rooms with themes from nautical to equestrian (The Ascot Suite), to a Parisian Artist's Loft. Most have private decks and ☛ superb views. And since it *is* fabled, sybaritic Marin, there are luxurious tubs for two (sometimes elevated and open to the room), refrigerators stocked with fruit juice and mineral water, and fresh flowers. (But no peacock feathers.)

If you're indifferent to unique rooms surrounded by lush gardens, exotic bougainvillea and trumpet vine spilling over decks and walkways, perhaps ☛ elegant food will ring your bell. A beautiful wine bar and uncluttered dining room in the old house on top of the hill are lighted and decorated to enchant. Only white linen on round tables and fresh flowers compete with the view from the deck beyond . . . that is, until the food is served.

We began with a California cuisine standard, radicchio and Belgian endive salad with baked chevré (goat cheese). Perfection. Our waiter was agreeable when I ordered another first course (angel hair pasta with roasted peppers and mussels) instead of an entrée. (I love places that encourage you to order by *your* appetite instead of *their* rules.) Others at our table raved about grilled swordfish with a red pepper butter and poached salmon in a tarragon, leek, tomato sauce. The meal could not have been lovelier.

How to get there: Cross the Golden Gate Bridge; take third Sausalito exit (Bridgeway) down to center of town. Inn is on the right. San Francisco Airport pickup available. Ferry service from San Francisco.

♓

J: *If this inn can't rekindle a dying ember, no place can.*

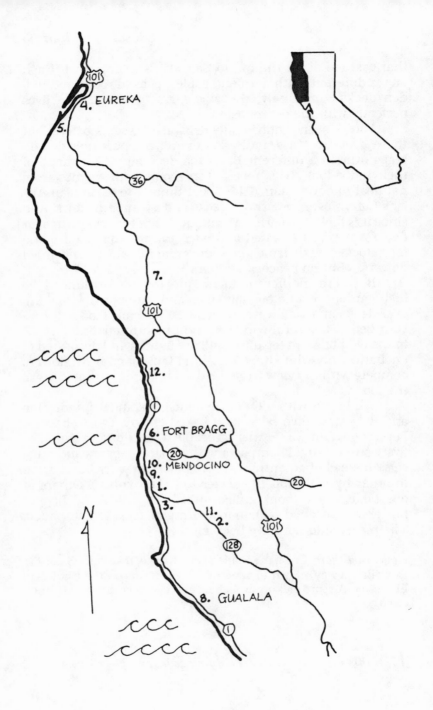

California: The North Coast

Numbers on map refer to towns numbered below.

Olive Metcalf

Fensalden
Albion, California
95410

Innkeepers: Jane and Bob Casey
Address/Telephone: Highway 1 (mailing address: Box 188); (707) 937–4654.
Rooms: 5 rooms, all with private bath.
Rates: $70 to $90 for suite, including breakfast. Prefer no smoking.
Open: All year.
Facilities and Local Attractions: Seven miles from Mendocino for fine restaurants, shopping, art center, galleries, theater. Near Albion and Navarro Rivers for swimming, fishing, canoeing. Hiking, biking terrain.

Humming down California Highway 1, roof back, sea breezes blowing, and Willie Nelson on tape singing his heart out, I nearly ignored a small sign that read "Fensalden." Fortunately, I followed the narrow road back into the hills and discovered a ☞ stunning new inn.

It belongs to Jane and Bob Casey, who flew out from Denver several years ago to look for an inn to buy and fell in love with two dilapidated old buildings sitting on twenty acres. No wonder! The rolling, wooded land is on the spectac-

140

ular Mendocino Coast, and the ramshackle buildings were once an 1860s stagecoach stop and a tavern. What could be better?

With a year's hard work, Jane and Bob transformed the now-connected buildings into a handsome country inn that ☛ blends naturally into the land. It is two storied, cedar shingled, with dormers and balconies, looking out to the ocean. Every step of renovation and decorating has been done with reverence for this beautiful site. They've named it Fensalden (accent the middle syllable), which in Norwegian means "home of the mist and the sea."

You enter a small parlor with a fireplace, Jane's loom, and Bob's telescope in front of a window wall. The interior walls have been left white, with window frames, doors, and beams of redwood. To the right is a large common room, striking because of the view, and wisely left ☛ uncluttered. A few dramatic pieces of local art, a comfortable sofa, and at one end a large dining-room table and chairs are all that's on the soft blue carpet.

The five bedrooms are beautifully simple. Down comforters are inside colorful cotton covers—such a fresh, clean idea, I wonder why more innkeepers don't use them, instead of quilts that can't be laundered after each guest. The baths are particularly attractive. Ceramic tile showers and ☛ sinks made by local potters are works of art.

Bob is the breakfast cook. He'll make muffins, scones, or coffeecakes, depending on his mood, to go with the fresh eggs, coffee, and fresh fruit. For other meals, there are excellent restaurants within a short drive.

How to get there: Driving north on Highway 1, the inn is 1 mile past Albion, on the right.

☗

J: *Away from highway noise here, you can stand among the wildflowers or tramp over the meadows and hear only ocean and wind.*

Olive Metcalf

The Toll House
Boonville, California
95415

Innkeeper: Beverly Nesbitt
Address/Telephone; 15301 Highway 253; (707) 895–3630.
Rooms: 5, 2 with private baths.
Rates: $40 to $93, including country breakfast and complimentary
    wine. Each additional person, $15. No pets; no young children.
    Smoking discouraged.
Open: All year. Evening meals by special arrangement.
Facilities and Local Attractions: Large yard with gazebo, hot tub,
    barbecue. Television in sun parlor. Short drive to wineries and
    fine restaurants.

The Toll House, a picture of apple-pie rural America, sits
in the beautiful, secluded Bell Valley in the heart of Mendocino County. The 1912 house is six miles up the road from
Boonville and was once the headquarters for the vast sheep
grazing Miller Ranch. It became known as Toll House because the family that maintained the road charged loggers to
haul their redwood over it to the inland mills.

In Beverly Nesbitt's hands it has become a well-maintained inn that draws you into its homey atmosphere. The big
shaded yard with a hammock, gazebo, and a hot tub are wel-

come sights to city-weary eyes. Guests have the run of the kitchen during the day to help themselves to coffee and snacks. In your room, more relaxing spirits await: a carafe of local Parducci wine.

The sunny bedrooms have a refreshing absence of frills. Two rooms upstairs with a shared bath are done in pastels, with windows situated to let the sun spill in. The large Blue Room is even more inviting—to masculine tastes, perhaps—with a private bath and a fireplace. All the rooms have queen-sized beds with an additional daybed. Everybody loves the main floor's library, which features a private bath, a fireplace, and book-lined walls. Behind the house is the Bicycle Shed, a captivating room with twin beds and wood paneling—though you do have to cross the patio and enter the house to use the bathroom.

A big country breakfast starts the day in the dining room, on the patio, or in the delightful sun parlor. Fresh juice and fruit are followed by one of Beverly's specials: omelets, waffles, or pancakes, and warm gano sauce (see J's comment). The atmosphere here is so cozy that you may want to request dinner when you make your reservation. With advance notice you can have an intimate dinner for two or a five-course feast, often featuring local lamb. If you go out for dinner, try the sophisticated cooking at the Floodgate in Navarro, just a fifteen-minute drive to the coast.

Getting there: Traveling north from San Francisco, take Highway 101 to Cloverdale. Turn west on Highway 128 and follow to Boonville and Highway 253. Turn northeast. The inn is about six miles up the road. Or take Highway 101 to Ukiah and then Highway 253 (Boonville Road) as it twists over the mountains to Boonville.

☙

J: *This valley is the home of "Boontling," a peculiar, contrived jargon spoken here and even taught in the schools between 1880 and 1920. A sprinkling of it survives today. A cup of coffee at a Boonville café is a* horn of Zeese. *The* Buckey Walter *is a pay telephone. At* The Toll House *you might have* florries *(light biscuits) or* gano sauce *(applesauce made from the apple orchards of Anderson Valley).*

Elk Cove Inn
Elk, California
95432

Innkeeper: Hildrun-Uta Triebess
Address/Telephone: 6300 South Highway 1 (mailing address: Box 367); (707) 877–3321.
Rooms: 8, 6 with private bath; some with fireplace.
Rates: $106 to $148 weekends and holidays, AP; $52 to $98 midweek, breakfast included. No pets.
Open: All year. Dinner on weekends.
Facilities and Local Attractions: Beach walks, secret caves, seals, exotic birds. White-water tours. Restaurants nearby.

Elk is a small village on a bluff overlooking the ocean, as fresh as the winds that blow over it. There are a few surviving Victorian houses, as is this 1883 inn, but it is ocean lovers who come to Elk. From the bluffs behind the inn there is a ☞ spectacular everchanging view of the Pacific.

The main house is where all meals are served. Adjacent to it are four individual units, recently remodeled. Two of these have fireplaces, high, beamed ceilings, and skylights. All of them have bay windows looking out to the ocean view.

Hildrun-Uta's décor is nicely done, with appealing individual touches in each cottage. One has handmade doors more than one-hundred years old; another has bits of stained glass worked into the framework; still another has a sunken bedroom from which the bay window looks to the ocean. Decanters of sherry or wine and fresh flowers welcome you.

Three fourths of a mile north of the main house is the Sandpiper guest cottage with four bedrooms. You enter a living room with books, games, and a big fireplace ready for the first arriving guest to light. Redecorating this rustic cottage is Hildrun's next project. *Nothing* outside needs changing. A windblown ☛ natural garden leads to the cliffs and a path down to the sheltered cove.

Breakfast and dinner at Elk Cove are part of the experience. Hildrun cooks everything herself. With the help of two daughters, she serves on fresh linens and pretty china in her newly remodeled dining room that runs across the ocean side of the cottage. Her German background is reflected in the French and German specialties she prepares. The breakfast star is ☛ Eierkuchen, an impressive German pancake served with fresh berries, applesauce, or raspberry syrup. Weekend dinners might include Sauerbraten, Rouladen, Coq au Vin, Ling Cod Veracruz, or Veal Ragout. A good selection of wines is available, many of them local and unique to the inn.

How to get there: From San Francisco, take Highway 101 to Cloverdale, then Route 128 to the coast. Turn left on Highway 1; go 5 miles to Elk. The inn is on the ocean side of the highway.

☒

J: *Take your sneakers and a sweater for brooding and usually blustery beach walks.*

Olive Metcalf

Carter House
Eureka, California
95501

Innkeepers: Mark and Christi Carter
Address/Telephone: 1033 Third Street; (707) 445–1390.
Rooms: 7; 5 with private bath, 2 sharing a bath.
Rates: $45 to $125 double occupancy; breakfast included.
Open: All year.
Facilities and Local Attractions: Dinners and special events catered at the house. Walk renovated Old Town waterfront, shops, restaurants. Victorian architecture tours; salmon fishing; Fort Humbolt. Drive south to Avenue of the Giants; north to Redwood National Park.

Sitting in the splendid parlor of Carter House sipping wine, I listened as a guest from Ohio declared that he had "built a good many houses in my time" and this house couldn't possibly be new. "No one *does* work like this anymore."

It *is* hard to believe, but Mark Carter built this grand Victorian only five years ago. Growing up in Eureka near the famous Carson Mansion, probably the single finest example of Victorian architecture in the country, Mark admired the architects, Samuel and Joseph Newsom, and worked on renovating other houses they built. When he came across an old book of their designs, he decided to construct one himself, from scratch. Records show that a house following the same design had been built in San Francisco once but was evidently destroyed in the '06 fire.

With a crew of three, Carter built the four-story redwood mansion, handcrafting the intricate wood moldings and detailings. His only deviation from the Newsom plan (aside from modern baths) was a bay window that splashes light into the entryway. Instead of heavy Victorian décor, Mark and Christi kept the walls white (allowing the beautiful wood to stand out even more), put down white marble in the hallway, and decorated with a few outstanding antiques and Oriental rugs on polished oak floors. A 🖙 changing gallery of paintings and ceramics by local artists, plants, and fresh flowers complete the remarkable, light-filled *new* Victorian.

One of the seven guest rooms is a suite, complete with sitting room, fireplace, private bath, and Jacuzzi. Three rooms with high-vaulted ceilings, designer linens, and antiques are on the top floor; three more rooms and a sitting room with a TV are below the parlor.

Mornings begin with a newspaper at your door, then a lavish breakfast served in the dining room. On my visit, we stared with fresh raspberries and juice, proceeded to hot breads and eggs Benedict, and finished with Christi's 🖙 wonderful apple tart.

What a hospitable place to get acquainted with Eureka—and you should. Mark smiles at people who think that because the town is remote, it must be a cultural wasteland. The truth is, it's a stimulating community of writers, artists, and craftspeople, with five theater companies and higher theater attendance per capita than in San Francisco!

How to get there: Highway 101 into Eureka becomes Broadway. At L Street, turn left. Inn is on the corner.

🝊

J: *A friend of Mark's tells that a few years ago he'd often lock up the restaurant he managed and see Mark drive by—at 2 A.M. He wondered what his married friend was doing out at that hour and learned later that new father Mark, rather than have his guests disturbed, lulled his crying son back to sleep out driving. Is that an innkeeper?*

olive Metcalf

Old Town Bed & Breakfast
Eureka, California
95501

Innkeepers: Carolyn and Floyd Hall
Address/Telephone: 1521 Third Street; (707) 445–3951.
Rooms: 5; 3 with private bath, 2 sharing a bath.
Rates: $45 to $55; singles deduct $10. Includes full breakfast. No
smoking.
Open: All year.
Facilities and Local Attractions: Walk to waterfront, Old Town, Victorian architecture, Carson Mansion, shops, restaurants, Theaters, museums. Fishing; bicycles loaned.

With children grown and gone, Carolyn and Floyd Hall
decided they were ready for a new adventure and chose innkeeping. It brought them 300 miles from the valley town of
Stockton to Humboldt County, the far northern part of California, and to this 1872 Victorian. The house is the one-time
residence of William Carson, a local lumber baron. Its location at the entrance to Old Town is ideal for walking that ambitious waterfront revival of Eureka's Victorian past.

Carolyn and Floyd have obviously found a new life they
love. Their inn is neat as a pin, with a ☞ friendly, down-to-

earth atmosphere. Floyd says that he and his guests do so much talking over the wine and cheese spread in the afternoon, they frequently end up going out to dinner together. Since breakfast is the only meal provided, the Halls like to keep up to date on all the restaurants in town so they can help their guests choose one.

Bedrooms are spacious, airy, and attractively decorated. The largest room is The English Ivy, just as fresh as its name implies. But it's hard to resist one called Raspberry Parfait, with a raspberry carpet, lace curtains, and pretty floral wallpaper.

This is one of the few inns that give a break to the solo traveler. A deduction of $10 from the rate schedule offers an attractive package to a single traveler who wants an inn rather than a hotel atmosphere.

Carolyn serves a full breakfast in the formal dining room or sometimes in the kitchen, warmed by its wood-burning stove. Eggs, homebaked muffins, and a variety of fresh fruit are typical fare.

How to get there: Going north on Highway 101, proceed through Eureka and turn left on R Street. Go two blocks to Third Street; turn left. The inn is one-and-one-half blocks on the right.

ⵊ

J: *Floyd Hall has a wonderful quality for an innkeeper: the enthusiasm of a man who is giving a party and can hardly wait for his guests to arrive.*

olive Metcalf

The Gingerbread Mansion
Ferndale, California
95536

Innkeepers: Wendy Hatfield and Ken Torbert
Address/Telephone: 400 Berding Street; (707) 786–4000.
Rooms: 8; 5 with private bath, 3 sharing 2 large baths.
Rates: $55 to $85, double occupancy; singles deduct $10. Includes
    generous continental breakfast. No pets, no children under 10.
    No smoking.
Open: All year.
Facilities and Local Attractions: Walk Victorian Ferndale, theater,
    art galleries, shops, restaurants. June Scandinavian Festival,
    August Ferndale Fair, May three-day World Champion Kinetic
    Sculpture Race (in which "cheating is not a right—it's a privi-
    lege"). Bird-watching reserve at Russ Park; walking tours of
    Pacific Lumber Co.; Humbolt Redwoods State Park.

The Victorian village of Ferndale is far enough off Highway 101 to have remained a secret for a long time. Now, however, increasing numbers of travelers are discovering it and
experiencing that special pleasure of finding a still-little-
known treasure.

Except that every owner of a Victorian has obviously

hired a color consultant and a painstaking crew with brushes to decorate his or her fairy-tale house, ☞ the town has virtually not changed since the 1800s. There are no traffic lights, no parking meters, no mail delivery (citizens pick up at the post office). A village blacksmith is more than local color for the tourists; he uses his hammer and anvil to fabricate practical tools and decorative items. And one of the few remaining Carnegie-endowed public libraries is still in business, circulating books.

Visitors can sample this slice of old-time Americana from a ☞ spectacular turreted, gabled, and elaborately trimmed Queen Anne inn. The Gingerbread Mansion is renowned for being one of the most photographed Victorians in northern California, but fame hasn't turned its head. Wendy and Ken run a first-class inn, paying ☞ attention to little things that you'll remember: robes and luggage racks, a turned-down bed at night, and a hand-dipped chocolate on the table. They'll provide boots and umbrellas if you forget yours, and they'll lend you a bicycle too.

Rooms are decorated romantically and amusingly. Even if you stay in a smaller room, be sure that you ask to see the Gingerbread Suite if it's unoccupied. It has a proper, pretty sitting area, *and* ☞ twin claw-footed bathtubs sitting toe to toe—with reading lights!

I'm a fan of inns like this that have coffee ready and a newspaper for early risers. When breakfast is served, you'll have homemade muffins and cakes along with juice, fruits, cheeses, and jams. Wendy also serves an afternoon tea and cake spread in one of the downstairs parlors.

How to get there: Exit Highway 1 at Fortuna, west to Ferndale. Cross over Eel River Bridge, and proceed 5 miles to center of town. At the green Bank of America, turn left. Go one block to inn on corner.

⧖

J: *Ferndale threatens to become an art colony—God help it—with a significant population of painters, potters, and sculptors.*

Olive Metcalf

The Grey Whale Inn
Fort Bragg, California
95437

Innkeepers: John and Colette Bailey
Address/Telephone: 615 North Main Street; (707) 964–0640.
Rooms: 14 rooms, 12 with private bath. Two penthouse suites share 1 large bath. One room adapted for handicapped.
Rates: $50 to $75, double occupancy; $40 to $65, single; $90, three people; $100, four people. Continental breakfast. Cribs not available; well-behaved children welcome. No pets.
Open: All year.
Facilities and Local Attractions: Walk to depot for Skunk Train, shops, restaurants. Drive to redwood forests, hiking trails, state parks, beaches, Noyo Harbor fishing. Local events: March Whale Festival; July Salmon Barbecue; September Paul Bunyan Days.

The Grey Whale was the first bed and breakfast in Fort Bragg, and many people still think it's the best. The weathered redwood building has the spare, straight lines of New England architecture, and looks suitably sea-bleached and salty. The perception is enhanced by the ☞ hand-carved whale on the front lawn created by Byrd Baker, artist and leader in the "Save the Whales" movement.

152

The inn was originally built in 1915 as the Redwood Coast Hospital. Owners John and Colette Bailey converted it to an inn in 1976, adding their own warm, colorful touches. They have a deeply felt interest in the community and its artists, reflected in the local work decorating the walls.

Wide, carpeted hallways and spacious rooms afford unusual privacy and quiet. Both the prices and the variety of facilities make it a ☞ convenient inn for families. Some rooms sleep up to four and have kitchenettes, some have a fireplace, and others have ocean views. A small sitting room on the first floor is stocked with magazines, scrapbooks of information about the area, and games.

On the second floor, the breakfast room has a refrigerator that guests can use. A morning buffet is spread here of fruits, breads, custard or yogurt, and boiled eggs. You can eat here and meet other guests, or after sizing up the conversational possibilities, you can take a tray back to your room.

Straight directions don't begin to tell the story of driving to the North Coast. One suggestion is to take Highway 128 west out of Cloverdale over to the coast. You'll maneuver steep climbs and tight curves before dropping down into beautiful Anderson Valley with many wineries to explore. Once through the redwood groves along the Navarro River, you'll meet Highway 1 and climb to the headlands looking out at the Pacific. Don't take your eyes off the road until you pull over, but the views are breathtaking. The point is . . . *great scenery takes time.* If you drive Highway 1 all the way from San Francisco, allow about six hours to Fort Bragg.

How to get there: In Fort Bragg, Highway 1 becomes Main Street. Driving north, the inn is on your left.

Olive Metcalf

Pudding Creek Inn
Fort Bragg, California
95437

Innkeepers: Marilyn and Gene Gunderson
Address/Telephone: 700 North Main Street; (707) 964–9529.
Rooms: 10, all with private bath.
Rates: $45 to $65, double occupancy; includes continental breakfast.
Open: All year.
Facilities and Local Attractions: Western depot for Skunk Train; walk to Glass Beach, shops, restaurants. Party boats at Noyo Harbor; July Salmon Barbeque. Mendocino Coast Botanical Garden three miles south. Pudding Creek State Beach open for picnicking, swimming, fishing.

What's an inn without a story? Pudding Creek's tale is that a Russian count with a mysterious past came to the area in the mid-1800s, bringing money that everybody assumed to be ill-gotten. He started a bottling plant, prospered, and built four houses in Fort Bragg, including this one. He changed his name to Mr. Brown, and took a bride who wore the first wedding dress advertised in the Montgomery Ward Catalog.

Pictures of the couple, and the wedding dress, are displayed in the parlor.

If this adds an information overload to your historical triva quotient, simply enjoy the cheerful, easy atmosphere you'll find here. The inn is really two houses connected by ☛ an enclosed garden. Even on the blustery day I visited, it was warm in the garden, and the fuchsias, begonias, and ferns were thriving. This is the choice spot, weather permitting, for afternoon wine and cheese.

On other days, guests gather in the parlor or poke around the country store on the first floor of one of the houses. The store stocks a jumble of souvenirs, local art, gifts, handcrafts, and a collection of depression glass.

Breakfast is served in the parlor or in the old-fashioned kitchen. Marilyn serves homemade coffee cakes along with fresh fruit and coffee. This is the only meal served, but she has plenty of suggestions for dinner at good local restaurants.

The bedrooms are decorated in a combination of early American and Victorian furniture, colorful quilts, and pretty flowered wallpaper. A room named for the count is, naturally, a touch more royal, with cranberry velvet accents, redwood paneling, a king-sized brass bed, and stone fireplace.

How to get there: Highway 1 becomes Fort Bragg's Main Street. Traveling north, the inn is on the right.

🍷

J: *If you don't know about the Skunk Train—it is a forty-mile trip on a standard gauge passenger railroad through mountainous terrain between Fort Bragg and Willits. A big tourist attraction.*

clive Metcalf

Benbow Inn
Garberville, California
95440

Innkeepers: Patsy and Chuck Watts
Address/Telephone: 445 Lake Benbow Drive; (707) 923–2124.
Rooms: 56, all with private bath; terrace- and garden-level rooms
   with TV.
Rates: $62 to $190, EP. Off-season rates: April 1 through June 15;
   October and November.
Open: April 1 to December 1; December 18 through January 2. Bar,
   dining room open to public for breakfast, lunch, dinner, Sun-
   day brunch.
Facilities and Local Attractions: Hiking, swimming, picnics at
   Benbow Lake; bicycles, boat rentals, tennis, horseback riding;
   nine-hole golf course. Scenic drives through redwoods. Shake-
   speare-on-the-Lake, mid-August. Special inn events: Hallow-
   een Ball. November wine tasting, Christmas and New Year's
   Eve celebrations.

   Californians call this territory the Redwood Empire, and
the Benbow Inn is surely one of its castles. Driving north on
Highway 101, you see it rising four stories high in ☛ Tudor
elegance, situated among tall trees and formal gardens on

156

the shores of Benbow Lake and the Eel River. It was designed in 1926 as an inn and enjoyed some grand years. In 1978, the Wattses rescued it from fading elegance and have been steadily restoring and improving it.

For all the fresh refurbishing and additions, Patsy and Chuck have managed to keep a kind of ☛ old Hollywood baronial feeling in the main lobby that's fun: a large stone fireplace, Oriental rugs, antiques, and grand-scale furniture. Tea and scones in the afternoon and an Afghan hound that lounges about looking elegant add to the Hollywood atmosphere. Looking at an old guest register, I saw that fifty years ago Mr. and Mrs. Basil Rathbone checked in—with valet/chauffeur. Charles Laughton stayed here, too, memorizing his lines for *Mutiny on the Bounty* and reading in the evenings to the Benbow family and staff.

Nostalgia stops when it comes to accommodations. New bathrooms, thick towels, great beds, and attractive décor are the rule in the main building. A nice touch in every room is a basket stocked with paperback mysteries. Garden- and terrace-level rooms are even more deluxe, all with decks overlooking the garden and river.

Dinner in the handsome dining room is a dressy (in California, that means shoes, no jeans), candle-lit affair. If you're a guest at the inn, you'll be greeted by name at the door. The menu is not trendy, but includes a variety of fresh fish, good beef, and veal in particular. Several ☛ low-fat entrées are offered with calorie count listed for guests who notice those things. For those who don't, there's a gorgeous ☛ white chocolate mousse with fresh berries.

How to get there: Two hundred miles north of San Francisco, 2 miles south of Garberville, on Highway 101.

☖

J: *The Benbow is not inexpensive, but it's not for snobs either. When I visited, it had a full house of mostly affluent-looking middle-aged couples and honeymooners. But when a party of latter-day hippies arrived for dinner, infant in arms, they were greeted as warmly as any other guests.*

Olive Metcalf

The Old Milano Hotel
Gualala, California
95445

Innkeeper: Kathy McCrea
Address/Telephone: 38300 Highway 1; (707) 884–3256.
Rooms: 9, including 2 cottages; 3 rooms with private bath, 5 share 2 baths.
Rates: $65 to $130, with generous continental breakfast. Two-night minimum on weekends. No children under under 16; no pets. No smoking.
Open: All year. Dinner.
Facilities and Local Attractions: Hot tub; massage therapy available. Beach walks, fishing; explore coastal towns.

The Old Milano Hotel has the right patina of age to look engagingly romantic. At the same time, it's a pleasure to stay where all appointments are fresh, clean, and where everything *works*. This well-maintained country inn has a special setting—three sprawling acres on the Mendocino Coast. You can stroll through the English gardens or relax on the broad lawn and watch the churning surf.

Two indoor sitting rooms have plants, fresh flowers, and cozy chintz-covered sofas to snuggle in by the huge stone fireplace. Afternoon wine tastings here give you a chance to sample some of Mendocino's vintages.

Guest rooms upstairs blend antiques, armoires, floral wallpapers, and handmade quilts. Five of them have ocean views, and one overlooks the garden. The rooms are refined, but not exclusively feminine. Men will enjoy the spacious master suite, which has a private bath and a separate sitting room with a superb view of the ocean and "Castle Rock."

Two cottages on the grounds give you the ultimate in privacy. The Passion Vine Cottage has a sitting area and Franklin stove. ☞ The Caboose, which really is an old caboose, is tucked among the cedars.

Continental breakfast is served in your room, outside on the patio, or by the fire in the wine parlor. Along with the standard fare of homemade breads, fresh fruits, and yogurt are the Old Milano's private blend coffee and unique teas.

Dinner, even though it is open to the public, has an intimate atmosphere. Only two or three entrées are offered each night, usually a fish, lamb and beef, or pork, so that the freshest foods can be used. Gretchen, the cook, is famous for her hors d'oeuvres, things like fresh mussels and ☞ miniature thick-crusted pizzas made with goat cheese and tarragon. Her desserts usually include a deep-dish fruit pie, triple-cream Brie with apples and nuts, and a hot fudge brownie.

Don't miss trying the ☞ terrific outdoor hot tub on a point overlooking the surf. Guests reserve it to assure privacy. Nearby are several skilled massage therapists whom the innkeeper will schedule for you also. Does this sound like a place to drop in for a few days and recharge your batteries? You're right.

How to get there: On the ocean side of Highway 1, 1 mile north of Gualala; 100 miles north of San Francisco.

Olive Metcalf

St. Orres
Gualala, California
95445

Innkeeper: Rosemary Campiformio
Address/Telephone: 36601 Highway 1 (mailing address: Box 523); (707) 884–3335 or 884–3303.
Rooms: 8 in the inn, sharing 3 baths; 8 cottages, each with private bath.
Rates: $50 to $65 double occupancy in the inn; $65 to $125 in the cottages. Breakfast buffet included. No pets.
Open: All year. Dinner, Sunday brunch. Beer and wine bar.
Facilities and Local Attractions: Hot tub, sauna. Beach access, walking, picnics. Visit Fort Ross.

Non-Californians see the ☛ spectacular Russian architecture of St. Orres tucked away above Highway 1 and tend to think it is another example of the native penchant for theater. Actually, a historical basis for the style is found only a few miles south at the trading fort the Russians built in the nineteenth century when they traded in furs and employed the Aleut Indians to hunt the sea otter.

Fort Ross is restored to look as it did while the Russians were in residence, but St. Orres stands as an architectural fantasy of the heritage. It's an intimate hideaway built of hundred-year-old timbers and hand-carved redwood, with stained-glass windows and onion-top turrets capped by copper, octagonal roofs.

You enter through a trellis-covered patio to a cedar lobby, an attractive bar, and plant-filled solarium. The dining room is in one of the stunning 🖝 domed towers that rise more than fifty feet, with row after row of windows and stained glass.

Each bedroom in the inn is a cozy redwood snuggery with a built-in double bed covered with a unique handmade quilt. The baths are "his," "hers," and "ours," the third one being a large, tiled tub with dual shower heads. Two front rooms have French doors that open onto ocean-front balconies.

The more spacious accomodations are the nine cottages surrounding the inn. The most rustic is The Wildflower, one of the original buildings on the property. It has a double bed on a sleeping loft, with a skylight above and a hideabed downstairs. There's a kitchen, bath, wood-burning stove, and an outdoor hot-water shower.

For more luxury, try The Rose Cottage, with architectural details similar to those of the inn. It has a carpeted living room with fireplace, kitchenette, and French doors opening onto a sun deck with an ocean view.

You should not be surprised that the food is as outstanding as the architecture. Begin with Russian caviar and close with Chocolate Decadence; in between, the menu is continental. It changes according to what is fresh and special, but the specialty is 🖝 rack of lamb with a Dijon mustard crust.

How to get there: On Highway 1, between Gualala and Anchor Bay, the inn is on the inland side.

🍺

J: *Gualala, by the way, is pronounced "Wallala." It's not Spanish, but rather a Spanish version of the Pomo Indian word meaning "where the waters meet."*

Olive Metcalf

Whale Watch Inn
Gualala, California
95445

Innkeepers: Irene and Enoch Stewart, and Aurora Hayes
Address/Telephone: 35100 Highway 1 (mailing address: Box 1141); (707) 884–3667.
Rooms: 18, in 5 buildings, including 3 suites; all with private bath.
Rates: $105 to $175 for two; $20 each additional person. Continental breakfast included. Smoking on decks only; no pets. Two-night minimum on weekends.
Open: All year.
Facilities and Local Attractions: Dinners catered by arrangement; selected wines and champagnes available. Whirlpool baths. Private stairway offers beach access. Hiking; nearby golf and tennis facilities.

If the quaint appeal of the North Coast's old accommodations escapes you, Whale Watch may be just the contemporary luxury answer to your desires. On two cliff-side acres, it consists of five architecturally striking buildings with spectacular ocean views. It is the ultimate adult getaway designed for privacy, personal service, and with incomparable scenic beauty.

Every bedroom is stunningly decorated with elegant

furniture, some custom-designed Queen Anne, some hand-carved pieces, a fine Bombay chest here, a yew-wood library table and chest there. Amenities? Merely fine linens and down comforters, ice makers, skylights, fireplaces in most rooms, and your private deck looking out at the rugged surf.

If sybaritic bathrooms are your thing, these take you to the outer limits of the bathing experience. In one, a spiral stairway flows from the bedroom up to the second level capped by a skylight roof to a two-person whirlpool, separate shower, and lounging area with a fabulous view of the Pacific below.

Many rooms are on two levels, and all of them are large. Some units are self-contained and designed for longer stays with fully equipped kitchens.

The original Whale Watch building was the former home of Irene and Enoch Stewart. The redwood-and-glass house has a huge, hexagonal living area with a circular fireplace and a sweeping Pacific view. The area is used as a gathering place for inn guests and has comfortable sofas and chairs, game tables, taped music, books, and wonderful spots to enjoy the view. The two bedrooms in this building open off of this impressive room.

Continental breakfast is served to guests in their rooms. If you would like to stay in for the evening, the innkeepers will arrange an intimate dinner for two, with advance notice. But a short drive up or down the coast brings you to some excellent restaurants—St. Orres, for one.

How to get there: Take Highway 101 to Petaluma and proceed west to Highway 1. Or, take Highway 101 to 4 miles north of Santa Rosa and proceed west to Highway 1. Follow Highway 1 north to Whale Watch at Anchor Bay, 5 miles north of Gualala on the ocean side. Fly-in: Ocean Ridge Airport.

Olive Metcalf

Glendeven
Little River, California
95456

Innkeepers: Jan and Janet deVries
Address/Telephone: 8221 North Highway 1; (707) 937–0083.
Rooms: 10; 8 with private bath, 2 sharing a bath.
Rates: $60 to $100; $15 less for single occupancy; two-night mini-
  mum on weekends. Continental breakfast included. Smoking
  only in sitting room after breakfast. Credit cards, children, by
  arrangement.
Open: All year.
Facilities and Local Attractions: Beach walks, picnics. Close to
  Mendocino galleries, restaurants, and shops.

The delights of California's North Coast have little to do
with sunshine and blue skies. It's the bluffs, the rugged
coastline, and the misty cool climate that seduce those of us
who love it. But unpredictable weather makes the comfort of
your lodging all the more important. Glendeven is an inn that
pleases, rain or shine.

It is an 1867 farmhouse of Maine-style architecture, set
back on a headland meadow from the Mendocino Coast, surrounded by fields and trees. The atmosphere in the pleasant
living room pulls you in to nestle before the fire and enjoy the

view through a wall of windows to a brick patio and the meadow beyond. A piano for impromptu musical urges, a good stereo for those of us less inclined, books, a tray of sherry, and a quiet rural setting—this is the stuff of a country inn.

The deVrieses have an eye for ☞ contemporary art—paintings and sculpture—that they display engagingly in their vintage house. I wanted to buy half a dozen pieces in the house—and they *are* for sale, even though price tags aren't on them. There are also some fine antiques and just comfortable furniture.

Most of the guest rooms have high, vaulted ceilings and French doors leading to private balconies. A favorite is ☞ The Garret, a large attic room with skylights, cozy slanted ceilings, and splendid vistas. A separate building in the back garden is called Stevenscroft, in honor of Isaiah Stevenscroft, who built the farmhouse. It has four elegant rooms, with big tiled baths, decks, pine furnishings, and commanding views.

Breakfast included excellent coffee (ready for the early risers), a fresh fruit bowl, boiled eggs, and just-baked raisin-bran muffins. Breakfast seems to be a good time to hear the latest reports on local restaurants. There are some outstanding choices in the vicinity that the innkeepers will tell you about.

A ☞ path to the beach is an easy walk and a wonderful place to spend the day. With notice, the innkeepers will prepare a picnic basket for you to take along.

How to get there: On California Highway 1 traveling north, just past Van Damme State Park, the inn is on your right.

⧗

J: If you don't enjoy Glendeven, you're just not inn material.

olive Metcalf

Heritage House
Little River, California
95456

Innkeeper: L. D. Dennen
Address/Telephone: 5200 Highway 1; (707) 937–5885.
Rooms: 64, all with private bath.
Rates: $95, one person, to $195 for two-person suite, MAP. Each
   additional person $45. No credit cards; no pets.
Open: Closed December and January. Restaurant serves breakfast,
   dinner; full bar.
Facilities and Local Attractions: Walking paths through woods,
   along beaches. Reading, relaxing. Mendocino nearby for art
   galleries, unique shops, restaurants, theater.

Above the dramatic Mendocino Coast in 1949, innkeeper Dennen and his late wife, Hazel, set about restoring
the original 1877 farmhouse of Mr. Dennen's grandfather.
Since then, Heritage House has become a classic. Without
ever advertising, defying time and fashion, it goes on pleasing and setting a ☛ high standard for a country inn.

The ☛ site is magnificent: forests of eucalyptus and
redwood meet green pasture lands with sheep grazing, and
then stretch to a rocky, churning sea coast. The present sedate atmosphere belies a fairly wild past. In the early 1930s,

Baby Face Nelson used the cove below the house for his bootleg operations, concluding one of his last deals in the house. As late as the 1940s, Chinese immigrants were smuggled into the country here. Today it is one of the more formal inns along the coast, with gentlemen "encouraged" to wear jackets and ties at dinner.

A few guest rooms are in the main building, but most are in cottages tucked into the landscape. As the rooms were built and remodeled through the years, the spirit of 1877 has been kept with furnishings and names inspired by early-day buildings of the area, like Scott's Opera House and Schoolhouse. A two-story unit, The Watertower, has a circular stairway leading from a living room to a bedroom. Most rooms have fireplaces or Franklin stoves.

A glass-domed dining room (one area is nonsmoking) has superb ocean views and a fresh, airy feeling that make it as inviting at breakfast as it is for candle-lit dinners. Breakfasts are hearty: a cereal, fruit and juice buffet, followed by eggs Benedict, a choice of breakfast meats, and dollar-sized pancakes. By the time you return to your room, the sharp staff has made the bed and refreshed your bathroom. Dinner menus change nightly. Perhaps a creamy potato soup, greens mixed with pine nuts and Smithfield ham, rare beef tenderloin or Pacific snapper with sauce mousseline, fresh vegetables, and fettuccine, ending with an almond cream cake. The wine list is extensive.

The comfortable lounge has an enormous fireplace and sweeping views of the rocky coastline. Don't expect TV or video games; you come here to read, look, and relax. And the walks are major pleasures.

How to get there: On Highway 1, the ocean side, between Albion to the South and Little River to the North.

※

J: *Anyone who gets bored on the Mendocino Coast should apply for a new soul.*

olive Metcalf

Little River Inn
Little River, California
95456

Innkeepers: The Charles D. Hervilla Family; Bert Davis, general
 manager
Address/Telephone: Highway 1; (707) 937–5942.
Rooms: 53 accommodations, all with private bath: inn rooms, cottages, motel-type units.
Rates: $56 to $70 in the inn; cottages $70 to $100; fireplace units
 $85 to $175; EP. $10 per extra adult; ☞ no charge for children
 under 12. No credit cards; no pets.
Open: All year. Breakfast, dinner daily. Bar.
Facilities and Local Attractions: Golf course (nine holes), pro
 shop, putting greens; hiking, bicycling Van Damme State Park;
 beachcombing, good tide-pool exploring. Minutes from Mendocino art galleries, antique shops, restaurants.

  Anyone who has driven north on Highway 1 along the
dramatic Mendocino coastline has seen this rambling white
inn off on the right. It looks "New England" because it was
built in 1853 by a pioneer from Maine, Silas Coombs.
  Three generations later, the parlors are lobbies and dining rooms, and the conservatory is the bar. The long front
porch used to be the place to watch for arriving schooners.

168

Now it's where you follow the movements of the salmon fleet, and during the winter months, a favorite place for watching the migration of gray whales.

The range of accommodations here means you can have exactly what tickles your fancy. Rooms in the inn are decorated in early California style with antiques. If you prefer more modern appointments, try the motel wing. The pleasant, single-story rooms have big decks looking out at the ocean. Quiet spots to read are interrupted occasionally by deer wandering in the meadow below.

The cottages are especially cozy when you want to snuggle in for a few days. They have one or two bedrooms, some with sitting areas and fireplaces. One of my favorites for many years and through several refurbishings is called the ☛ Van Damme Property. Across the road from the inn, there are three units sitting directly above the rugged coastline.

Little River's dining room is known up and down the coast for fine cooking. ☛ Whatever is freshest from the sea will be on the menu, along with good steaks and other choices. Salmon, abalone, snapper, and ling cod are specialties, and they are prepared with the delicate touch fresh fish deserves. (It ought to be a crime for kitchens to *claim* that they specialize in seafood when their only technique is to beat, batter, and deep fry!)

There's a down-to-earth quality about food here that you get only when things are homemade. This kitchen makes soups from scratch and its own breads. For dessert, try a fresh berry cobbler with tender crust and softly whipped cream.

How to get there: Three hours north of San Francisco on Coast Highway 1. The inn is on the right just south of Mendocino. Fly-in: Mendocino County Airport, 2 miles from the inn.

Olive Metcalf

Rachel's Inn
Little River, California
95460

Innkeeper: Rachel Binah
Address/Telephone: 8200 North Highway 1; (707) 937–0088.
Rooms: 5, each with private bath. Access for the handicapped.
Rates: $85, double occupancy; $14 for third person. Full breakfast
    included. Two-night minimum on weekends.
Open: All year. Dinners by special arrangement.
Facilities and Local Attractions: Walk fields, headlands and beach;
    whale watching; skin diving cove; Van Damme State Park;
    Fern Canyon. Close to Mendocino restaurants, galleries,
    shops, theater.

If you like the wild, natural Mendocino atmosphere, but
still want comfort, even elegance, in light-filled space, try Rachel's Inn. What a pleasure to see someone with Rachel
Binah's talent and flair go into the inn business. She had
been catering for 10 years when she found a dishearteningly
ramshackle 1870s house on the Mendocino Coast and decided to make it an inn. It took the confidence of a riverboat
gambler to believe that an inn was hiding in that ruin, but
Rachel has accomplished an impressive renaissance of the
house.

The ☞ site is very special—ocean views, tall trees, and wind-swept meadows. And adjoining her property are one hundred acres of state-owned land running right down to the coast, which will remain in the natural state it is now.

The interior of the inn is as fresh and airy as the outdoor Mendocino breeze. Each room's construction and décor reflect a feeling for the coast setting and make the most of the superb ocean views. ☞ High, vaulted ceilings, white walls, and redwood trim detailings are in the large living/dining room. A crackling fire felt good, even on an August morning.

The bedrooms have the same uncluttered good looks as the rest of the house. Linens on the queen-sized beds are in soft muted colors—mauves, grays, and sea green. The Parlor Suite has a cushioned window seat, a separate sitting room with a piano, and an ocean view. The Blue Room has a private deck, a fireplace, and an outside entrance, convenient for a wheelchair. Several rooms have an extra single bed.

For someone with ☞ Rachel's catering experience, breakfast is a piece of cake. She offers juices, fresh fruits, homemade sausage or bacon, muffins, and an egg dish. But give her an event and she'll really start cooking—buffet receptions or a seven-course dinner, like the one she was preparing this day. Her guests were bringing their own rare wines to accompany her menu.

How to get there: On Highway 1 immediately north of Van Damme State Park and 2 miles south of Mendocino, the inn is on the ocean side.

J: *Your first sight of this inn, painted a daring soft mauve, will tell you that there's a stylish innkeeper at work.*

Olive Metcalf

The Victorian Farmhouse
Little River, California
95456

Innkeepers: Carole and George Molnar
Address/Telephone: Highway 1 (mailing address: Box 357); (707) 937–0697.
Rooms: 4, all with private bath.
Rates: $65, with generous continental breakfast. No children; no credit cards.
Open: All year.
Facilities and Local Attractions: Walk to ocean; whale watching; picnics. Two miles to Mendocino restaurants, galleries, shops, theater.

When the Molnars were looking for an inn to buy, Carole favored gold rush country, but George had his heart set on the Northern Coast of California all along. When he talks about "the historic North Coast," you hear real feeling for the beauty and history of this rugged area. The Molnars had long collected antiques, so when they found this picture-perfect Victorian farmhouse near Mendocino, it was kismet.

The house was built in 1877 by John Dennen as a home for him and his wife, Emma. The Molnars' pride in it is ap-

172

parent, and they've lavished their time and attention on making it a completely captivating inn. With just four guest rooms, it is as intimate and cozy an atmosphere as you'll find. Each room is a picture of Victorian charm with period antiques, white eyelet dust ruffles, quilts on the beds, and wicker furniture. One room has an appealing cushioned window seat and a small sitting room that opens onto a deck. The Garden Room looks onto an old-fashioned flower garden that is lighted at night. The views from upstairs are of apple orchards and ocean.

Each room has a small, round table set with white eyelet cloth and pretty china where you'll be served breakfast. The tray brought to your room will have whatever beverage you want—tea, coffee, hot chocolate—juice, fresh fruits, perhaps baked apples, yogurt, and homemade muffins and breads. Carole never wants guests to have the same breakfast twice during a visit, and when people settle in for a week or more, she laughs that she has to get creative.

In the small downstairs parlor, sherry is offered in the evening, and you'll see some of the clocks George has restored. Carole and George will show you menus of nearby restaurants, and there are some fine ones on this part of the coast. When I was there, an antique desk in the room held wine, stuffed animals, and family photographs—all recent gifts from guests who left feeling they had found a home away from home with the Molnars.

How to get there: Driving north on Highway 1, the inn is on your right between Heritage House and Little River.

J: *The Molnars say you should see it in the spring when the daffodils flower and the orchard is in bloom.*

olive Metcalf

The Headlands Inn
Mendocino, California
95460

Innkeepers: Kathy Casper and Pamela Lopresto
Address/Telephone: 44950 Albion Street (mailing address: Box
   132); (707) 937–4431.
Rooms: 6, all with private bath, and fireplace or parlor stove.
Rates: $65 to $85, double occupancy. Two-night minimum on
   weekends; three nights on holiday weekends. No credit cards;
   no pets; no children under 16.
Open: All year.
Facilities and Local Attractions: Hiking the Mendocino Headlands;
   walk to galleries, shops, restaurants, Art Center, theater. Mendocino Botanical Gardens.

   The lumber industry flourished along this coast a century ago, leaving this all-wooden New England–style town as
a legacy. Among the remaining buildings is The Headlands
Inn, named for the spectacular bluffs above the rocky shore.
The shingled, rather stern exterior belies an ☞ exceedingly
warm and well-furnished interior.
   The building began in 1868 as a small barbershop on
Main Street. The barber, John Barry, added the second story
as living quarters for his family. It also had a history as a

"high class" restaurant, The Oyster and Coffee Saloon. In 1893, the house was moved to its present location on the corner of Howard and Albion Streets by horses pulling it over logs used as rollers. From here, it has ☞ unobstructed views of the Big River inlet and the tree-covered mountains beyond.

I could happily move into any one of these guest rooms. The décor is restful—fresh flowers, good furniture, tasteful appointments—with ☞ impeccable housekeeping. Everything from bed coverings to upholstery looks fresh and inviting. Most of the rooms have wonderful views, and each has a fireplace or country stove. Some furniture is antique, and other pieces, like several of the beds, are handsome products of contemporary craftsmen.

A delightful sitting room is on the second floor, with games, books, and good reading lights. You can breakfast here, but most guests prefer having it brought to their room. In comfortable surroundings like these, it's an indulgence that pleases. The innkeepers make their own breads or muffins every morning to serve with freshly ground coffee, teas, juices, and the best fresh fruit they can find. For lunch and dinner, you can walk to a dozen good possibilities, including the renowned Café Beaujolais.

How to get there: Entering Mendocino from Highway 1, proceed one block on Main Street to Howard Street. Turn right, go one block to inn on the left corner.

J: *The flower gardens, like so many in Mendocino, are very English and quite special. They appear to be completely natural, as if the flowers had popped up spontaneously.*

Olive Metcalf

Joshua Grindle Inn
Mendocino, California
95460

Innkeepers: Gwen and Bill Jacobson
Address/Telephone: 44800 Little Lake (mailing address: Box 647);
   (707) 937–4143.
Rooms: 9, all with private bath. Access for the handicapped.
Rates: $62 to $76, single or double occupancy; includes breakfast.
Open: All year.
Facilities and Local Attractions: Walk to coast headlands or beach;
   all Mendocino activities, shops, restaurants, Art Center, the-
   ater.

The beautiful Joshua Grindle Inn looks every bit as New England as it sounds. It is named for the man who built it in 1879, situated on two acres several streets above the bustle of Main Street, Mendocino. The white house is a picturesque sight itself, but from the slight hill it sits on, ☞ the views of ocean and rocky coast are glorious.

New England flavor at its best is throughout the house—comfortable, tasteful, and immaculate. Antiques that decorate each room are early American rather than Victorian. Fine woods and pieces from the Jacobsons' own collection lend a classic, unfussy feeling to the décor.

176

Guests are invited to use the light, airy living room with a fireplace. There sits a fine piano that Gwen identifies as her mother's engagement ring. (Her independent-thinking mother scorned a traditional ring and opted for a grand piano instead.)

Gwen serves a full breakfast at an antique 12-foot-long, pine refectory table. A fine old hutch and a grandmother's clock make exactly the kind of cheerful, cozy ambience that draws people to country inns. Conversation hums over fresh fruit, eggs, and homemade coffeecakes and breads.

It is a short walk to explore the town's galleries and excellent restaurants, but you might choose this inn merely to experience the misty air of Mendocino in a comfortable, country atmosphere. All the guest rooms are appealing. The Library is a warm room with a four-poster double bed and a fireplace trimmed with tiles depicting Aesop's *Fables*. The Grindle, with a view of town and ocean, has a queen-sized bed and, for a third person, a twin bed. In the grounds behind the main house are two additional buildings with accommodations: two rooms in the cottage, and two in the newest addition, The Watertower. The décor is early American with pine antiques and beautiful quilts. Some rooms have fireplaces.

Fleet Admiral Chester W. Nimitz is a friendly presence around here, too—that's Chester, the inn dog, who was found abandoned on the Oakland, California, Nimitz Freeway.

How to get there: Going north on Highway 1, turn off to Mendocino at Little Lake Road (the exit past the main road into town). Inn is on your right in the first block.

J: *Even with the crowds that flock to Mendocino during summer tourist time, the atmosphere here is tranquil and rural.*

olive Metcalf

MacCallum House
Mendocino, California
95460

Innkeeper: Patti Raines; owners, Joe and Melanie Redding
Address/Telephone: 45020 Albion Street (mailing address: Box
    206); (707) 937–0289.
Rooms: 21 rooms, 7 with private bath; other rooms share bath-
    rooms; some rooms have sinks.
Rates: $45 to $165 for 4-person suite. Special family and mid-week
    rates. Continental breakfast. Prefer cash or checks. Children
    welcome; no pets.
Open: All year. Restaurant serves dinner; full bar.
Facilities and Local Attractions: Walk to everything in Mendocino:
    restaurants, shops, galleries, theater. Whale watching, fishing,
    hikes.

Daisy MacCallum was the lucky bride who in 1882
moved into this beguiling New England–style Victorian
house, a gift from her father. Gingerbread trim, gables, and a
white picket fence decorate the yellow house that sits on
three acres.

This is an inn for lovers of flowers and flounces, quilts
and old trunks. In the old house, the rooms have been cheerfully preserved, many still containing the 🖝 original fur-

nishings, Tiffany lamps, and Persian rugs. Facilities are down the hall, but most rooms have a sink. The third floor is a cozy haven with walls papered with rotogravures of the period, and has a small parlor with splendid views of the town.

Other accommodations are in cottages around the garden. Among these, The Watertower and The Green House have private baths and wood-burning stoves. The Carriage House is convenient for families or two couples, with two separate units, each with a Franklin fireplace and an adjoining bath. The most luxurious rooms are those in The Barn. The ☛ upstairs unit has a private deck with sweeping views and a sitting room with a massive stone fireplace.

The Gray Whale Bar and sun porch are additions so skillfully done you would think they were part of Daisy's house. Remember, a bar means music and laughter (naturally), so if you plan to rise early for bird watching, you might want one of the garden or barn suites, a little more removed from the action.

Tim Cannon oversees the restaurant. Dinners are served in the book-lined dining room at tables set with fresh flowers and oil lamps, before a huge cobblestone fireplace. Like all good chefs, he cooks what is freshest, and in season. No cans in this kitchen. Poached salmon with Béarnaise sauce, bouillabaisse, beef Bordelaise, and veal and champignons are typical fare. On the porch off the bar, you can order light items rather than a full dinner. I had tasty homemade linguine with red peppers and snow peas. A continental breakfast is served strictly for house guests.

How to get there: From Highway 1, enter Mendocino on Main Street. On Howard, turn right and go one block to Albion; then turn left. The inn is on the right in the center of the village.

clive Metcalf

Philo Pottery Inn
Philo, California
95466

Innkeepers: Judy and Bill Hardardt
Address/Telephone: 8550 Route 128 (mailing address: Box 166);
    (707) 895–3069.
Rooms: 4, 2 with private bath.
Rates: $65 to $70, including continental breakfast. Smoking only
    on decks. No children or pets.
Open: All year.
Facilities and Local Attractions: Explore Anderson Valley wineries.
    Pottery Studio. Nearby Boonville restaurants, shops. Ocean
    forty-five minutes away.

If you like an atmosphere more laid back than elegant, prefer ingratiating cats and dogs to sybaritic facilities, favor conversation, wine and good music rather than fine antiques and solitary splendor, you'll find a haven at the Philo Pottery Inn.

Fannie, the house dog, will meet you at the driveway and guide you up the walk to the picturesque redwood house. Photographs don't do justice to this old-fashioned log cabin, complete with smoke trailing out of the chimney.

The 1888 house was once a stage-coach stop. The setting is still rural with tall trees, a flower and vegetable garden, and one of the largest blackberry patches in Mendocino County. The main house is an intimate lodging with high-ceilinged common rooms, antique furnishings, a piano, and an extensive library that guests can use. Former owners Jan Wax and Chris Bing were ceramic artists who added decks, stained-glass windows, and floor tiles made in their backyard pottery studio.

There are only two bedrooms downstairs, each with private bath, and two bedrooms upstairs sharing a bath. All the better to enjoy chatting in the parlor with the innkeepers. Chris brings out wine, a few hors d'oeuvres, and turns on some classical music. As other guests arrive, they drift in to join the relaxed gathering. Evening plans are tested, rejected, and enhanced with suggestions from Bill and Judy: a hearty trucker's dinner across the street at Janie's, wonderful gourmet fare at the Floodgate in Navarro, or perhaps a jazz group playing in the coast area. The innkeepers know what's going on and will make any reservations you need.

At the round dining-room breakfast table, you compare notes over fresh fruit cups, croissants, homemade yogurt, cheese, crackers, and jams. Then a tour of the pottery studio and gallery behind the main house is in order. Yes, the pottery *is* for sale, and you may not be able to leave without, at least, an original sugar bowl and cream pitcher.

How to get there: From San Francisco, take Highway 101 north to Cloverdale; follow Highway 128 west through the Anderson Valley to Boonville, then Philo. Driving south on Highway 101, exit at Highway 253, and drive through the Bell Valley to Boonville and Philo. Both are beautiful drives.

Olive Metcalf

DeHaven Valley Farm
Westport, California
95488

Innkeeper: Wayne Zion
Address/Telephone: 39247 Highway 1; (707) 964–5252.
Rooms: 5, sharing 2 baths; 2 suites, 1 with private bath, 1 with half-bath, sharing shower. Two cottages, each with private bath, fireplace, wet bar, refrigerator.
Rates: $55 to $110, including full breakfast.
Open: All year.
Facilities and Local Attractions: Hot tub; bicycling, riding, hiking, picnicking. Picnic baskets and dinners available on request.

Along the Mendocino Coast, an 1870s farmhouse sits on forty acres of hills, woods, meadows, and streams sloping down to the ocean. You can walk the beach and explore life in a tide pool, tramp the hills and chase butterflies, or sit on the front porch and brood as the ocean mist rolls in. Talk about getting away from it all for a few days! If you're a city person, you may not know that places like this exist, but it cozily fills that sometime need for a little isolation.

All the while your creature comforts are being provided for by innkeeper Wayne Zion. A dining room with bright blue tablecloths and with windows open to the meadows is the scene of a breakfast to get you started—unless you elect to have it delivered to your room. Farm-fresh sausage or bacon, eggs, homebaked bread and muffins, and sometimes grits will steel you for the nerve-racking day of tranquility ahead.

The setting may be rural, but down comforters on the beds, along with robes in every room, are pleasant, hardly rustic, touches. One of the simply furnished rooms opens onto a deck that has a ☞ spectacular view of the coastline and surrounding hills. If the day is raw, you'll be comfortable in the living room by the fire, with games, a well-stocked library, or old movies on the VCR. For major chills, Wayne keeps a table full of aperitifs for sipping.

The staff here (Wayne and the chef) are open to doing ☞ guest dinners if you wish. Not only is it nice to stay in on a foggy night, but these two really know their food. They grow their own vegetables, take advantage of the fresh fish in the area—and I mean caught that morning—and do all the baking. Dinner on a recent night was fresh minted pea soup, blanquette de veau, fresh vegetables, and blueberry cassis. Not too shabby for rural life.

One sidelight of the atmosphere here is that you begin to feel that it's *your* country house. After the second day, Wayne says, people start acting funny. They'll come into the kitchen to help, or ask if they can mow the grass or feed the animals. He thinks that maybe he's doing something right.

How to get there: From San Francisco, take Highway 101 to Cloverdale, then Highway 129 to Highway 1. Past Fort Bragg and 1⁷/₁₀ miles north of Westport, inn is on the right.

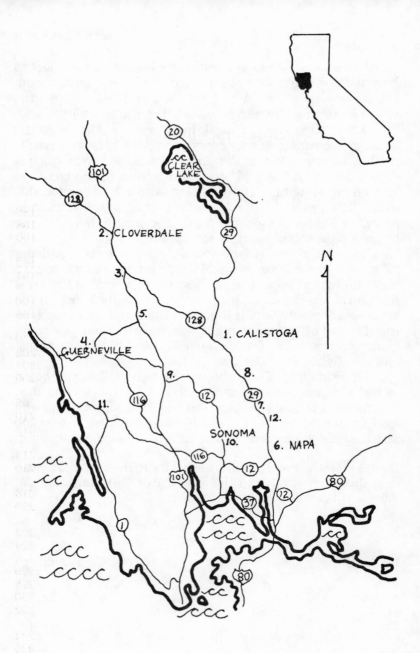

California: The Wine Country

Numbers on map refer to towns numbered below.

olive Metcalf

Calistoga Country Lodge
Calistoga, California
94515

Innkeepers: Tom and Linda Scheibal
Address/Telephone: 2883 Foothill Boulevard; (707) 942–5555.
Rooms: 6; 3 with private bath, 1 common bathroom.
Rates: $75 to $85, with generous continental breakfast.
Open: All year.
Facilities and Local Attractions: Swimming pool. Visit neighboring
    wineries; hike; bicycle; picnic.

The silhouette of a weary Indian warrior on his tired
horse is on the sign at the lodge's entrance. It is an unusual
but fitting theme for an inn situated in the heart of Napa
Valley wine country; the ☛ beautiful wooded property prom-
ises a peaceful retreat at trail's end. Tom Scheibal, who divides his time between here and his Bale Mill Inn a few miles
south, has designed it with great style.

When you open the door to the rambling, white 1930s
stucco house nestling in trees, you enter a thoroughly ☛
uncommon common room. Scheibal has removed all distrac-
tions to create one long open-beamed space, as clean and
bleached as a desert scene. The floors are wide planks of
whitewashed pine with textured rugs scattered about. At one

end is a grand piano and an old stone fireplace with a moose head over it surveying the room.

The ☞ rustic pine furniture arranged in several groupings down the room was designed and built by Tom. Chairs and settees are softened with pads and pillows covered in natural canvas. On some he has splashed the fabric with ragged black splotches to resemble cowhide. The only color in the room comes from ☞ vivid Indian rugs on the walls and leafy green potted trees. Some aptly chosen black-and-white photos are a wonderful touch: Gary Cooper in a cowboy hat; Georgia O'Keeffe and Alfred Stieglitz.

A marble-top table is used for a generous continental breakfast buffet served on bright pottery. Very pleasant to help yourself and mosey out to the swimming pool terrace.

Bedrooms down the hall keep the southwest feeling with Indian artifacts and rugs and Tom's four-poster pine beds. The Mt. Helena room has a fireplace with deer antlers, Indian baskets, and a beige-and-carmel-spotted calfskin rug. The ☞ common bathroom in the hall will make you smile. It looks as if it is lined with cowhide. Every surface, walls and porcelain alike, is spotted with black and outlined with rope. Downstairs, a low-ceilinged room with a stone fireplace is quiet and cozy, but you do have to go upstairs for the bath.

A basket of local restaurant menus is in the common room. The valley has such an embarrassment of famous places that you may arrive with several names you want to try. The innkeepers are glad to help with reservations.

How to get there: Follow Highway 29 through the Napa Valley to Calistoga; at the intersection of Highway 128, continue straight ahead a mile. The Inn is on the left side of Highway 128.

Olive Metcalf

Culver's, A Country Inn
Calistoga, California
94515

Innkeeper: Scott Harring
Address/Telephone: 1805 Foothill Boulevard; (707) 942–4535.
Rooms: 6; each 2 rooms share a bath. Air conditioning.
Rates: $65 to $85, single or double occupancy; continental break-
    fast included and evening wine. No children under 12; no pets;
    no smoking in bedrooms.
Open: All year.
Facilities and Local Attractions: Catered dinners arranged. Swim-
    ming pool, Jacuzzi, sauna. Winery tours arranged. Mineral wa-
    ters and mud baths nearby. Biking; hot-air ballooning;
    Calistoga restaurants, shops.

Calistoga has been famous since the nineteenth century
as a health-spa town with mineral waters and mud baths.
One of the mansions built in the resort community then was
that of editor and publisher John Oscar Culver. His large,
three-level Victorian is now an ☞ immaculate, well-decorated inn.

The inn sits on a hillside with a view of the Napa Valley
and Mount St. Helena from the big covered front porch. The
grounds are dotted with old shade trees, and a path leads

around to a new 🖝 swimming pool, sun deck, and Jacuzzi elegantly nestled into the back hillside.

Inside, Scott Harring has created a comfortable, inviting sitting room with mellow, pine floors, vivid Oriental rugs, cushy sofas, antiques, and a fireplace. Beside it is a formal dining room where 🖝 special Thanksgiving and Christmas (very Dickensian, with roast goose) dinners are done for house guests by the chef for the Beringer Winery.

At breakfast, guests gather at round tables in a light-splashed room adjoining the spiffy kitchen that recklessly sports an Oriental rug. French doors open onto a patio for summer breakfasts. It is a fresh, appealing atmosphere with a dividend to the arrangement: While you sip juice, you can savor the aroma of homemade goodies baking and get Scott's ideas on restaurants and local attractions. Sometimes he makes scones or pastries, and he modestly admits he has an "amazing" muffin repertoire. Fresh fruit, coffee, and a variety of teas are accompaniments.

Bedrooms are as light and airy as is the main floor. The upstairs four are furnished in Victorian and early-twentieth-century style. The three on the lower floor are in authentic Edwardian, Art Deco, and Art Nouveau. They are uncluttered and simply done, each benefiting from a few carefully selected furniture pieces and accessories.

At the end of the hall on the lower level is a 🖝 first-class sauna with a shower beside it. Scott says that guests enjoy hopping from one to the other. For really major body rejuvenation, he will arrange for massage or mud baths—"the works"—at a nearby spa.

How to get there: Follow Highway 29 through the Napa Valley to Calistoga and intersection of Highway 128. The inn is ¾ mile north of Calistoga on the west side of Highway 128.

Olive Metcalf

Larkmead Country Inn
Calistoga, California
94515

Innkeepers: Gene and Joan Garbarino
Address/Telephone: 1103 Larkmead Lane; (707) 942–5360.
Rooms: 4, each with private bath; air conditioning.
Rates: $88, including continental breakfast and early evening re-
    freshment.
Open: Year round.
Facilities and Local Attractions: View vineyards from porch. Visit
    wineries, Calistoga restaurants, shops, mineral waters, mud-
    bath spas.

Between the Silverado Trail and the Sonoma Mountains
runs the fertile Napa Valley. Acres of vineyards are crisscrossed with lanes. On one of them is a splendid white clapboard house with broad porches. You will not find a fluttering
flat or a cute sign announcing the inn, merely a burnished
brass plate with "Larkmead" on it. Drive through the old
fieldstone gates and around the house to a 🖙 wisteria-covered loggia.

The main-floor living room and bedrooms are really on
the second floor. Early in the century, the house was pur-
posely built high by the Swiss owner, says Joan Garbarino, in

order to catch the evening breezes and look out over his vineyards.

Guests are encouraged to enjoy the ambience of the sprawling house and grounds. The large living room is beautifully furnished with the Garbarinos' collection of antiques, handsome upholstered furniture, books, and paintings. Their Persian rugs are brilliant contrasts to dark wood floors. A crackling fire and a decanter of sherry invite arriving guests to a ☞ private, tasteful world.

The house is large, but Joan offers only four bedrooms. It is a matter of high standards ("I'm death on cleanliness!") and wanting to give personal attention to every guest. Bedrooms, named for Napa Valley wines, all overlook the vineyards and hills beyond. Beaujolais uses the open porch over the loggia. Chenin Blanc has a fresh green-and-white floral print on the walls, draperies, and a chaise. Chardonnay is decorated in Art Deco, and Chablis has an enclosed sun porch.

You breakfast in the formal dining room on ☞ Imari china with Grand Baroque sterling. Joan serves a beautiful arrangement of fresh fruit followed by individual baskets of hot breakfast breads with freshly ground coffee.

This is the only meal served, but the recent appearance of some exceptional restaurants in the valley attracts many people. The Calistoga Inn is a great favorite, with fresh menu changes daily and an adjoining pub.

How to get there: From San Francisco, take Highway 101; or from the East Bay, take Highway 80 to Highway 37. At Highway 29 continue north, and turn right on Larkmead Lane between St. Helena and Calistoga. For a more picturesque route, take any cross-valley road from Highway 29 to the Silverado Trail; follow north, turn left on Larkmead Lane.

J: *You can step right next door to the Hans Kornell Winery and see the process of making bottle-fermented champagnes.*

olive Metcalf

The Old Crocker Inn
Cloverdale, California
95425

Innkeepers: Jamie and Jennifer McIntosh
Address/Telephone: 26532 River Road; (707) 894–3911.
Rooms: 9, all with private bath.
Rates: $75 to $120, including continental breakfast and afternoon wine and cheese. No pets. Children welcome.
Open: Year round. Lunch and dinner by arrangement.
Facilities and Local Attractions: Swimming pool, barbecue facilities, badminton, volleyball. Hiking. Winery visits. Four miles to Cloverdale restaurants, shopping. Airport pickups.

What a perfect place for a family get-together! The Old Crocker Inn is situated on five quiet, shaded acres in the beautiful hills of Asti. The location among huge old oaks, pines, and some redwoods is secluded, but there is plenty to do for entertainment.

A big swimming pool with a cabana and a barbecue area is the lure on hot days. There are also volleyball, badminton, and beautiful trails to hike. If the weather is cool, you can stay in and snuggle up by a fire in the main lodge, read, and enjoy the complimentary afternoon wine and hors d'oeuvres.

Philosophical types who seek quiet will find the space to be alone and superb views for inspiration.

Farther afield is the opportunity of visiting more than thirty nearby wineries, or enjoying the Russian River, and Lake Sonoma attractions.

The four buildings on the property are the large main lodge, with two large common rooms, and three cabins, one of them a honeymoon suite. Rooms in the main lodge are built around a garden court and have French doors that open to a veranda encircling the building. There are wonderful views from here of the Alexander Valley. The rooms have queen-sized beds and a turn-of-the-century feeling with antiques and 12-foot ceilings.

A "whatever you want" attitude about food here is very appealing. Do you like juice, a cup of coffee, and solitude in the morning? Or are you ready for pastry, muffins, fresh fruit, and company? Whatever your choice, you can enjoy it by the pool, on the veranda, or in the dining room by a fire. If you want to stay in for dinner, just tell the innkeepers what you would like and it can be arranged.

Jamie says that a new restaurant, the Russian River Yacht Club, at the bottom of the hill, is pleasing many of his guests with great steaks, chicken, ribs, and inexpensive prices. For more choices you have only a four-mile drive to Cloverdale for Zola's continental fare or Catelli's Italian.

How to get there: At Cloverdale, leave Highway 101; follow First Street east through town across the river to River Road. Continue on, turning left as road winds south. At KOA Campground sign (Old Crocker Inn sign is below it), proceed 1 mile to another Old Crocker sign. Follow drive up ¼ mile to the inn. Fly-in: Asti or Santa Rosa Airports.

olive Metcalf

Vintage Towers
Cloverdale, California
95425

Innkeepers: Lauri and Dan Weddle
Address/Telephone: 302 North Main Street; (707) 894–4535.
Rooms: 8, 6 with private bath. Air conditioning.
Rates: $45 to $80, including full breakfast. No chidren; no smoking.
Open: All year.
Facilities and Local Attractions: Russian River six blocks away for
    canoeing, swimming, tubing. Lake Sonoma boating, fishing,
    skiing. Equestrian trails, hiking. Bicycles available.

Vintage Towers is another of those grand Victorians
built by a lumber baron for himself. Simon Pinschower built
this Queen Anne in 1901, and it's had loving care through
the years, most recently with innkeepers Lauri and Dan
Weddle.
They've remembered Pinschower by naming one of the
tower suites for him. A settee and chair upholstered in royal
blue sit in the bay window formed by the tower. The bedroom
furniture has belonged in Cloverdale families for more than
one hundred years. The tower suites are choice, but each one
of the antique-appointed rooms is pleasant.

194

One owner of the house had a penchant for adding 🖝 huge floor-to-ceiling, many-drawered cabinets to the bed-rooms. An overnight guest is hardly going to use them, but I enjoyed just thinking about how I could fill them if they were in my house.

Pinschower did not scrimp on space. At the top of the stairs, what could have been an ordinary landing is, instead, an entire sitting room furnished with a wood-burning stove, a Victorian sofa, and a barber's chair. Dan says that wedding parties who have booked the whole house often set up the ironing board here and scurry back and forth between rooms in a flurry of activity.

The 🖝 library is fascinating. More than 1,000 volumes are in the house, including handsome old sets of Dickens and Carlyle. Across the hall is the Music Room with a piano and a collection of offbeat instruments. The most unusual is a 🖝 piano player—no, that is *not* a player piano. The old Chase-and-Baker oddity is fitted up with a roll of music, say a Scott Joplin rag, rolled up next to the piano, and its wooden fingers dash over the keyboard banging out the tune.

Breakfast is a substantial meal here: fresh fruit, eggs, and hot breads. As an afternoon refreshment, Lauri and Dan pour a 🖝 velvety, thirty-year-old August Sebastiani sherry. For dinner, they will suggest several restaurants in town, or you might want to drive to Healdsburg for a big splash at Madrona Manor.

How to get there: From San Francisco, follow Highway 101 to cen-ter of Cloverdale. At first stoplight in town, turn right on First Street. Go one block to North Main; turn left. Inn is three blocks on the right.

olive Metcalf

Hope-Merrill House and Hope-Bosworth House
Geyserville, California
95441

Innkeepers: Bob and Rosalie Hope

Address/Telephone: 21238 Geyserville Avenue (mailing address: Box 42); (707) 857–3356.

Rooms: 5 in Hope-Bosworth, 2 with private bath, 1 with half-bath, 2 share common bath; 5 in Hope-Merrill, 2 with private bath, 3 with sinks in room share common bath.

Rates: $45 to $75, double occupancy; continental breakfast included at Hope-Bosworth; full breakfast at Hope-Merrill. Not suitable for children; smoking discouraged.

Open: All year.

Facilities and Local Attractions: Picnics, vineyard tours arranged. Explore backroads, many small wineries. Russian River, redwoods, Lake Sonoma, Warm Springs Dam close by.

Geyserville is a small town in the Alexander Valley, one of the most beautiful—and least traveled—areas of California wine country. On the first day of September, the vines were hanging heavy with ripe grapes, and the aroma of the crush just begun pervaded the valley.

This pair of houses, facing each other across Geyserville's main street, was restored as inns by the Hopes in 1980. The Hope-Merrill is the more splendid of the two, a redwood Victorian of the Eastlake Stick style popular in the 1880s. It was once an early stage stop. It has exceptionally beautiful dining and living rooms, with 🖝 handsome silk-screened wallpapers, antique furniture, and a collection of Victorian curiosities. The five bedrooms are strikingly decorated.

Both houses retain an atmosphere of the time they were built—old-fashioned yards, grape arbors, and at Hope-Merrill, a white gazebo. Ceiling fans are a modern touch that *look* old but do a good job of cooling on hot days.

The Hopes have devised a tour they call 🖝 "Stage a Picnic" to show guests the wine country. Two strawberry-roan draft horses pull a ten-person antique open-air stage right through the vineyards. You visit three wineries while your driver tells you about the grapes and relates tales of this old community. If your tour includes Trentadue Winery, the stage approaches it down a long grape arbor thick with green leaves and hanging bunches of grapes. People who have never before visited the wine country can't take pictures fast enough; and for those who are familiar with it, it's still a spectacular excursion.

Then comes Rosalie's gourmet picnic of local cheeses and smoked meats, seasonal fresh fruits and vegetables grown in Sonoma County, and her own prize-winning breads. She's well known as 🖝 an outstanding caterer, and the lunch is as beautiful to look at as it is to taste.

How to get there: From Highway 101, take Geyserville exit to 128; follow it into town past the Bank of America. Check in at Hope-Merrill on the left.

J: Get a map and drive or bike as many of these back roads as you can. They're special.

olive Metcalf

Ridenhour Ranch House Inn
Guerneville, California
95446

Innkeepers: Robert and Martha Satterthwaite
Address/Telephone: 12850 River Road; (707) 887–1033.
Rooms: 8, 5 with private bath. Wheelchair access.
Rates: $50 to $85, including tax and complimentary breakfast.
    Children over 10 welcome; no pets.
Open: Closed December and January.
Facilities and Local Attractions: Quiet retreat; hot tub; croquet
    court. Hiking, bicycling, winery visits. Close to Russian River
    beaches; good restaurants.

The Russian River winds over two hundred miles of
northern Sonoma County. Near Guerneville (pronounced
Gurn-ville, please), it flows west through wooded mountains,
redwood forests, and vineyards to the Pacific. In this beautiful countryside, Louis Ridenhour built a ranch house in 1906
on part of the 940-acre spread that his family had on both
sides of the river.

The Satterthwaites have owned the house since 1977.
They have succeeded in creating a quiet country inn that
blends comforts and conveniences with the atmosphere of a
private home. There is a large country kitchen, a formal din

ing room, and an especially appealing redwood-paneled living room. This is the kind of room that invites you to relax by the fireplace, with lots of comfortable furniture, Oriental rugs, and greenery.

Each bedroom has individual touches that please, along with decanters of sherry, fresh flowers, and tranquil views of the wooded setting. Some rooms have an early American look with brass beds and quilts; others have English antiques.

You can enjoy a light breakfast in the big kitchen or out on the patio: freshly ground coffee, fresh juices and fruits, cheeses, nut breads, muffins, and hard-cooked eggs. During the day, guests are free to help themselves to coffee, tea, or chilled white wine from the refrigerator.

Paths meander around the inn's informally landscaped grounds, under oak and redwood trees, and past a hot tub. One can walk to the neighboring Korbel Winery and visit their champagne cellars, or to secluded river beaches nearby.

The Satterthwaites know an abundance of good restaurants to recommend. In Santa Rosa, they like the continental fare at Matisse and La Garre. At Jenner-by-the-Sea, they say River's End not only has good food but also a spectacular ocean view.

How to get there: From Highway 101 north of Santa Rosa, take River Road exit. Drive west 12½ miles to entrance to the inn on the right, just 500 yards east of Korbel Winery.

J: Your fresh breakfast fruit is often from the inn's own orchards: figs, pears, plums, apples, and, oh joy . . . fresh raspberries!

Olive Metcalf

Camellia Inn
Healdsburg, California
95448

Innkeepers: Ray and Del Lewand
Address/Telephone: 211 North Street; (707) 433–8182.
Rooms: 7, 5 with private bath.
Rates: $40 to $75 double occupancy; rate includes full breakfast
  buffet, afternoon wine. No pets; children not encouraged;
  smoking in designated areas only.
Open: Year round.
Facilities and Local Attractions: Swimming pool. Two blocks from
  town plaza's shops, restaurants. Visit Russian River wineries.
  Canoeing, fishing, swimming on the river.

This graceful Italianate Victorian is a wonderful setting
for indulging fantasies of the leisurely "good old days," with
you starring as master or mistress of the mansion.

Because you're decently rich, you have not one, but *two*
connecting parlors with ☞ twin marble fireplaces. The
rooms have long elegant windows, 12-foot ceilings featuring
medallions and other architectural details. Oriental rugs, and
inviting sofas and antiques fill the rooms, which are decorated in warm salmon tones. A crystal decanter of sherry and
fresh flowers are appointments you insist upon.

As the proper owner of one of the finest houses in town, you must perambulate the grounds to see that the roses and camellias are thriving and to pause by the tiled fishpond to count the stock. After a vigorous property inspection, you rest by the villa-styled swimming pool—just the shady spot for a sip of something bracing.

If your fancy today is a winery tour or dinner at a restaurant, your household staff is knowledgable about both. For dinner, a suggestion might be that you leave the carriage at home and stroll to the Plaza Grill on the town square. Most agreeable.

Later that night you step from an upholstered footstool to your four-poster, canopied, queen-sized bed and slip between crisp sheets. You prop yourself up on fluffy pillows and survey your big bedroom with lace at the windows and antiques. Soothing music lulls you to a well-deserved sleep. In the morning, confident that someone *else* is grinding Viennese coffee and squeezing fresh juice, you linger in your private bath with its marble shower, antique sink, and thick towels.

What a pleasure to enter a dining room that looks the way God meant it to look—spacious and substantial, with a massive hand-carved mahogany mantel surrounding a tiled fireplace. Help yourself from the buffet offering fresh fruit, just-baked breads, soft-boiled eggs, and homemade jams. Have another cup of coffee and, if you *must* spoil the dream, face the morning newspaper.

How to get there: Driving north on Highway 101, take the second Healdsburg exit. Follow Healdsburg Avenue to North Street, and turn right. Inn is on the left.

J: *I can't see why some people are always complaining about life's hardships. The world seems altogether orderly and pleasant to me at Camellia Inn.*

Olive Metcalf

Grape Leaf Inn
Healdsburg, California
95448

Innkeeper: Kathy Cookson
Address/Telephone: 539 Johnson Street; (707) 433–8140.
Rooms: 7, each with private bath. Air conditioning. Wheelchair access.
Rates: $55 to $95, including full breakfast and complimentary local wines and cheeses. No smoking.
Open: All year.
Facilities and Local Attractions: Walk to Healdsburg Square; restaurants, shops. Wine touring. Bicycling. Russian River boating, rafting, fishing.

This sedate, lavender Queen Anne with the grape color trim is a gingerbread deceiver. Who would think that behind its Victorian façade are seventeen skylight roof windows, air-conditioned bedrooms, and seven private bathrooms, each with a ☞ two-person whirlpool tub/shower?

The 1900-vintage home has undergone major renovations, including the addition of an entire second floor under the existing roofline. The four bedrooms and baths up here have an abundance of appeal, due in large part to all the ☞ natural light from the roof windows. They can be opened for

202

fresh air, but even when closed, you have magnificent views of the trees, mountains, and blue sky of Sonoma.

Each of the guest rooms has a sloping roof, and you know how cozy that is. They are named and decorated after the varietal grapes grown in the surrounding countryside: Chardonnay, Cabernet Sauvignon, Merlot, Zinfandel, Pinot Noir, and Gamay Rosé. Colorful linens and puffy comforters decorate the iron and brass beds, all king- or queen-sized. The Chardonnay has a separate sitting area with a daybed covered in white eyelet and two stained-glass windows in shades of blue and purple.

Downstairs guests can enjoy a colorful parlor with a blue-floral-patterned sofa before the fireplace, as well as a living room, dining room, and kitchen. They are fresh, pleasant rooms to relax in, read, or sip a glass of wine. Outdoors under the trees, the umbrella tables are inviting, too.

A full breakfast is served in the dining room at a lace-covered table with fresh flowers. Fresh juice and fruit, home-baked breads and muffins, and an entrée, such as a frittata, are typical.

For dinner, stroll to the square and try the Plaza Grill's mesquite-broiled fresh fish and meat. Also on the square is the Salame Tree Deli. It's a good supply station for picnickers. Choose from an assortment of cold cuts, cheeses, and wines; then head for the back roads—on bikes if you've brought them. And who would go to Sonoma without a bicycle!

How to get there: Driving north on Highway 101, take the second Healdsburg exit and follow into town. At Grant Street, turn right two blocks. The inn is on the right at the corner of Johnson Street.

J: *Can anyone doubt that we Westerners are ready for hardship and sacrifice when necessary? The popular duo-bathing phenomenon proves we'd do* anything *to conserve water!*

olive Metcalf

Healdsburg Inn
on the Plaza
Healdsburg, California
95448

Innkeeper: Genny Jenkins
Address/Telephone: 116 Matheson Street (mailing address: Box
     1196); (707) 433–6991.
Rooms: 8, each with private bath; air conditioning.
Rates: $75 to $95; substantial discounts mid-week and off-season.
     All rates include full breakfast, afternoon refreshments. No
     children under 7; smoking only on roof garden.
Open: Year round; closed first two weeks in December.
Facilities and Local Attractions: Walk to Healdsburg restaurants,
     shops. Wine tours; Russian River nearby for canoeing, fishing;
     picnics; good bicycling area.

    Genny Jenkins looks around the small Victorian hotel
she has restored, shakes her head, and grins. "I didn't *need*
this!" She already owns a small B&B in Sonoma, but given
her enormous energy, the beautiful old Krause building on
the Plaza had too much potential to pass by.
    Healdsburg is a 🖙 heart-tugger of a town, built around
a Spanish-style plaza with quaint storefronts and historic

houses on its backstreets. Genny has decoratively painted and trimmed her building with bright colors, divided the lower floor into attractive shops, and created a comfortable inn upstairs. A paneled stairway leads up to a wide, tall-ceilinged hallway with ornamental architectural details, period lighting fixtures, and a cozy parlor with a TV.

Rooms facing the plaza have graceful bay windows that make delightful sitting areas. Genny is constantly decorating with an eye for turn-of-the-century furniture and whimsy. Several bathrooms have new ☞ spectacular skylights over big, claw-footed tubs. "We really go in for an abundance of plush towels, bubbles, and rubber ducks," she says.

The room that captivated me is in back. Long ago, it was a ☞ photography studio. An entire wall—and these are 12-foot ceilings—is a slanted skylight. Besides the large bath and queen-sized bed, at no extra cost, you get a ceiling of clouds and sky. Imagine it for full moons!

A large ☞ flower-filled roof garden is one of Genny's best innovations. Breakfast is usually served out here at fancy, white iron tables and chairs: fresh fruit and juice, homemade goodies, and an entrée of cheese, eggs, or meat combination. Hot popcorn and wine constitute the afternoon refreshment.

Most guests walk across the square to the Plaza Grill for dinner. The innovative mesquite grill cooking, with the freshest ingredients, is winning many fans.

How to get there: Driving north on Highway 101, take second Healdsburg exit; turn right on Matheson Street, follow to town plaza. Inn faces the plaza. Coming from the north, take Mill Street exit to the plaza.

J: *In 1901, the local paper said that this building was "a substantial ornament to the town." Healdsburg is lucky that the description holds true once again.*

olive Metcalf

Madrona Manor
Healdsburg, California
95448

Innkeepers: John and Carol Muir
Address/Telephone: 1001 Westside Road (mailing address: Box 818); (707) 433–4231.
Rooms: 14 and 2 suites, all with private bath.
Rates: $75 to $140 double occupancy; full breakfast included.
Open: All year. Dinner nightly, Sunday brunch.
Facilities and Local Attractions: Swimming pool. Convenient to golf, tennis, hiking, canoeing, fishing. Winery tours and picnics.

Country inns are springing up in northern California faster than you can spot a yuppie, but Madrona Manor stands alone. First, it is a truly ☞ dramatic Victorian mansion sitting in the midst of landscaped grounds and eight wooded acres. But even more notable is its ☞ outstanding California restaurant, the only one in Sonoma County rated 3-stars by *Chronicle* food critic Patricia Unterman.

Approaching the Italianate mansion up the long driveway brings feelings of pleasant anticipation. Elegant accommodations await inside: antique furnishings, period wallpapers and rugs, and rooms with original plumbing and

206

lighting fixtures. Less opulent but more modern rooms are in the Carriage House and two other outbuildings.

The fine cooking is served in two high-ceilinged, attractive dining rooms. The kitchen is run by an ex–Chez Panisse cook, Todd Muir, with a staff that includes his sister, who apprenticed with the Stanford Court's pastry chef. They work in a modern kitchen (contrasting with the rest of the 1881 setting) complete with a wood-burning oven for bread and pizzas, a mesquite grill, and a smokehouse in back that produces smoked trout, chickens, and meats.

During the week, salads, pastas, and grilled main courses are served. On weekends they offer a $25 (at this writing) prix-fixe menu. As a first course, my individual goat-cheese soufflé was perfectly crusty on top with a softly oozing middle. Every element of the meal, down to dessert of amaretto-soaked cake with chocolate-ricotta filling, was meticulously prepared.

The wine list is both interesting and reasonably priced, which, even though this is the heart of the wine country, is not always true up here. Some selections from small local wineries are at near-retail prices.

Breakfast for guests is as carefully done as dinner. It includes their wonderful house bread, toasted, a perfectly timed soft-boiled egg, ripe, room-temperature cheeses, and house-smoked meats. When the weather allows, take this meal outside on the palm terrace.

How to get there: From San Francisco, drive north on Highway 101, 12 miles north of Santa Rosa; take the second Healdsburg exit; follow Healdsburg Avenue north to Mill Road, which becomes Westside Road. Inn is on the left. From the north, take Westside Road exit from Highway 101.

❋

J: *What a beautiful place for a special celebration.*

olive Metcalf

Beazley House
Napa, California
94559

Innkeepers: Carol and Jim Beazley
Address/Telephone: 1910 First Street; (707) 257–1649.
Rooms: 9, 4 in main house sharing 3 baths, 5 in the Carriage House, each with private bath. One room with wheelchair facilities.
Rates: $70 to $105, including expanded continental breakfast.
Open: All year.
Facilities and Local Attractions: Jacuzzi tubs. Wine touring, hot mineral baths, ballooning, bicycling. Close to Napa shopping, restaurants.

The blue-and-white striped awnings take your eye immediately. They give this shingled Colonial Revival the look of a grand English vacation house. It is an old Napa landmark and sits on half an acre of lawns and gardens within walking distance of the town's shopping area.

The solid-looking house is beautifully symmetrical, with an especially wide staircase at its center. A beveled- and stained-glass doorway opens to the entry and music room. To the right is a formal dining room; to the left is a long, gracious living room with polished, inlaid wood floors and large bay windows at either end, one with a padded window seat. Brightly upholstered sofas and chairs are arranged in several groupings. There are a fireplace, bookcases, and a basket of Napa restaurant menus to peruse. A teacart arranged with china cups and saucers, tea, coffee, and sherry looks very civilized and Edwardian.

Halfway up the stairway is a window seat and a ☞ spectacular half-round stained-glass window. The bedrooms are pleasantly spacious. Carol has made most of the comforter covers herself in big, English floral prints with matching draperies. The Master Room, with a fireplace, and the Wine and Roses Room have a common bath. They make a comfortable suite for couples traveling together.

At the back of the property, the old carriage house has been rebuilt from the ground up, modeled after the original barn. These rooms have fireplaces, high ceilings, and Jacuzzi tubs. The ☞ fresh scent of cedar comes from the bathrooms that are lined with tongue and groove cedar paneling.

The Beazleys set out a generous continental breakfast on the dining-room buffet for guests to help themselves and make return trips. Carol is proud that three of her muffin recipes are included in a recently published collection of country-inn recipes. A typical breakfast has large platters of sliced fresh fruit, yogurt, a cheese board, and homemade breads and muffins.

How to get there: From San Francisco, drive north on Highway 101 to 37 East, then north on 121 to 121 East; follow to Highway 29. Proceed north to the First Street/Central Napa exit. Follow exit all the way to the end; then turn left at Second Street. Continue $3/10$ mile to Warren Street. Turn left to the inn on corner of First and Warren.

♉

J: *Jim Beazley will make arrangements for his guests to visit and taste at wineries that are not on the regular tourist routes. And he also knows the best picnic spots in the valley.*

Olive Metcalf

La Residence
Napa, California
94558

Innkeeper: Barbara Littenberg
Address/Telephone: 4066 St. Helena Highway N.; (707) 253–0337.
Rooms: 15, 4 in farmhouse with private bath, 3 rooms sharing 2
 baths; 8 rooms in the "Barn," all with private bath. Air conditioning; wheelchair access.
Rates: $65 to $115, including continental breakfast. No children;
 no pets.
Open: All year.
Facilities and Local Attractions: Spa. Elegant dining room available for parties, catered dinners. Wine tours, ballooning, bicycling. Close to fine restaurants, shopping. Concierge service
 for all area activities.

The two buildings that together are La Residence are
different, but both are so delightful that it is hard to decide
which to choose. The inn began with the Gothic Revival
mansion Harry C. Parker built in 1870 when he moved to
Napa County to farm. He was a river pilot from New Orleans,
and the house shows a distinctive Southern character, with
all the winning features of a fine Victorian home.

If you like Victoriana, the farmhouse will delight you. It

has antique furniture and lighting fixtures and flamboyant period colors. It is a comfortable combination of period charm in a gracious house that has been well cared for. There are a parlor and a light-filled sun porch used as common sitting rooms.

A few yards across the yard, innkeeper Barbara has added a handsome shingled building with eight additional bed/sitting rooms in elegant English/French décor. With amusing understatement, she calls it the "Barn." Let me assure you, the only animals to roam these elegant rooms are a few porcelain geese decorating the dining room.

The Barn was a true labor of love for Littenberg—and it shows. Individuality is apparent when someone with talent takes on a major project like this, rather than hire an outfit to whip up a décor for a new inn. Barbara bought the furniture in England—country French and English, pine beds and chests—and chose marvelous soft-colored floral fabrics for comforter covers, draperies, and upholstery. She took fabric samples to a Napa craftsman to design matching decorative tiles for a border on the bathroom floors. Each room is a beauty, with a fireplace, sitting area, and French doors opening out to verandas that give the entire house a sunny, open feeling.

A brick terrace surrounds the Barn. The brick continues into the wide entry and leads into a large dining room. Bleached pine chairs around draped tables, a big fireplace, and other French country touches set the atmosphere. Straw wreaths, a porcelain swan centerpiece on a buffet, and a huge basket filled with crusty baguettes are the accents.

How to get there: Drive north on Highway 29, the main thoroughfare of the Napa Valley. At the north end of Napa, pass Salvador Street and look for the inn sign on the right. Turn onto a side road running parallel to the highway; follow around to the inn.

⏳

J: *When I visited, Barbara was in the farmhouse wallpapering a bathroom and a third-floor bedroom that already looked terrific to me. Why? "I like to keep things fresh."*

Olive Metcalf

The Old World Inn
Napa, California
94559

Innkeepers: Janet and Geoffrey Villiers
Address/Telephone: 1301 Jefferson Street; (707) 257–0112.
Rooms: 8, all with private bath, air conditioning.
Rates: $55 to $100, including substantial continental breakfast. No
　　pets or children; no smoking.
Open: All year.
Facilities and Local Attractions: Large Jacuzzi. Walk to Napa res-
　　taurants, shopping. Winery tours, ballooning, bicycling, pic-
　　nics.

　　There are no better innkeepers than the British. Their
impeccable manners, that wonderful sense of fun, the ever-
ready cup of tea or glass of sherry all seem to project an atmosphere that says you're going to be well looked after. Or is
it that confident accent? Before I ever saw The Old World
Inn, I had only to hear Janet Villiers' crisp voice over the telephone telling me about her "letting rooms" to be won over.
　　If you prefer to tour the wine country from a base in the
town of Napa rather than out in the countryside, this is an
engaging choice. The handsome, old house is a mélange of
wood shingles, wide shady porches, leaded and beveled glass,

dormers, and bays. I wouldn't dream of putting a label on its architectural style; let us just say "eclectic."

In addition to its British innkeepers, the inn's outstanding feature is its ☞ lovely décor. The entire house has been decorated with gorgeous fabrics inspired by the Swedish artist Carl Larsson—French blue, French pink, soft peach, and green. Painted Victorian and antique furniture accent these fresh colors. The parlor invites you with plump upholstered furniture, a tile fireplace, and tall ceilings whimsically painted with sunny quotations.

The individually decorated bedrooms have ☞ full or half canopied queen-sized beds and coordinated linens. Fresh flowers are everywhere—that's another thing the British have a special flair for. Most of the private baths have a Victorian, claw-footed tub and a shower.

At breakfast, a buffet is spread on a romantically draped table in the sunny Morning Room. Janet says, "Geoffrey really does the *most* beautiful fruit platters of six or more fruits." There is also a hot dish (perhaps a quiche) and homemade breakfast breads. Guests help themselves and sit at individual tables by a huge bay window.

In the early evening, wine is served and an ☞ international cheese board is offered in the Morning Room. The Villiers are well acquainted with reasonable restaurants you can easily walk to, and more lavish ones are only a short drive away. When you return to the inn, they will have homemade sweetmeats (their own almonds) and dessert wines waiting.

After dinner is when most guests like to use the large custom Jacuzzi. It is open to the stars but surrounded by vines and trees.

How to get there: From San Francisco, drive north on 101; exit onto 121 at Sears Point. Turn left on Highway 29; take Lincoln East exit in Napa, and turn right on First Street. Inn is on the right.

Olive Metcalf

Auberge du Soleil
Rutherford, California
94573

Innkeeper: Adair Borba-Thoms, general manager
Address/Telephone: 180 Rutherford Hill Road; (707) 963–1211.
Rooms: 36, all with private bath, fireplace, television, deck or patio.
Rates: $170, double room, to $410 for 2-bedroom suites; rate includes continental breakfast and use of tennis and swimming facilities.
Open: All year. Lunch, dinner, bar. Reservations advised.
Facilities and Local Attractions: Swimming pool, Jacuzzi, tennis courts, bikes for rent. Visit wineries, picnic; nearby hot springs, restaurants, shops.

First, there was the prestigious Auberge du Soleil Restaurant; then two years ago it expanded into a chic, country inn comprising nine two-story Mediterranean-style villas. The entire resort is nestled into thirty-three acres of olive groves spread over a hillside looking down on the Napa Valley.

The ☛ atmosphere here is quite simply . . . luxury. Oh, it may be understated and unfussy, but this is *major* luxury. On each level of the villas are two bedrooms, two baths, two fireplaces, and a large living room with a ☛ stocked refrigerator—liquors, champagne, wine, pâté, and aged cheeses. Each suite converts to a one-bedroom unit and a one-bedroom suite keeping the amenities. From each private deck is a perfect view of the Napa Valley with the Silverado Trail winding through.

The décor is a blend of European sophistication and California informality—sort of an ☞ earthy elegance. Floors are covered with Mexican tiles, and furniture is kept to a minimum, but much of it is bold, like Mexican pigskin chairs and concrete stone-roller lamps. Walls are the same rough, adobe-colored plaster as in the restaurant, with white framed, French glass doors and casement windows with heavy, white louvered doors and inside shutters. The only splash of color comes from fresh flowers and oversized pillows on sofas and chairs. Sheets are percale, towels the thickest; and bathrooms are big enough for small meetings.

One look at the elegant dining room and terrace overlooking the valley tells you this is *not* the place to order anything you ever cook at home . . . not that you're going to find meat loaf on the menu. Liberate your plastic card and wallow in the chic California cuisine. Try salad of ☞ duck with mangoes, curry-and-lemon linguine, or braised pheasant with crayfish and truffles. The wine list is a catalog of California's finest. Some of the grapes came from the very valley you look over.

How to get there: From San Francisco, take Highway 80 northeast to connect with Highway 37, then Highway 29. From Highway 29 in Napa Valley, follow any of the cross-valley roads west to the Silverado Trail; continue north to Rutherford. The inn sits above the trail. Fly-in: Napa County Airport.

Olive Metcalf

Rancho Caymus Inn
Rutherford, California
94573

Innkeeper: Mike Halfhill; owner, Mary Tilden Morton
Address/Telephone: Rutherford Road (mailing address: Box 78); (707) 963–1777.
Rooms: 26 suites, all with private bath, air conditioning, color television, wet bar, refrigerator.
Rates: $85 to $295, including continental breakfast. Two-night minimum for weekends. No pets; no children.
Open: All year. Breakfast, lunch.
Facilities and Local Attractions: Ideal location for wine touring; easy bicycling; hot-air ballooning. Interesting restaurants, shops close by.

This luxurious new inn with red tiled roofs and rough stucco walls ☛ captures the feeling of early California. It's a two-story building with colonnades and open balconies, shaped around a central garden court in the Spanish style. Each room has a sitting area with either a wet bar or a complete kitchen; bed and bath are up two steps to another level. Most have fireplaces and balconies. Hand-hewn beams and planking from an old barn give the rooms a warm, western feeling.

216

The concept of a handcrafted hacienda was a five-year labor of love for owner Mary Tilden Morton. She is a third-generation Californian, a sculptor, and grape rancher who has spent most of her life in the arts. Morton also designed Rutherford Square, a dining-entertainment complex next door to the inn.

Morton has made the inn a showplace for artisans and carpenters. Sausalito artists made the ☞ hand-thrown stoneware basins that sit in counters made from slabs of black walnut. Parota-wood chairs and matching dressers were carved in Guadalajara. A Napa artist created the stained-glass-window murals behind the Jacuzzi tubs in the bathrooms.

Much of the inn's character comes from the ☞ handcrafted furnishings and appointments done by Ecuadorian artists: hand-carved, black walnut queen-sized beds and wrought-iron lamps, vibrantly colored bedspreads, rugs, and wall hangings dyed and woven by South American Indians.

The Caymus Kitchen serves only breakfast and lunch at this point. Continental breakfast of freshly baked breads and fresh fruit can be served in your room or in the garden. For lunch there are excellent sandwiches (smoked turkey and avocado), fresh daily soup, Mexican specialties like quesadillas and chicken enchiladas, and changing chef's specials.

Sampling all the many superb dinner places in the valley is a gourmet adventure. One of them in Yountville is Mustard's, one of the great restaurants in the country—innovative, fresh, and fun! It's also popular, so be sure to ask the innkeeper to make your reservation.

How to get there: On Highway 29 through the Napa Valley, turn east at the crossroads of the highway and Rutherford Road, south of St. Helena. The inn is on the left, just past Rutherford Square complex.

olive Metcalf

Bale Mill Inn
St. Helena, California
94574

Innkeepers: Tom and Linda Scheibal
Address/Telephone: 3431 North St. Helena Highway; (707)
    963–4545.
Rooms: 5, with 2 community baths.
Rates: $60 to $65, including generous continental breakfast.
Open: All year.
Facilities and Local Attractions: Next door to Bale Gristmill State
    Historic Park. Wineries all around; picnics; bicycling; hiking.

The gigantic water wheel and restored old grain mill of
the State Park draw most of your attention at this section of
highway through the Napa Valley. The next time you pass,
pause and look at the rustic two-story roadside building just
beyond advertising antiques for sale and lodgings.

The Bale Mill Inn was once a railway depot and then a
tavern, but today the upstairs is a country inn that from the
outside you wouldn't guess existed. A sunny sitting room
draws you into a friendly setting of plants, an iron stove, and
an amusing conglomeration of furniture and antiques.

French doors open wide onto a large, 🖝 unexpected
deck comfortably outfitted with umbrella tables, padded

218

chaises, and an antique carriage filled with potted flowers. The wooded hills you look out at stretch to a 🖝 trail that connects the three-hundred acres of the Bale Grist Mill Park. This is beautiful hiking territory.

Tom Scheibal has shown a refreshing wit for using many of the 🖝 authentic antiques from his shop downstairs in guest rooms. He chose a legendary-figures theme for decorating the five rooms and has characterized the furnishings around that person. The Emily Dickinson Room looks like a New England summer porch with original, natural wicker. The cat box is a nice touch. The Hemingway Room is filled with memorabilia relating to the author, like mounted bull's horns and a safari hat; it opens onto the patio through French doors.

The Jack London Room is the most startling. A wolf's head eyed me fiercely from under a rare, antique brass bed, but just before yelping, I realized it was a rug, recalling the adventurer who built his Wolf House in nearby Glen Ellen. A hilarious fur coat hanging in the closet looks as if London had just dropped in from Alaska. These are small rooms, and guests share a bathroom with an old fashioned claw-legged tub upstairs and a shower and toilet downstairs.

Tom and Linda spread a breakfast buffet on a long, marble-topped table in the common room: an abundance of fresh pastries, scones, cinnamon-nut-raisin bread, freshly squeezed juice, a fruit plate, and coffee.

Colorful and friendly describes the atmosphere. *National Geographic* thought so, too, when it chose this little inn to photograph for a recent story on the Napa Valley.

How to get there: From Napa, take Highway 29 north to St. Helena. Inn is just past the Bale Gristmill Park on the left.

Olive Metcalf

Wine Country Inn
St. Helena, California
94574

Innkeeper: Jim Smith
Address/Telephone: 1152 Lodi Lane; (707) 963–7077.
Rooms: 25, all with private bath. Wheelchair access.
Rates: $88 to $153, including continental breakfast. No children
under 12.
Open: All year.
Facilities and Local Attractions: Swimming pool. Walk country
lanes. Close to tennis courts, hot-air balloon rides, mineral
baths, many wineries, antique stores, restaurants.

The Wine Country Inn has grown the past dozen years,
along with the tremendous popularity of the Napa Valley. It
has added buildings, patios, and, most recently, a swimming
pool, but it is still a family operation. You can hear Jim Smith
describing a room to a guest over the telephone, adding,
"And my mother made the quilt on the bed."
Unlike many inns in the area, this one was built new
from the ground up. The Smiths borrowed ideas from historic buildings in the valley, making their three-story stone-
and-wood inn look right at home in the vineyards.
Each room is individually decorated, combining old and

new. There are fresh, pretty color combinations, floral wall-papers, carpeting, and modern baths. Most rooms have a fireplace and vineyard view. ☛ Patios and intimate little balconies invite you to sit and appreciate the beautiful surrounding hills. Early on weekend mornings, you can usually see vividly colored hot-air balloons wafting their passengers over the vineyards.

Coffee is always ready in the large country-style common room. Make yourself at home in the comfortable sofa or wingback chairs beside an iron stove. Attractive books about wine and the area are all about, along with all the local restaurant menus. In St. Helena, La Belle Hélène is my long-time favorite restaurant, partly because of its ambience in a lovely, old stone building.

Guests gather at a ☛ long refectory table, or at individual tables throughout the room, for continental breakfast. Along with juice and fruit, the substantial fare includes two nut breads, several pastries, butter, and jams. French doors lead to a deck, which is the best breakfast spot of all with views of vineyards and hills. These are pleasant, friendly mornings, always with some of the Smith family there to refill your coffee cup and help you with plans for your day.

How to get there: From Napa, take Highway 29 2 miles past St. Helena. Turn right on Lodi Lane. The inn is on the left.

J: *Take your bikes to St. Helena. If you ride early in the morning on the lanes that wind through still-dewey vineyards, you will begin to understand how the wine country can become a passion.*

Olive Metcalf

Melitta Station Inn
Santa Rosa, California
95405

Innkeeper: Diane Jefferds
Address/Telephone: 5850 Melita Road; (707) 538–7712.
Rooms: 6; 5 have private bath; 1 shares bath with innkeeper.
Rates: $55 to $65, with full breakfast.
Open: All year.
Facilities and Local Attractions: Wine touring. Visit Jack London
    State Historical Monument, Annadel State Park. Spring Lake
    sailing, fishing. Hiking, bicycling, picnics.

Ever heard of the Valley of the Moon? There is such a
place in the rolling Sonoma countryside, and it is as poeti-
cally beautiful as its name. Jack London called the area "my
paradise" and built his famous Wolf House here.

The Melitta Station has been a part of Sonoma's history
since the late 1800s as a stagecoach stop, then a railroad
depot, a general store, and post office. The Jefferds have converted the long redwood barn into a homey inn. It has that
☛ winning country charm that magazines love to photograph, but in this instance it is less slick, more genuine, and
ever so much more warm.

You step into the sitting room and find a large wood-burning stove, wood floor with colorful rugs, baskets of kindling, and rough beams contrasting with white walls. Diane and a local artisan have stenciled a border of folk-art designs around the room.

Bundles of drying herbs hang from the rough-beamed high ceiling. A red-and-white quilt hangs on one wall. Furniture is American Country, featuring a mellow pine sideboard and a wicker sofa with bright print pillows. The cozy bedrooms are also furnished with antiques and collectibles, and all but one have private baths.

The Melitta's location wins my heart. It is rural and quiet, but with all the advantages of being in the very center of Sonoma County's abundant attractions. You are surrounded by outstanding wineries, close to the historic town of Sonoma, and near elegant Santa Rosa restaurants. John Ash is very hot at the moment and just a mile and a half from the inn. Specialties include *rillettes* of duck with bitter greens, California nut torte, and dinners featuring local wines and wine makers.

A hearty breakfast is the only meal served regularly, but everything is homemade, from quiches and tortes to baked apples and muffins. Diane also makes a big, puffy Dutch Baby topped with fruit. But this is a ☞ very personal inn, and the Jefferds will arrange just about anything you want: unique luncheons, champagne tours, mud baths and massages, hot-air ballooning, or glider rides. Let the good times roll.

How to get there: From Highway 101, exit at Highway 12 exit and follow signs to Sonoma for 5 ½ miles. Cross Calistoga Road; turn right at Melita Road, first road on the right. Continue about a mile to the inn.

Olive Metcalf

Vintners Inn
Santa Rosa, California
95401

Innkeepers: Francisca and John Duffy
Address/Telephone: 4350 Barnes Road; (707) 575–7350 or California only, (800) 421–2584.
Rooms: 45, including 1- and 2-bedroom suites, all with private bath; each with color TV, radio, telephone; facilities for the handicapped.
Rates: $78 to $250, including continental breakfast.
Open: All year.
Facilities and Local Attractions: Conference facilities. Ideal location for wine touring. Russian River water sports, fishing.

Four creamy-pink stucco buildings with red tiled roofs around a ☞ plaza complete with fountain comprise the splendid Vintners Inn. It rises in the ☞ center of a forty-five-acre vineyard (French Colombard, Pinot Blanc, Sauvignon Blanc), the picture of a village (although a new one) in the South of France. Actually, it is just sixty miles north of San Francisco at the crossroads of the Sonoma County wine country.

The European concept was carefully planned by the Duffys when they determined that a luxury country inn was needed in the Sonoma and Alexander valleys. "We tried to design it to be the way we like things when we travel," says Francisca. They went to Europe, Francisca's original home, and studied Provence marketplaces, plazas and architectural details, then came home to re-create the feeling in the middle of their own vineyard.

The forty-five rooms were individually decorated in French Country fashion after a meticulous search for authentic details. Chairs at writing desks and in the dining room are from a factory in France; outdoor lamps and standards are from a foundry near Brussels that has been in business 200 years. ☛ The exceptional antique, European pine armoires and desks were collected in East Germany, refinished in Antwerp, and then shipped to the United States. The queen-sized pine beds are new, but they were designed by John from sketches made in France and custom made by a local craftsman.

There are ☛ no small rooms. Their airy spaciousness includes sitting areas, dressing rooms, and elegant bathrooms with brass and porcelain fixtures. Most have a fireplace. Provincial wallpapers with matching draperies decorate all the rooms. Pleasing tall arched windows look out at vineyards or the plaza.

A library and a dining room, both with fireplaces, are in the common building, which is tiled throughout and decorated with more Old World accents. A continental breakfast of fresh fruit and homebaked rolls is served here. Other meals—gourmet dinners, wine-bar receptions with local wines—are done by prior arrangement.

Francisca and John give their guests personal attention by making wine-tour arrangements and reservations, along with personal suggestions, at a variety of fine restaurants nearby: Madrona Manor, Matisse, and John Ash are just a few they recommend.

How to get there: Just north of Santa Rosa, exit Highway 101 on River Road. Follow west to the corner of Barnes Road. Inn is on the left. Fly-in: Sonoma County Airport.

Olive Metcalf

Au Relais Bed and
Breakfast Inn
Sonoma, California
95476

Innkeepers: Harry, Nancy, and Dorothie Marsden
Address/Telephone: 691 Broadway; (707) 996–1031.
Rooms: 4, 2 with private bath. Wheelchair access.
Rates: $70 to $80, includes tax and continental breakfast. No credit
    cards; no children or pets; no smoking.
Open: All year. Lunch, dinner, bar.
Facilities and Local Attractions: Walk to Sonoma Plaza, the Mis-
    sion, unique shops, galleries, restaurants. Winery tours, pic-
    nics, bicycling.

　　The Au Relais Restaurant has been an award-winning
favorite for many years, serving outstanding food in handsome redwood surroundings. Its ☞ garden patio has long
been my preference for starry Sonoma nights.
　　Recently, the proprietors redecorated and appointed as
an inn a charming 1880s Victorian house just a few stepping
stones from the restaurant. Besides being an utterly delightful retreat, its location has some distinct advantages: It is

completely removed from the comings and goings of restaurant patrons, but close enough to have drinks and hors d'oeuvres available at the touch of a button. And when you're ready for company and a first-rate meal, you need only step next door. Not bad.

The Marsdens decorated the entire inn, even the woodwork, in restful, soft shades of rose and peach with touches of a misty aqua. Relaxing by the fireside in the common sitting room, ☞ you feel wrapped in a rosy cocoon. Comfortable upholstered furniture and antiques accent the tranquil surroundings.

The bedrooms are all a generous size and are romantically decorated with pretty bed linen and tables draped in fabric and lace. Some have beautiful quilts hanging as wall accents, armoires, and brass beds. Dishes of potpourri are a nice touch.

The restaurant features fresh fish and local ingredients, but with a bent toward those authentic, long-simmering classics of southern France. Harry's bourride, a whitefish stew from Provence, is redolent with garlic; the cassoulet and bouillabaisse are positively comforting. For a lighter touch, during warm weather he makes a ☞ Salade Niçoise—the way you always hope it will taste.

Inn guests step over to the restaurant for their complimentary breakfast consisting of fresh juice and fruits, muffins, croissants, and freshly ground coffee.

How to get there: From San Francisco, drive north on Highway 101 to 37 East, then 121 north to Sonoma. The highway becomes Broadway. The inn is on the left, just before the Sonoma Plaza.

J: *Remarks in a guest book can often tell the tale. This one was filled with sentiments like "The cuisine was only exceeded by the hospitality."*

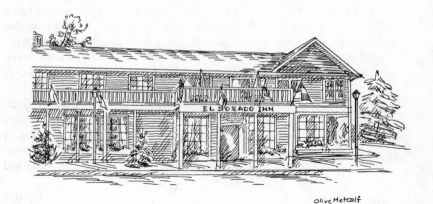

Olive Metcalf

El Dorado Inn
Sonoma, California
95476

Innkeeper: Paul Sosnowski

Address/Telephone: 405 First Street West (mailing address: Box 463); (707) 996–3030.

Rooms: 30, 19 with private bath; 4 rooms with access for the handicapped.

Rates: $50 (winter mid-week) to $95 (summer weekend), including continental breakfast.

Open: All year. Lunch, dinner, Sunday brunch; bar.

Facilities and Local Attractions: Located on Sonoma's historic plaza; walk to shops, restaurants, galleries, General Vallejo's home, the mission, Sonoma Barracks. Wine tours, bicycling, picnics. Inn's annual Oktoberfest.

The patio here just might be the prettiest spot in downtown Sonoma to lunch. A ☞ giant fig tree rises in the center of the courtyard surrounded by tables and chairs. Brick planters are filled with blooming azaleas and camellias, and vines climb up to the second-floor balcony that looks down on the garden.

A balmy, sunny day and a pretty patio tend to soften my critical barbs every time, but I can report my lunch took no back seat to the ambience. I had one of the inn's specials, Chicken Salad Helene, a poached boneless breast, glazed in a spicy curry sauce, surrounded with fresh fruit. Pasta was the choice of most of those around me—tortellini, linguine with sausage and red peppers, and chicken Tetrazzini. Luscious, first-of-the-season strawberries was the most sensible dessert choice, but the cheesecake clamored for attention too.

This handsome inn is a reconstruction of one of Sonoma's earliest adobe structures. The downstairs public rooms include an elegant saloon with its original Brunswick Bar, a spacious lounge with a fireplace, and a large dining room. The feeling is quite grand, with a lot of leaded and beveled glass, antique fixtures, and glowing brass.

There are ☛ garden cottages, but most of the rooms and suites are up the wide oak staircase. They are decorated in muted shades of burgundy and rose. Ten of the rooms look over the courtyard greenery, and others look out at Sonoma's hills and the plaza.

The location right on Sonoma Plaza is a joy. This is where the California Bear Flag was first raised in 1846. The restored Sonoma Barracks and the beautiful old mission will interest history buffs, too. For a really good shopper it can take most of the day to make one trip around the square: Boutiques, delis for picnic supplies, the Sonoma French Bakery, the Cheese Factory, art galleries, and Fantasie au Chocolat all call for a stop.

How to get there: From San Francisco, take Highway 101 to 37 East and then on to 121 north to Sonoma. Entering Sonoma on Broadway, turn right at Sonoma Plaza, circling around it to the third side. The inn is on the corner.

J: *On the February day I visited, the temperature was a heavenly 80 degrees, a testament to Sonoma's famous climate.*

Olive Metcalf

Sonoma Hotel
Sonoma, California
95476

Innkeepers: John and Dorene Musilli; Joanne Nagel, restaurant
    manager
Address/Telephone: 110 West Spain Street; (707) 996–2996.
Rooms: 17, 6 with private bath, 11 sharing baths at end of hallways.
Rates: $49 to $68, including continental breakfast.
Open: All year. Lunch, dinner, bar.
Facilities and Local Attractions: Located on Sonoma's historic
    plaza with Mission San Francisco de Solano, Sonoma Barracks,
    boutiques, restaurants, galleries.

My affection for this old hotel stems from the morning I
was coming down the steps from my room and recognized
(before I saw her) the unmistakably rich voice of Maya Angelou. She was lingering over conversation and coffee with
the elderly man on duty at the desk and, as she told me with a
smile, delaying the moment when she would have to climb
the stairs and begin work in the tiny third-floor room she kept
for writing. From that morning on, I've always thought of the
colorful 1870s hotel as having an especially authentic, literary atmosphere. Indeed, Room No. 21 on the third floor is the
Maya Angelou Room.

Sonoma is a delightful town to explore, with its history as a distant outpost of the Mexican empire, the northernmost of the California missions, and General Vallejo's barracks and home. At the Sonoma Hotel, you are directly on the historic plaza and can walk to all the attractions in town.

John and Dorene Musilli have recently restored and re-furnished the entire inn so that the 🖙 authentic early California atmosphere is more fresh and comfortable than ever. Dorene says there is not a reproduction in the place. The furnishings came from private homes, antique stores, and loans from the Sonoma League for Historic Preservation. You can sleep in a carved rosewood bed from the Vallejo family, a unique, solid-oak bed inlaid with ebony, or in impressive brass beds.

Third floor rooms are smaller, lower in price, but still have some choice antiques. The innkeepers are starting a clever ploy to take the sting out of the European custom of sharing bathrooms. They are hiring a European helper to be the floor director up there, to handle the bathroom traffic flow, keep wine cold, do touch-up ironing, and polish shoes left outside the door. I predict that guests will be clamoring to be on the third floor.

A new restaurant and long bar gleam with beveled glass and polished wood. Menus change weekly, and the cooking has been winning raves. A recent favorite was pork loin stuffed with pancetta, onions, and dry Vella Jack, the local cheese. Dessert specialties include a Queen Mother Torte, and—steady on, you chocoholics—a 🖙 white-chocolate cheesecake.

Continental breakfast specialties—like Italian wheat bread made with apples, raisins, and nuts—and superb bran muffins are baking while guests still sleep. A pleasant change of taste from excessively sweet breakfast breads, they are served along with fresh fruit, juice, and coffee and tea.

How to get there: From San Francisco, take Highway 101 north to Ignacio; then take Highway 37 east to Highway 21, which leads to Sonoma Plaza. The hotel faces the plaza.

Olive Metcalf

The Inn at Valley Ford
Valley Ford, California
94972

Innkeepers: Sandra Nicholls and Nicholas Balashob
Address/Telephone: 14395 Highway 1 (mailing address: Box 439);
     (707) 876–3182.
Rooms: 4 rooms, sharing 2 baths.
Rates: $47.50 to $58.30, including tax, full breakfast, wine in room.
Open: All year.
Facilities and Local Attractions: Bicycles, sun deck. Minutes from
     Bodega Bay fishing, boating, beach walking. Nearby historic
     towns, art galleries, antiques, restaurants.

In this age of specialization, here's an inn for lovers of
literature. Innkeeper Sandra Nicholls is a romantic with an
M.A. in English literature and an inn to indulge her fantasies.

Her guest rooms are named for Virginia Woolf, Colette,
and Molly Bloom; the fourth is "a room for the muse." Each
is decorated in a style that reflects the writer or character for
whom it's named, and stocked with a 🖝 library of the lady's
work or of the author who wrote about the character.

The house is late-1860s vintage and retains that era's

feeling, even with the architectural changes that the inn-keepers have made. Rooms are decorated with flair—beautiful fabrics, lace, big puffy comforters, and wicker. The two bathrooms—one with a claw-footed tub, the other with an enormous sunken shower—are as efficient as one could ask.

The wallpaper in the light-filled dining-room sitting area is wonderful. It has a black background with big colorful flowers blooming over it, reminiscent of a gaudy English chintz. You'll have a Sandra–style continental breakfast here: fruit compote, fresh juice, and just-ground coffee. You'll also see something made with the farm-fresh eggs she gets, and when it's berry time (as it was during our visit), she just *has* to do a "little something" with them . . . perhaps cobbler or coffee-cake.

The cheerful dining room looks into a dream of a kitchen. Outside is an English–style flower garden, a broad deck (a sunny spot to read) that overlooks the Sonoma countryside, and a yard in the process of change. Recently completed is a new accommodation to be called the W. Somerset Maugham Cottage. Besides Maugham's books, it will include a travel library. On the way are an arbor and a gazebo for summer concerts.

Merely the address of Highway 1 tells you that this is beautiful, peaceful territory. A hundred years ago, Valley Ford had 126 people living here; 126 people live here today—reportedly not the same people. Only ten minutes away by car are restaurants and pubs in Bodega Bay.

How to get there: From San Francisco, follow Highway 1 north to Valley Ford, 5 miles past Tomales. The inn is on the left.

J: *Attention, English majors of ages past: When did you last have a serious conversation about literature? There is every possibility that the atmosphere at this inn could start one.*

Olive Metcalf

Burgundy House and Bordeaux House
Yountville, California
94599

Innkeepers: Mary and Bob Keenan
Address/Telephone: 6711 Washington Street (mailing address: Box
    2766); (707) 944–2855.
Rooms: 6 at Burgundy House, 1 with private bath and 5 rooms
    sharing 2 baths; 6 rooms at Bordeaux House, all with private
    bath. Air conditioned.
Rates: $35 to $120, including continental breakfast.
Open: All year.
Facilities and Local Attractions: Yountville is a town for walking,
    and its back roads are good for bicycling. Good shopping, Vin-
    tage 1870 complex. Winery visits, picnics.

My back-roads sidekick and I discovered Burgundy
House before Napa Valley knew it was chic. The tiny, fieldstone country inn by the side of the road winding through
the undiscovered town of Yountville seemed terribly European. During our visit, innkeeper Mary was in Europe on an
antique-buying trip, and Bob looked after us like an anxious
father.

From cushy loveseats in the small sitting room, we

chatted with Bob and locals who dropped in, enjoying the ambience of 22-inch-thick walls around stout hand-hewn posts and beams, and the stylish collection of antiques and art objects. At breakfast, we gathered around the hearth for fresh fruit and juice, coffee, and wonderful, fresh pastries. It didn't matter a whit then or now that spaciousness was sacrificed for the sake of charm. When I soaked in the big claw-footed tub upstairs while gazing out at vineyards, it was the beginning of a love affair with country inns.

Since those quiet days, Burgundy House has kept its innocence, but Yountville has become a favorite stop for tourists to the valley—and it's partly Bob's fault, too. He is the architect who designed the restoration of Vintage 1870, a stunning conglomeration of specialty shops and restaurants housed in a core of 110-year-old winery buildings.

Across the road from Vintage 1870 and just two blocks south of Burgundy House is Bordeaux House, a sister inn designed by Bob and decorated by Mary. The formal, red-brick structure nestled under tall pine trees seems half English, half French. Bordeaux House has an atmosphere completely different from that of Burgundy House: sleek, modern furnishings kept to a minimum give each room an uncluttered elegance. Here, the six bedrooms are spacious, each with a fireplace, private bath, and individual patio. There is a comfortable combined lobby and sitting room, but for breakfast, guests walk down to Burgundy House to join others in the hearth room.

You can walk to several fine restaurants from these two inns. The French Laundry is one of the most admired—and has one of the longest reservation lists. Dinner is served in one of several small dining rooms in a stone and timber building. It is a wonderfully relaxed affair, allowing you to stroll in the English garden, even between courses.

How to get there: Yountville is 10 miles north of Napa on Highway 29. The inns are on the main street through town, past Vintage 1870. Bordeaux House is on the right; Burgundy House is on the left.

J: *Mary's favorite subjects are antiques, travel, and Bob; his are wine, polo, children, and Mary. That's nice.*

Magnolia Hotel
Yountville, California
94599

Olive Metcalf

Innkeepers: Bruce and Bonnie Locken
Address/Telephone: 6529 Yount Street (mailing address: P.O. Drawer M); (707) 944–2056.
Rooms: 12, all with private bath.
Rates: $85 to $155, with full breakfast. No credit cards; no children; no pets.
Open: All year.
Facilities and Local Attractions: Swimming pool; Jacuzzi spa. Walk to all Yountville shops, restaurants, galleries. Wine tours; hot-air ballooning; picnics.

In the '70s, before the Napa Valley became a bigger tourist attraction than Disneyland, "quaint lodgings" meant the Magnolia Hotel. The first time I stayed there, our party booked the entire hotel—all four rooms—for a birthday celebration. Some of us were enchanted with the ☞ old stone building behind an iron gate entwined with roses, but others in the party failed to see any charm in small rooms and doors that didn't lock. The experience was an early indication of which of us would become country inn fans and which would settle only for efficiency.

The valley has grown, and so has the Magnolia, but the outside appearance is as picturesque as ever. Now there are twelve antique-decorated rooms ranging from tiny to spacious, all with a private bath, and some with fireplace, sitting area, and king-sized bed. Second- and third-floor rooms have views and access to several balconies and sun decks.

Only breakfast is served in the little dining room where once were served fine dinners. The innkeepers say that most people come to the valley looking forward to trying some of its famous restaurants; therefore, they would rather concentrate on feeding guests a good breakfast and then help them choose which restaurant to sample from among the riches. In Yountville, you can walk to half a dozen choices, including Aneste's (continental), Mama Nina's (Italian), or the elegant French Laundry.

Through the back courtyard, past the pool and spa, are several interesting shops—one almost impossible to ignore is a designer chocolate place.

The courtyard comes out on Washington Street and Vintage 1870, a brick complex of restaurants, unique shops, galleries, and a little theater you should visit. A ☞ beautiful fifteen-minute entertainment there is well worth your time. Photographer Keith Rosenthal captures the spirit and changing beauty of the valley's vineyards with a combination of dramatic music and spectacular photography, from spring's yellow mustard carpet to fall's harvest magenta.

How to get there: Follow Highway 29 through the Napa Valley to the Yountville exit. You will see the red brick and flags of Vintage 1870. The inn is opposite the complex, one street farther east on Yount Street.

ᵍ

J: *Attention all "Falcon Crest" junkies: The Rosenthal show includes an exclusive* inside *look at the Spring Mountain Vineyard mansion used on the show.*

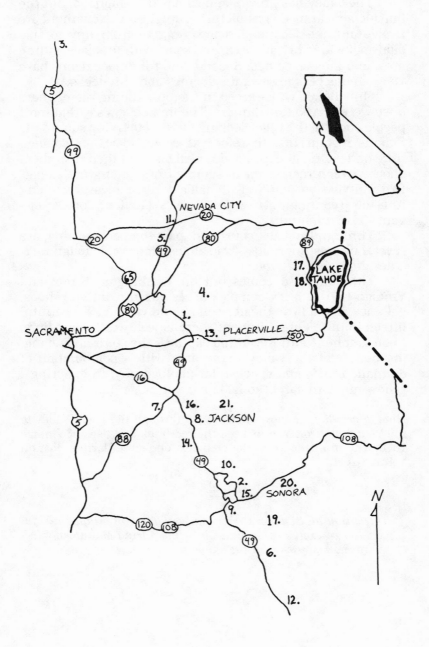

California: The Mother Lode and Sierras

Numbers on map refer to towns numbered below.

Olive Metcalf

Vineyard House
Coloma, California
95613

Innkeepers: Gary, Frank, and Darlene Herrera, and David Van-Buskirk

Address/Telephone: Cold Springs Road (mailing address: Box 176); (916) 622-2217.

Rooms: 7, all sharing 1 bath.

Rates: $43 to $54, double occupancy, continental breakfast included. No children under 16.

Open: All year. Breakfast, lunch, dinner, saloon, Sunday brunch. Closed Monday and Tuesday.

Facilities and Local Attractions: Gift shop; live entertainment in saloon weekends. White-water rafting, fishing; California State Gold Discovery Park, museums, antiques.

   Naturally, there's a story behind a four-story house with a ballroom (totaling 11,000 square feet) sitting in the rolling hills of the gold country. Robert and Louisa Chalmers, vintners of fine wines of the era, built the house in 1878. The wines and brandies of Vineyard House pleased even that noted tippler, President Ulysses S. Grant, who visited twice. When a blight wiped out Robert's 500 acres of vines, the poor man went insane, finally starving himself to death, and penniless Louisa opened Vineyard House as a boarding house.

The present owners rescued the house in 1975 from total neglect. Stripping floors and walls, they completely refurbished the house. Today they have seven comfortably furnished bedrooms on the second floor, all with fine views of the mountains surrounding Coloma. Authenticity is maintained with one bathroom at the end of the hall.

This is a 🖝 friendly, family operation marked by enthusiasm rather than elegance. Homemade and hearty describe most of the dining-room specialties: tureens of soup, big bowls of help-yourself-salad, freshly baked wheat bread, honey, and special desserts. The absolute favorite that keeps bringing the locals back is 🖝 chicken and dumplings—slow-simmered chicken with a 2-inch topping of dumplings and gravy. A summertime Sunday brunch treat is waffles, piled high with fresh strawberries and whipped cream.

The old wine cellar downstairs is now a saloon. Cool brick walls make it an inviting retreat on a hot day. It also contains the remains of a late-nineteenth-century "stopover" jail. The parlor and a long veranda are two more spots where guests can relax.

Bay Area weekenders in gold country will appreciate a Sunday dinner that is served beginning at 4:00 P.M., allowing time to still drive home that night. River rafters often stop at Vineyard House before a trip and for a quiet recovery after the adventure.

How to get there: From Sacramento, take Route 50 to Placerville; exit at Highway 49; continue north to Coloma (Cold Springs Road). Watch for the Vineyard House sign on the left, just before Coloma.

☒

J: *An old graveyard across the road is fascinating for the story its markers tell about the days of gold fever.*

olive Metcalf

City Hotel
Columbia, California
95310

Innkeeper: Tom Bender
Address/Telephone: Box 1870; (209) 532–1479.
Rooms: 9 rooms, each with private half-bath, showers down the
hall.
Rates: Balcony rooms $65; parlor and hall rooms $55, double occu-
pancy. Ski package in season. Continental breakfast included.
Children welcome.
Open: All year. Lunch, dinner, What Cheer Saloon. Saturday and
Sunday brunch.
Facilities and Local Attractions: Stroll the town with its restored
buildings, working weavers, blacksmith, harness, and saddle
shops. Stagecoach rides. Fallon House Theatre. Special events:
Fire Muster in May; old-fashioned Fourth of July Celebration;
eight-day Miners' Christmas Celebration.

Early one morning in Columbia, I walked alone down
Main Street's boardwalk, passed a stagecoach and team
standing by the Wells Fargo Office, saw a woman in pioneer
costume opening her candy store, and listened to the barber
outside his shop playing a tune on a harmonica. This is the
heart of gold rush country, and no town captures that spirit
better than Columbia.

In its gold-fever days, Columbia had forty saloons, 150 gambling houses, and eight hotels. Today the entire town is a state park, with tree-shaded Main Street barred to cars during the day to enhance the 1850–1870 atmosphere. But this is no static museum ghost town. Columbia is alive and bustling, and the jewel of the town is the City Hotel.

The two-story red-brick building has an upstairs parlor opening onto a wrought-iron balcony. A continental breakfast is served here each morning. Bedrooms are furnished with unusually impressive antiques, massive Victorian bedsteads, and marble-topped bureaus. Half-baths in each room are restoration additions, but showers down the hall are scarcely a hardship when you're provided with a wicker basket to tuck over your arm holding robe, slippers, and all the essentials.

The handsome, high-ceilinged dining room is an improbable surprise. Gold-rush-country explorers usually don't expect white linen, silver napkin rings, and haute cuisine. Try escargots or fresh bluepoint oysters while sipping a selection from the outstanding wine list. Then choose from twenty-four elegant entrées such as chicken poached in wine with oranges and mushrooms, or rack of lamb stuffed with spinach. Complete your feast with a divine lemon soufflé that must be ordered ahead. That most necessary of mining-town establishments, the What Cheer Saloon, is the place for a nightcap and the local news.

How to get there: From San Francisco, take Highway 580 to Tracy, then 205 to Manteca. Take Highway 120 east, past Knights Ferry, to Highway 108 intersection. Continue on 108 east to Sonora; then Highway 49 to Columbia.

J: *I know a man who insists that eating the lemon soufflé is like looking into the face of God. Understatement, apparently, is not his style.*

clinc Metcalf

French Gulch Hotel
French Gulch, California
96033

Innkeepers: Dominic and Judi D'Innocenti
Address/Telephone: Box Drawer 6B; (916) 359–2114.
Rooms: 7, 1 with private bath, 6 sharing 2 baths.
Rates: $45 to $60, including expanded continental breakfast; guests staying Saturday night have Sunday brunch included. Smoking in bar or outside.
Open: All year. Dinners Friday, Saturday nights, Sunday brunch by reservation. Wine and beer bar.
Facilities and Local Attractions: Panning for gold; hiking wilderness area of Trinity Mountains; boating, fishing, swimming in Whiskeytown Lake.

Whiskeytown ... Jackass Springs ... Black Bart ... French Gulch—all names associated with this remote area of the northern gold mines. If you get a kick out of the romance of the gold rush, this hotel and town on the California portion of the Oregon Trail are survivors of it, and not as frequently explored as some other gold-rush towns.

The town's name came from French Canadians who mined gold here in 1849. The hotel has seen the boisterous gold-rush days when French Gulch was a boom town; in the twenties, it became a haunt for bootleggers; and throughout its past history, it has had its share of ladies dispensing hospitality for a price.

It's now a quiet, tree-shaded hamlet in ☞ an uncrowded, unspoiled area of historic California. Just enough restoration has taken place to offer comfortable accommodations and good food, but you're not likely to forget that you're in the ☞ Old West.

Upstairs are three clean, simple bedrooms and a bath opening off a parlor. Downstairs are four more rooms (much cooler choices in the summer), one with a private bath and the rest sharing a bath.

The walls of the large, high-ceiling dining room are decorated with an array of old photos and post cards, yellowed newspapers, and memorabilia of the area's early days. Dom and Judi serve a generous continental breakfast here on tables covered with cotton, printed tablecloths: fresh fruit and juice, homemade cinnamon rolls, boiled eggs, and plenty of coffee or tea. The Sunday brunch is special enough to attract locals from a wide surrounding area. Start with champagne and orange juice, or a French Gulch Jamoca Fizz (their very special coffee), and go on to eggs Benedict or a variety of omelets, potatoes, sausage or ham, country gravy, and biscuits.

Weekend dinners feature homemade soups served with gold rush sourdough bread, and hearty entrées such as prime ribs, steak, spaghetti, or chicken (either cacciatore-style or pan-fried Dijon breasts).

How to get there: From I–5 at Redding, take Highway 299 west 14 miles to French Gulch turnoff. Turn right (north) 3 miles; inn is on left. From Highway 101 at Eureka, take 299 east to French Gulch turnoff, 30 miles east of Weaverville. Proceed as above.

J: *For a weekend trip with gorgeous scenery, drive from San Francisco to Eureka (stay overnight); then route 299 to French Gulch (stay overnight); then home down I–5 from Redding.*

olive Metcalf

The American River Inn
Georgetown, California
95634

Innkeepers: Will and Maria Collin, Neal and Carol La Morte
Address/Telephone: Orleans Street at Main (mailing address: Box 43); (916) 333–4499.
Rooms: 12, 4 with private bath, 4 additional baths shared. Queen Anne House separate from main inn, with 5 bedrooms, bath, living room, and kitchen. Facilities for the handicapped.
Rates: $57 to $67 double occupancy. Full breakfast included.
Open: All year.
Facilities and Local Attractions: Pool, Jacuzzi. Bicycles provided. Explore the gold country. Rafting, kayaking, fishing on American River. Hot-air ballooning. Antique shop.

    This is upscale, beautiful lodging for the gold country. But that's only fitting for a town that in 1853 estimated it had mined two million dollars in gold since the discovery in 1848. Once-rich, booming Georgetown, which then enjoyed the more picturesque name of Growlersburg, is now the setting of an ☞ impressive inn. There's no escaping the fact that a lot of money has been spent restoring the original American Hotel, but the four young innkeepers have also lavished love, hard work, and attention to detail on the effort.

246

Antiques, polished pine floors, and bright provincial fabrics invite you into the attractive common rooms. In the late afternoon, the innkeepers serve local wines and hors d'oeuvres in the tasteful parlor. They'll also tell you about restaurants you can stroll to for dinner, or others a short drive away. Tall, handsomely draped windows, and antique tables and chairs are in the light-filled dining room. Breakfast here is a full production: fresh fruit (from the inn's own garden), juice, quiche or other egg dishes, Canadian bacon, berry muffins, and freshly ground coffee.

The spacious bedrooms have each been individually decorated and have luxurious bathrooms with thoughtful touches like robes. Rooms that open onto porches are especially pleasant. On a mid-week visit, when the town is quiet, these are delightful spots for reading.

Besides the fresh mountain air and the clear rivers and lakes, history's footprints are everywhere in these foothills of the Sierra Nevada. ☛ Georgetown, itself, is well worth your time. It's a pleasure to see some of the stately homes built in the '70s and '80s, surrounded by well-tended gardens. Georgetown is one of those gold towns with charm but few tourists . . . always a winning combination.

If you're looking for adventure, the innkeepers will arrange hot-air ballooning, rafting, or kayak trips down the American River. They'll even provide the bicycles and pack you a picnic basket to take along while you explore. But a look at the beautiful ☛ natural stone swimming pool or the Jacuzzi could easily persuade you that relaxing right here has a lot of merit.

How to get there: From Sacramento, take Interstate 50 or 80 to Highway 49. Follow the signs to Georgetown. The inn is two short blocks from the junction of California 93 and Main Street. Fly-in: Georgetown Airport.

Annie Horan's
Bed and Breakfast
Grass Valley, California
95945

Innkeepers: Ivan and Bette Nance
Address/Telephone: 415 West Main Street; (916) 272–2418.
Rooms: 4, all with private bath.
Rates: $54 to $81, continental breakfast included. No smoking; no
    pets or children.
Open: All year.
Facilities and Local Attractions: Easy walk to Grass Valley shop-
    ping, restaurants, pubs. Nearby fishing, boating, skiing. Sum-
    mer local Blue Grass festivals, fairs, Victorian home tours.
    Antique shows. Cornish Christmas celebration.

    Ivan Nance likes to tell the story that his wife, Bette,
went shopping for dresses in Sacramento one day, so he
bought an inn. His offhand façade doesn't stand up long,
however, when you see the warm, interesting rooms he has
created and the enthusiasm they both bring to innkeeping.
    Previous owners called the inn Gunderson House. It
was built in 1874 for Annie Horan by her husband, James, a
builder and investor in the local mines. The Nances thought

the beautifully designed house should have the name of its original owner, since she lived in it for more than seventy-five years.

The Nances have lived on a boat and traveled widely, collecting ☞ antiques and accessories from London to West Virginia to Hong Kong. Much of their collection is now displayed in this Victorian house and seems to be quite at home in true eclectic style.

Bedrooms are sunny, comfortable, and neat as a pin, each with its private bath. Speaking of his remodeling work in the house, Ivan's conversation still reflects his former boat life when he says that it had to be "yachtie."

Guests will enjoy an inviting sitting room opening to the dining room. Ivan has an easel set up here with a calendar of events, soirées, forums, and happenings in the area. The social and ☞ cultural whirl in these little mountain towns is astonishing. "You can do everything here," says Nance. "Why, we have all kinds of theater, ☞ Bluegrass festivals, and serious music that gets better reviews than the Carmel Bach Festival. We even have [I *think* he was kidding me] geriatric drill teams!"

The Nances' favorite restaurant in town is Michael D's, which serves a "combination French and San Francisco cooking." They also recommend the newly restored Holbrook Hotel as another good option in town.

Whenever the weather allows, continental breakfast is served outside on a pleasant deck—fresh fruit salad, croissants, and German pastries from a local baker. In warm weather, guests enjoy sitting on the deck late into the evening.

How to get there: Northbound on Highway 49, take 174 Colfax/Central Grass Valley off ramp. Turn left on South Auburn; then left on West Main. Inn is on the left. Southbound on Highway 49, take East Main off ramp; turn left on Main Street.

Olive Metcalf

Murphy's Inn
Grass Valley, California
95945

Innkeeper: Marc Murphy
Address/Telephone: 318 Neal Street; (916) 273–6873.
Rooms: 8, 6 with private bath; 3 with fireplace; air conditioning.
Rates: $48 to $88 with full breakfast.
Open: All year.
Facilities and Local Attractions: Airport shuttle. Located in the
heart of Grass Valley's historic district; walk to restaurants,
unique shops, saloons, historic landmarks. Arrangements
made for sporting activities. Minutes from Nevada City.

The Sierra foothills are ☛ a sportsman's paradise—fish
one day, ski the next. You can golf, pan for gold, go white-
water rafting, and hike beautiful trails.

Marc Murphy is an avid participant in all these sports,
and he also happens to have an inn. It's a great combination
for those who enjoy lodging in the luxurious comfort of historic California ambience, but who also appreciate the convenience of an innkeeper who shares their sporting interests.
☛ Marc will help you fit it all in, make the arrangements,
even shuttle you there if you wish.

Murphy's Inn is an elegant 1866 home built by one of

the gold barons, Edward Coleman, owner of the North Star and Idaho mines. It's immaculately maintained, from the manicured, topiary ivy baskets hanging on the wide veranda, to the handsome sitting rooms with fireplaces and sparkling decanters of sherry and Courvoisier set out for guests.

 Beautiful pine, oak, and mahogany antiques are in every room. Three of the bedrooms have fireplaces, some have private entrances. There are large bathrooms, some with skylights and double shower heads. A suite across the street in Donation Day House is the latest Murphy refurbishment. It consists of a queen-sized bed, sitting room, fireplace, and private bath.

A big, cheerful kitchen and dining area has been added to the house. Marc can chat with guests while he makes "innkeeper's choice" breakfasts. There's always freshly squeezed juice, fruit, home-baked breads, and then whatever inspires him, maybe eggs Benedict, or sausage and hash browns.

Strangers are pleasantly surprised to hear about the many fine restaurants in Grass Valley and Nevada City. Among Marc's favorites are Michael D's for excellent California–French cuisine, and Andiamos for fresh pasta and entrées from a mesquite grill.

How to get there: From Highway 49, exit on Colfax (Highway 174), turn left at first stop sign. Turn left at second (two are close together) stop*light* on Neal Street. Proceed three blocks to inn on right corner of School Street. Fly-in: Nevada County Airport.

J: *The Grass Valley area is rich in gold-country lore. A few of the old residences remain, among them the frame house of the notorious Lola Montez.*

Olive Metcalf

Hotel Charlotte
Groveland, California
95321

Innkeepers: Ruth and Jim Kraenzel
Address/Telephone: Highway 120 (mailing address: Box 787); (209) 962–6455.
Rooms: 12, 4 bathrooms in hallway; 2 suites have bath in between; sinks in rooms.
Rates: $35 to $55, double occupancy, including continental breakfast. Ask about special package rates. Children welcome.
Open: All year. Breakfast, lunch, dinner.
Facilities and Local Attractions: Private dining room available for parties. Explore historic town, old mine shafts. Close to Pine Mountain Lake 18-hole golf course; rafting launch point. Pickup for van tour of Yosemite; airport pickup available. Direct route (25 miles) to Yosemite entrance; road open all year.

Garrote was the name of Groveland back in gold rush days, when town names told a story. A horse thief was hanged here, and the descriptive name hung on for twenty years. When the western-looking Charlotte Hotel was built here in 1918, more civilizing influences arrived. As "Groveland," the town had a second boom; it became the construction site for work on the Hetch Hetchy Dam, the system that brings water from the Sierras to San Francisco. When that flurry of activity ended, the town was deserted again.

Among the good reasons to seek out Groveland now is the Hotel Charlotte. Highway 120 through town is the most scenic and direct route to Yosemite from the Bay Area, and the hotel's fresh, homey guest rooms are a comfortable stop on your way to the park.

The lobby has white wicker furniture and books and games, and it also serves as the waiting room for the hotel dining room. Upstairs with the bedrooms is another sitting room. It's the kind of place you'll find comfortable when traveling with children. They can explore the hotel and the town on their own.

I arrived at lunch time on a beautiful, warm Halloween Day, which accounted for the creamy pumpkin soup on the menu. I tried and enjoyed. But the kitchen also turns out homemade biscuits, "beefalo" steaks, and a great Sierra-burger and fries. A continental breakfast is provided for hotel guests, but if you want to order from the menu, the popular favorite is Scramble of the Day: eggs with the chef's choice of additions.

Just a few miles away is the starting point for one of the great Sierra adventures—rafting the South Fork of the Tuolumne River. I hear that on an international scale of eight for rafting rivers, this trip gets a five—a white-water thriller.

Pine Mountain Lake is another attraction, only two and a half miles away. Its championship golf course has incredible views, and the air is wonderful.

How to get there: From Highway 120 or Sonora on Highway 49, follow signs to Groveland; drive into the town's one main street. Hotel faces the street. Fly-in: Pine Mountain Lake Airport. Hotel pickup in a '65 white Mercedes.

J: *A young man having the pumpkin soup told his dubious buddy, "Hey, this isn't so weird. I even had soup made out of watercress once, and it was really good!"*

Olive Metcalf

The Heirloom Inn
Ione, California
95640

Innkeepers: Patricia Cross and Melisande Hubbs
Address/Telephone: 214 Shakeley Lane (mailing address: Box 322); (209) 274–4468.
Rooms: 6, 3 with private bath.
Rates: $45 to $65, including generous breakfast. No credit cards; no pets or small children.
Open: All year.
Facilities and Local Attractions: Beautiful setting for receptions. Bicycles available. Walking tour of Ione, antiquing. Explore surrounding Mother Lode area, Amador County wineries. Good restaurants nearby.

The Heirloom's two innkeepers have a handle on every nuance of hospitality . . . and they dispense it with 👉 graciousness so genuine you'll know you've come across the real thing. Their thoughtful touches remain fresh and spontaneous—like appearing with a cold bottle of local white zinfandel and a couple of glasses while you're reading in the garden, or tucking a hot-water bottle in the foot of the bed on a cold night.

Their 👉 antebellum brick house with classic, white

Greek columns sits among towering old trees. It's filled with the innkeepers' personal furniture, china, silver, and antiques, including a splendid rosewood piano, said to have belonged to Lola Montez. The atmosphere is grand enough to be special, but so comfortable that perfect strangers feel quite at ease sitting in robes before the fire in the living room, sipping a late evening port.

Fireplaces, balconies, and private or shared baths are available in the four bedrooms in the house. In the springtime, we've often enjoyed the room with that name, with its private balcony surrounded by wisteria and magnolia.

A unique cottage with two accommodations is separate from the house. Its rammed-earth construction is as old as the Great Wall of China and as contemporary as environmental concern. All the earth scraped away to make room for the foundation makes up the walls and the sod roof. From the outside, the adobe house blends into its surroundings as if camouflaged. Cedar and redwood left in their natural finishes, skylights, wood-burning stoves, and handcrafted accessories give the inside a warm, tasteful ambience.

Breakfast is the leisurely, elegantly presented event that makes an inn visit memorable. Melisande and Pat, dressed in long skirts and pretty blouses, always look wonderful. They serve on beautiful china and pour from silver pots, and whatever the menu, the food is outstanding. There is always a fresh-fruit plate, homemade breads, muffins, and jams. The main dish might be blintzes, a quiche, or tender crêpes filled with cream cheese and topped with fresh strawberries. To breakfast on a summer morning under a huge shade tree in this lovely yard is my idea of inn-heaven.

How to get there: All highways into Ione lead to Main Street. One block north of Main on Highway 104, turn down Shakeley Lane to the Heirloom sign on the left.

☀

J: *Nobody does it better!*

Olive Metcalf

Gate House Inn
Jackson, California
95642

Innkeepers: Frank and Ursel Walker
Address/Telephone: 1330 Jackson Gate Road; (209) 223–3500.
Rooms: 5, all with private bath.
Rates: $50 to $75 weekdays; $65 to $85 weekends, two-night stay
    tied to Saturdays. Breakfast included. No credit cards; no chil-
    dren or pets.
Open: All year.
Facilities and Local Attractions: Swimming pool, screened-in bar-
    becue room. Walking tour of Amador County Museum, Jack-
    son's historic houses, churches, antique shops, restaurants.
    Explore nearby gold-rush towns, wineries. Skiing at Kirkwood.

      No really good innkeeper would bad-mouth another, but
lavish praise is not carelessly tossed around either. The Gate
House Inn is an exception. All around the Mother Lode, people speak of the handsome house, elegant décor, and the
"good job" the Walkers do.
      The buttercup-yellow Victorian mansion lives up to its
reputation. It epitomizes Victorian charm, with peaked roofs,
spacious lawns, rose gardens, and a wisteria-covered pavil-
ion. The summertime pool and ☛ quiet grounds look out on

the romantic rolling terrain of gold country—380 acres of it owned by the mansion's original family.

Through a beveled-glass front door is ☞ an interior grandeur matching that of the exterior. The original solid-oak parquet floors, Italian marble and tile fireplaces, an oak staircase, and many of the superb original wallpapers are in mint condition.

The Walkers have ☞ more than a hundred museum-quality antique clocks displayed throughout the house. The collection includes two rare grandfather clocks: one, with handpainted roses on the face, dates back to the 1700s; another, crafted of walnut burl, was created for Kaiser Wilhelm. More of their collection is at the Walkers' restaurant, The Sutter Creek Palace, in nearby Sutter Creek.

All five accommodations have queen-sized beds, private baths, and sitting areas, with antiques, fresh flowers, and decanters of sherry. The Woodhaven Suite, formerly a nursery, is especially winning. It's lined from ceiling to floor with pine and furnished with a brass bed. A bank of windows looks out over the garden.

In the garden, a grape arbor leads to the fifth suite, the Summerhouse, with a cast-iron, wood-burning stove and an immense ☞ cedar-paneled bathroom with stained-glass windows from the Comstock mansion in Virginia City. Across the lawn is a barbecue area you are welcome to use if you tire of Jackson's Italian restaurants.

☞ Breakfast is served on lace and linen, with Royal Albert china that Ursel acquired as a child in Canada. A typical menu includes fresh fruits, yogurt, freshly baked muffins, pastries, and coddled egg. In spring, a camellia is on each napkin; in summer, it's a rose.

How to get there: Turn off Highway 49 onto Jackson Gate Road, just north of the intersection with Highway 88 from Stockton. Follow to the inn on the left.

olive Metcalf

Jamestown Hotel
Jamestown, California
95327

Innkeepers: Marcia and Mike Walsh
Address/Telephone: Main Street (mailing address: P.O. Box 539);
    (209) 984–3902.
Rooms: 8, all with private bath; 7 are suites with sitting area.
Rates: $45 to $85 double occupancy. Continental breakfast in-
    cluded.
Open: All year. Lunch, dinner, Sunday brunch, full bar.
Facilities and Local Attractions: Outdoor sundeck. Walk historic
    Jamestown; shops, antiques. Mother Lode exploring, gold pros-
    pecting tours. Ride Sierra Railroad.

    Old West buffs come to Jamestown to walk picturesque
Main Street and to ride the Sierra Railroad's steam-powered
locomotives that pull tourists through the Sierra foothills.
The Jamestown Hotel is still another attraction, an absolutely
☛ smashing restoration accomplishment.
    The Walshes have completely redone the hotel, from the
old brick exterior to the flamboyant gold-rush-style interior. A
tidy lobby, dining room, and inviting cocktail lounge are on
the first floor. Upstairs are eight antique-decorated bedrooms, all named for personalities associated with the area's

past—Jenny Lind, Lotta Crabtree, Black Bart, Joaquin Murietta.

These are quaint Victorian-style rooms (seven are suites with sitting areas) with the distinct advantage of not *smelling* old. They're comfortable and immaculate, qualities that were, until recently, hard to find in the Mother Lode. Marcia has chosen colorful wallpapers as backgrounds for antique furnishings. Black Bart's floral bouquets on black and a black, claw-footed bathtub look particularly Victorian.

The handsome dining room's wall covering is a fresh floral print on ivory with matching balloon draperies. Fresh linen, plants, and touches of etched glass fill the room with light at lunch time; during candle-lit dinners, the atmosphere is romantic. The dining room opens onto an attractive lattice-covered patio used for summer dining and special parties.

At lunch, you start with a ☞ basket of hot, puffy sopapillas. (*Try* eating just one!) Seafood salads, fresh, poached red snapper in white wine sauce, and spinach pasta with linquica and garlic sauce were the specialties the day I visited.

A small plant-filled sitting room at the end of the upstairs hall opens onto a deck area with umbrellas and tables. This is a pleasant place to sit and sip on a summer evening while watching shadows on the foothills.

How to get there: From the San Francisco Bay Area, take Highway 580 to Manteca turnoff. Continue on Highway 108 30 miles past Oakdale to Jamestown. The hotel is on the right in the center of town.

ᵇ

J: *As you gaze at the foothills surrounding Jamestown, remember: There are those who claim there's still "gold in them thar hills!"*

clive Metcalf

The National Hotel
Jamestown, California
95327

Innkeeper: Steve Willey

Address/Telephone: Main Street (mailing address: Box 502); (209) 984–3446.

Rooms: 11, 5 with private bath; 6 have antique washbasins and share 2 bathrooms. Rollaways, TVs available.

Rates: $45 to $55, including generous continental breakfast. Ask about lower mid-week and winter rates. Children under 10 by arrangement only.

Open: All year. Lunch, dinner, Sunday brunch; full bar.

Facilities and Local Attractions: Explore old gold-rush town, antique stores; home of steam-operated Sierra Railroad, Railtown 1897 State Park. Near cross-country skiing, backpacking trail heads.

When you reach Jamestown, you get the 🖝 full flavor of what a Victorian-era gold-rush town was like. It was one of the boom towns, swarming with a sudden population bent on quick riches. If it looks familiar to you, it's because it's been used in hundreds of feature films, including *High Noon* and *Butch Cassidy and the Sundance Kid.* Our romantic attraction to those old towns continues, partly because of the picturesque buildings that remain and partly because of the natural loveliness of the Sierra foothills.

Like all gold towns, Jamestown has burned countless times, but the National Hotel is one of its survivors, operating since 1859. The Willey brothers have been working on its gradual restoration for over a decade, matching the façade to photos from the 1800s. Happily, it still looks much like the typical Old West hotel we've seen in movies—two stories with a balcony overlooking Main Street and a wooden sidewalk.

Inside is a ☞ massive, long bar (the original) with a brass rail and a splendid 1882 cash register; a large dining room, and a stairway up to the bedrooms. The rooms are clean and cheerful with quilts, brass beds, and other antique furnishings. The atmosphere is a combination of nineteenth-century charm—pull-chain toilets—with twentieth-century comfort—modern stall showers.

The dining room serves lunch and dinner to the public, everything from gazpacho to steaks, but continental breakfast–fruit, breads, coffee, and tea—is for guests only. Photographs of the hotel and Jamestown's earlier days decorate the walls. Adjacent to the dining room is ☞ a hundred-year-old grape arbor, a pleasant place for breakfast or for enjoying a bottle of wine after a day of exploring.

How to get there: From Manteca on Highway 99, take Highway 120 to Jamestown. You enter on Main Street. Hotel is on the right. Fly-in: Columbia Airport; hotel pickup service.

olive Metcalf

The Palm Hotel
Jamestown, California
95327

Innkeeper: Jacob Barendregt
Address/Telephone: 10382 Willow Street; (209) 984–3429.
Rooms: 9, 5 with private bath, 4 with sinks in room sharing a large bath plus half-bath. Wheelchair access.
Rates: $55 to $100, including breakfast. No smoking preferred.
Open: All year. Beer and wine bar.
Facilities and Local Attractions: Explore Jamestown, antique shops, Railtown 1897 State Historic Park. Ride Sierra Steam Train; gold-prospecting trips from livery stable. Near ski areas. Seven miles to Columbia State Park.

This old private home and one-time rooming house, situated a block off Jamestown's historic Main Street, is completely remodeled and newly decorated. It's had the happy fate of being rescued by Jacob Barendregt, a young innkeeper who has lived all his life in this most western of gold-rush towns, but whose taste in décor runs beyond that narrow trough into more cosmopolitan pastures.

Try to picture a dusty miner riding up Main Street past the balconied buildings and heading for some R and R at The

Palm. He bellys up to the elegant marble bar in the reception room and growls, "Espresso, please."

Maybe in a "spaghetti western," but surely not in old "Jimtown" ... not in the "Gateway to the Gold Country"! But where is it written that you have to put up with nine-teenth-century comforts just to explore the picturesque charms of an old town? The Palm is an attractive option for travelers who take their lodging seriously.

The inn's architectural flourishes give it an interesting exterior and an expansive, light-filled interior. The attractive lobby room (yes, there really is a marble bar and an espresso machine) is also where continental breakfast is set out. Two bedrooms are on this floor.

Up a broad, handsome stairway are the other seven bedrooms. Four of them have washbasins and share ☞ an elegant marble shower. ☞ A Thai canoe hangs over the stairwell like an enormous mobile. The rooms are attractively decorated with some wonderful antiques, and most have a sitting area. Amenities in the larger rooms include a TV and a small refrigerator. The innkeeper's keeness for marble is seen again in the palatial bathrooms.

☞ Intriguingly different windows are a feature of the restoration design. Small ones in various shapes are placed unexpectedly; large, tall arched ones have a stunning visual impact.

Jacob maintains that continental breakfast is the custom here, but conversation reveals that he is a pushover for guests' wishes, and he usually cooks whatever people ask for. He knows the Mother Lode scene and can help you choose interesting places to dine. He'll also cater special parties at the house.

How to get there: On State Highway 49, 3 miles south of Sonora. From Main Street, turn up Willow Street one block to inn on your left.

olive Metcalf

Murphys Hotel
Murphys, California
95247

Innkeeper: Robert Walker
Address/Telephone: (mailing address: Box 329); (209) 728–3454.
Rooms: 9 historical rooms sharing 4 baths; 20 separate motel units
  with private baths.
Rates: $35 to $47; continental breakfast included in historical-room
  rate.
Open: All year. Breakfast, lunch, dinner, full bar.
Facilities and Local Attractions: Walk the town; visit its museum.
  Explore surrounding historical towns, Mercer Caves, Cala-
  veras Big Trees.

On a cold December morning, a fire burned cheerily in
the pot-bellied stove in Murphys Victorian lobby. A
Christmas tree filled the room with the fresh aroma of pine.
In the dining room, platters of sausage and hot bowls of oatmeal were bustled to the tables as waitresses and locals ban-
tered about weather and horses, dogs, pickup trucks, and
foaling mares.

On crisp, clear winter days like this, when tourists are
back in the city, old gold-rush towns show their true character. If authenticity is your delight, then 🖝 quiet, little

264

Murphys, "Queen of the Mother Lode," is a must. It was once a major stagecoach route. A few old stone buildings survive and stand near the hotel in the center of town. Winding roads leading out to Angels Camp and Sheep Ranch are ☞ beautiful mountain drives.

But historic lodgings aren't for everyone. You have to be amused with floors that slant; tolerant of shared facilities; fascinated with walls of old photographs; and prefer stick-to-the-ribs fare instead of California cuisine. The picturesque hotel looks very little different today from the way it did when Ulysses S. Grant, Samuel Clemens, Horatio Alger, Henry Ward Beecher, and Black Bart were guests.

Grandest of all the historic bedrooms is the General Grant Room, with a splendid antique bed and a square piano that has been there as long as anyone can remember. The other bedrooms are smaller and are simply furnished with antique beds, dressers, and quilts.

The saloon and dining room on the main floor remain much as they were originally. The no-nonsense menu features steaks and chicken dinners. A continental breakfast delivered to guests (along with the morning paper) in the old historic rooms consists of coffee or tea, juice, and a homemade cinnamon roll.

The Mark Twain Ballroom upstairs opens onto a balcony with the original cast-iron railing. The Victorian room, with flamboyant cranberry red chandeliers, was decorated this day for a Christmas party.

A longtime citizen of the town, Elizabeth Kaler, wrote about the hotel in *Memories of Murphys:* "I think ☞ the balcony was the most charming. It has an old world air to it that has helped to make Murphys different. It was a rendezvous for friends both far and near."

How to get there: From Highway 49 east of Stockton, take Highway 4 east at Angels Camp to Murphys.

Olive Metcalf

The National Hotel
Nevada City, California
95959

Innkeeper: Tom Coleman
Address/Telephone: 211 Broad Street; (916) 265–4551.
Rooms: 43; 10 share bathrooms.
Rates: $35 to $75; EP.
Open: All year. Breakfast, lunch, dinner, full bar.
Facilities and Local Attractions: Swimming pool. Live music Saturday, Sunday nights in bar. Walk Nevada City, shops, restaurants, antiques, American Victorian Museum. Cross-country skiing nearby.

The old National Hotel is the centerpiece of the town. The ☞ broad veranda across the front of the building is the place to be for gala celebrations and parades on the Fourth of July and Constitution Day. Sitting out here in the summer under an umbrella with a cool drink is the perfect cat-bird seat for watching the passing scene.

Nevada City was originally called Nevada before the state came along and took possession of the name. Then the outnumbered citizens of the gold town had to add "City" to their town's name. It still has much of the ☞ character of an

1850s mining town with many old buildings and picturesque gas lamps along Broad Street, the town's main street.

The atmosphere in the Victorian Dining Room and bar is decidedly Gold Rush—chandeliers, period floral wallpapers, velvet and satin love seats and chairs. The ☞ ornate bar was originally part of the dining room buffet in the San Francisco Spreckels mansion. In the old days, gold dust was the medium of exchange in the bar. It could be traded for tokens, some of which can be seen in the lobby and hallways along with other artifacts from the era.

The menu includes many seafood dishes, as well as prime rib, steaks, lobster tail, and always some house specialties of whatever is fresh and best at the time. At dinner your table is lighted by attractive coal oil lamps.

You'll be pleasantly surprised at the size of some of the suites—big bordering on huge—with a few of the bathrooms as large as an ordinary bedroom. Massive antique beds and armoires, floral wallpapers, and chandeliers give the rooms a Victorian feeling. As befitting the large rooms, some fairly sizable projects have been hatched in them, too: Pacific Gas and Electric (PG&E) was organized in suite 74.

Recent additions to room appointments are direct-dial telephones and TVs. Although some people feel that they detract from the old-fashioned ambience, Tom says there's a vocal guest list that feels shockingly deprived if they're absent.

How to get there: Follow Gold Rush Highway 49 north past Grass Valley. Take Sacramento Street off ramp to downtown Nevada City. The National is on the left.

☐

J: *Nobody asked me . . . but isn't there something contradictory about seeking out historic lodgings with authentic antique charm, and then wanting a TV beside the marble fireplace or dear little Victorian settee?*

Olive Metcalf

The Red Castle Inn
Nevada City, California
95959

Innkeepers: Mary Louise and Conley Weaver
Address/Telephone: 109 Prospect; (916) 265–5135.
Rooms: 8, 6 with private bath.
Rates: $55 to $95, including continental breakfast. No credit cards;
    children and pets discouraged.
Open: All year.
Facilities and Local Attractions: Walking path to downtown shops,
    restaurants, antiques in Nevada City. Walk to mountain creek
    for swimming; cross-country skiing twenty minutes away; pic-
    nic baskets.

    Almost fifteen years ago, a San Francisco architect and
his wife visited Nevada City and stayed at the Red Castle Inn.
She fell in love with the Victorian red-brick mansion, and
they continued to visit it through the years. The thought of
ever owning it was mere fantasy, but now that the Weavers
have bought it from their friends, the former longtime innkeepers, Mary Louise says it is a case of a dream coming true.
    High on a hill nestled among dense trees, The Red Cas-
tle is an 🖝 impressive sight from many places around Nevada City. The Gothic-revival mansion is wrapped in rows of

white, painted verandas and lavished with gingerbread trim at roofline and gables. It has changed very little since it was built in 1857. From the driveway, walk around a veranda, with stylish canvas draperies tied back at each pillar, to the front of the house, where you can survey the historic mining town's rooftops and church steeples.

Eight guest rooms range over the four floors, each one of them a vibrantly decorated, tasteful delight. Most ☞ furnishings are Victorian, but not fragile or frilly. An explosion of color from wallpapers, fabrics, and rugs has an engaging effect in combination with the dramatic architecture. Two garret rooms on the top floor share a sitting room, bath, and balcony. It was from here that the original owner's son used to serenade the town with impromptu trumpet concerts.

A cozy sitting room off the entry hall has cushy upholstered furniture, wingback chairs, and colorful lamps. On the grounds, you'll find a pond and ☞ tranquil outdoor sitting areas arranged in a series of terraced gardens.

The Weavers are proud of their vintage inn and are enthusiastic about Nevada City. They like to suggest restaurants and local events they think their guests will enjoy. A buffet-style continental breakfast is the only meal served here, but it is a fine one: homemade breads and muffins, fresh fruit, juice, and freshly ground coffee.

How to get there: From Highway 49 at Nevada City, take Sacramento Street exit to the Exxon Station; turn right and immediately left onto Prospect Street. The driveway takes you to the back of the house. Walk around the veranda to the front door.

Olive Metcalf

Ye Olde South Fork Inn
North Fork, California
93643

Innkeepers: Virginia and Darrel Cochran
Address/Telephone: 57665 Road 225 (mailing address: Box 731);
 (209) 877-7025.
Rooms: 9, sharing 3 bathrooms; cribs available.
Rates: $44 to $70 for family room that sleeps five; includes expanded continental breakfast. No pets; smoking outside only. Children welcome.
Open: All year.
Facilities and Local Attractions: Good water skiing at Redinger Lake; 8 miles to Bass Lake with all recreational facilities; 28 miles to Yosemite gate.

You may well wonder where on earth you are when you wind your way into this out-of-the-way village, but Virginia Cochran can tell you precisely. "We're in the exact center of California," she says. "People sometimes think we're gold-rush country, but we're not. This is the ☞ gateway to Yosemite."

The inn that she and husband Darrel have in this remote area is a dandy place to stop over before you head on to Yosemite Park. Or if you've been out camping for a few days, this is a convenient place to regroup, shower, and have a good night's sleep in a clean, comfortable bed.

By all means, bring the children—this is their kind of relaxed, easy place. The living room has a TV and opens into a large common room. When it's not being used for breakfast, all the tables and chairs are handy for games. A piano is here, too, and boxes of toys.

The nine bedrooms accommodate flexible sleeping arrangements for families, with daybeds and cribs. The rooms are simple and fresh, with country antiques and ceiling fans.

There's not an acorn-ful of pretension here. It's western-style comfort, where the beautiful scenery at hand overrides indoor décor. You're not going to find Ye Olde South Fork Inn in *House Beautiful,* but you will find comfortable beds and warm hospitality. Future plans for the inn include a deck (work has already begun) and a hot tub.

The Cochrans (Darrel is retired Navy) have lived in this foothill community for fourteen years. ☛ They know the area well and are helpful in directing you to mountain attractions you might otherwise miss. Virginia pointed out Redinger Lake, for instance. It is close by and offers excellent water skiing, yet it's relatively undiscovered.

How to get there: From Highway 99 at Madera, follow Highway 145 to Route 41. From Fresno on Highway 99, take Highway 41 immediately. Continue north toward Yosemite about 30 miles to O'Neals. Follow signs to North Fork. Proceed through village to South Fork. Inn is on the left.

☒

J: *Virginia sells her knitting to boutiques. If you arrive just before she sends off a shipment, as I did, you'll get first pick of some fine handmade sweaters.*

olive Metcalf

The Chichester House
Placerville, California
95667

Innkeeper: Nan Carson
Address/Telephone: 800 Spring Street; (916) 626–1882.
Rooms: 3, 1 with half-bath; all share bathroom with tub. Air conditioning; no smoking.
Rates: $55 to $60, double occupancy. Full breakfast included. No
credit cards.
Open: All year.
Facilities and Local Attractions: Elegant library and parlor for relaxing. Historic Placerville, Gold Bug Park, and Gold Bug Mine
and Park. Short jaunt to Sutter's Mill, foothill wineries. Antiques, shops, and restaurants.

"Woody and I want to have an inn where people want to
come back" and "I don't like to sit someone down with a
croissant and call it breakfast." Nan Carson says that these
are her and her husband's two philosophies of innkeeping.
You just *know* you're going to be well taken care of when you
hear sentiments like these.

The Carsons' ☞ handsome Victorian home was built in
1882 to be the finest residence in Placerville. It's believed to
have been the first house in town with built-in plumbing.

Some grand houses of this vintage are interesting but a little musty and dusty. Not Chichester House. The antiques are the real McCoy, and they, like the house, are beautifully restored and well maintained.

The Yellow Rose Room is the largest of the three and has a half-bath. There's a wonderful old Pullman car fold-up sink that Woody has polished within an inch of its life. A sunny sitting area in the bay window, in a corner a dress-maker dummy in vintage costume, great robes to relax in, and little touches that delight the eye are everywhere in the room. On the blazing hot day of our visit, we had no quarrel with a departure from authenticity by way of air conditioning.

As for that breakfast *sans* croissant, it begins with a knock on your door and a tray of freshly brewed, especially aromatic coffee. Downstairs in the dining room, fresh flowers and gleaming silver accent the bounty: a beautiful fresh-fruit plate, eggs Benedict so good they make you remember why they became popular, and Nan's county-fair blue-ribbon prize muffins.

For dinner, the Carsons will help you choose from a variety of restaurants within walking distance. We tried Mama D. Carlo's and had good pasta. As Woody says, Placerville is not a gourmet capital, but the food is hearty. "The trick is to find someplace that serves small portions."

Back at Chichester House, enjoy the library and parlor and have a nip of wine. When you retire, you'll find that Nan has turned down your bed. You never get that kind of attention at Motel Six.

How to get there: From Sacramento, take Highway 50 to Placerville. Exit at Highway 49 North (Spring Street). Make the next three right turns on Coloma, High, and Wood streets to parking behind the house.

J: *Nan hangs "little surprises" everywhere around the house or tucks them in drawers to amuse you when you explore—like a dainty old-fashioned, batiste romper suit with drop-seat.*

Olive Metcalf

The Combellack-Blair House
Placerville, California
95667

Innkeepers: Jim and Cec Mazzuchi
Address/Telephone: 3059 Cedar Ravine; (916) 622–3764.
Rooms: 2, sharing a bath.
Rates: $59.40 (tax included) double; $54 single. Full breakfast included. No credit cards or smoking. Not convenient for children.
Open: All year. Closed Monday and Tuesday.
Facilities and Local Attractions: Relax on the porch swing and appreciate this house. Walk to town with parks, shops, and restaurants. Visit nearby Gold Discovery Park, foothill wineries.

This ☞ elaborate, late Victorian, Queen Anne home is too special to miss if you are in the area. Do two guest rooms make an inn? Perhaps not, and even Cec Mazzuchi herself says, "This is more a home than a business. But I didn't want to get too commercial. If I only use two rooms for guests, I can take care of everybody the way I like to."

The Combellack-Blair House was just recently placed in the ☞ register of National Historic Houses, and it is a jewel. The Mazzuchis have lived here thirteen years but have been innkeeping for only the past two.

274

Naturally, there are antiques throughout the house. The owners are completely aware of the responsibility of living in a masterpiece and have chosen the décor with care and taste. The two guest rooms have everything necessary for comfort, starting with good beds and pretty linen.

The full breakfast Cec serves features freshly ground coffee, juice, fresh fruit, and blueberry muffins with honey butter. Then there is bacon or sausage and sourdough pancakes made from her own starter. She also does a baked egg dish. Cec is so serious about authenticity that she even grinds her own flour for her home-baked breads.

Looking at a house like this seems always to bring Christmas to mind. Last year a local theater group decorated the house and did a Christmas program. It would be an especially pleasant time to visit.

How to get there: From downtown Placerville, follow Cedar Ravine Street north to the house on the left.

J: *Placerville started out as Dry Diggings and descended to Hangtown for awhile. The El Dorado County Historical Museum has some interesting exhibits of gold-rush times.*

olive Metcalf

River Rock Inn
Placerville, California
95667

Innkeeper: Dorothy Irvin
Address/Telephone: 1756 Georgetown Drive; (916) 622–7640.
Rooms: 3 rooms sharing one bath, with 3 lavatories and a stall
  shower; 1 suite with private bath. Air conditioning.
Rates: $55 to $80, single or double occupancy. Full breakfast in-
  cluded. Children welcome; pets discouraged. No credit cards.
Open: All year.
Facilities and Local Attractions: TV, books, games, in living room.
  Hot tub on deck. Rafting, fishing; touring gold country, Mar-
  shall State Park, antique stores, wineries, restaurants.

Some people might *tell* you their inn is on a river, when
you can see it from only an upstairs bathroom window;
Dorothy Irvin really *means* it. Her contemporary house is situated smack-dab on a glorious section of the American River.
And this is ☞ central-casting river: sparkling, white water
rushing over rocks and roaring in your ears. It's understand-
able that TV film companies like using it, most recently for a
commercial.

Every bedroom and the large deck are on ☞ eye level
with the river, perfect for uninterrupted viewing. Once down

the driveway, gate closed, you'll feel totally removed from the bustle of Placerville tourists. Ease into a large, beautiful hot tub on the deck, or walk down the expansive yard and put your feet into the water.

This is a comfortable, unpretentious house. Rooms are pleasant and nicely furnished, but if you aren't out watching the river, the hub of activity is the kitchen and living room. Some freshly baked treat is usually sitting there tempting you. The living room has a large fireplace, sofa and chairs to snuggle into, books, games, and a TV if you're at wits' end.

Breakfast here definitely falls into the category called "full." Dorothy calls it a gold-country breakfast. Typically, it might include fresh juice, apple crêpes, eggs Benedict, Dorothy's own baked rolls or baking powder biscuits, homemade jams, and fresh fruit. (Lunch, anyone?) This is served on the deck or in a glassed-in breakfast room that looks out at the river.

If you can tear yourself away from enjoying the river from the deck, Dorothy will help you arrange for one- or two-day raft trips with qualified guides. She'll also prepare a dinner or picnic lunch for you, by special arrangement.

It's not surprising that most of Dorothy's guests are repeaters. Some of them settle in for a week or two, leaving only for dinner at one of the nearby restaurants.

How to get there: From Placerville, take Highway 49 (Coloma Road) north to intersection of Highway 193 (Georgetown Road) leading to Chili Bar. Cross the American River and turn left immediately on first road, which leads to the inn.

J: *A stack of books, the American River, and thou.*

Olive Metcalf

The Robins Nest
San Andreas, California
95249

Innkeeper: Robin Brooks
Address/Telephone: Highway 49 (mailing address: Box 1408);
  (209) 754–1076.
Rooms: 8, all with private bath.
Rates: $55 to $85; mid-week winter rate $50 for any room available.
  Extended breakfast, evening wine and snacks included. Cash
  or personal checks. No children or pets.
Open: All year.
Facilities and Local Attractions: Central location for exploring en-
  tire Mother Lode. Year-round local events. Gold-panning tours;
  skiing, good restaurants nearby.

When Robin Brooks finished restoring this Queen Anne
Victorian, she had the original builder's ninety-year-old
daughter as her first guest and put her in the very same room
in which the woman had been born. The old lady recognized
the elegant old bathtub but insisted that the pull-chain toilet
must have been a recent addition. "Mother said that there
are *some* things you just don't do in the house!"
By those genteel standards, Robin made an aesthetic
mistake by having added five new bathrooms; by any other

measure, Robins Nest is an outstanding addition to gold-rush lodgings.

Robin left the world of Los Angeles real estate to turn the 1895 house—vacant for forty years—into a colorfully decorated inn. In the sitting room, she has mixed comfortable furniture with antiques, including a grand piano that gets frequent workouts.

Two bedrooms on the main floor and five new ones upstairs each have a ☞ unique decorating theme—a mode of transportation in California at the turn of the century. The carriage, balloon, bicycle, and train are all remembered with wall hangings, prints, and artifacts. The rooms are cheerful and spacious, with gabled ceilings and expansive views. The Steampship Room looks out at ☞ an old windmill on the property. In addition to the modern bathrooms, several rooms also have delightful brass lavatories, faithfully polished to a warm sheen.

Robin is an enthusiastic innkeeper brimming with ideas and a dash of the unexpected. Her breakfast buffet will almost always introduce you to something new. How about fresh plum juice for a change, or a ☞ frittata of apples and Monterey Jack cheese? She also makes a variety of homemade breads, quiches, and crêpes.

Evening wine in the sitting room is the time to look through Robin's collection of local restaurant menus for dinner suggestions. When you return to the inn, she'll have brandy waiting, a turned-down bed, and candy on your pillow. You're invited to find your own snacks in the kitchen if hunger strikes at odd hours.

How to get there: San Andreas is on Highway 49 between Angel's Camp and Jackson. The inn is on the west side of the highway at the north end of town; parking in back. Fly-in: Calaveras County Airport.

J: *Robin distributes a bimonthly newsletter keeping guests up to date on all the area's activities—and they're legion! Craft fairs, fiddle festivals, jumping frog contests, and Black Bart Day are just a few.*

olive Metcalf

The Carriage Farm
Sonora, California
95370

Innkeepers: Ron and Sue Snell
Address/Telephone: 21645 Parrotts Ferry Road; (209) 533–0501.
Rooms: 4, 1 with private bath, 3 sharing 2 baths. Air conditioning.
Rates: $50 to $70, including generous continental breakfast and
    evening social hour. Cash or traveler's checks preferred. No
    smoking in bedrooms; no children; no pets.
Open: All year.
Facilities and Local Attractions: Swimming pool, hot tub, bicycles,
    mopeds, table tennis, croquet, carriage rides. Explore nearby
    gold rush towns, antique stores; theater productions, restau-
    rants. Water sports on Melones Lake. Close to winter skiing.

      What could be a more idyllic setting than this 125-year-
old farmhouse on ☛ forty-three rolling acres of woods and
meadows? Chin deep in the pool or hot tub gazing out toward
the Sierras, you're likely to have a hard time remembering
why it's really necessary for you to get back to the city.
      The beguiling atmosphere begins with the immaculate
yellow-and-white farmhouse. A big country kitchen with an
☛ antique iron stove and stone fireplace is a cozy place for
sitting. A TV and comfortable chairs are there, and soft

drinks are in the refrigerator. A sensational red Victorian parlor features antique furniture and a piano with a chording device. It's a big hit at social hour, when the Snells pour wine and serve popcorn—their own home-grown product.

Three bedrooms on the main floor share two baths—one with a shower is a few steps out the kitchen door into another building. Ron takes credit for the farm's flamboyant (but effective!) red parlor and the downstairs bath. It took courage, but he's done the bath in purple and lavender, and it's absolutely right for the old-fashioned house. Up a steep stairway is a cozy slanted-roof retreat with its own bath. If you don't mind the steps, you are rewarded with panoramic views and privacy.

On the beautiful land surrounding the farm are countless diversions: swimming in the pool, croquet, horseback riding; there's even double lawn swing and hammock to relax in while you decide which to try. There's also Ron's collection of old carriages that he's restored. For a nominal charge, he'll hitch one to a couple of his horses and tour you around the countryside.

Near the swimming pool is a barcecue area and a screened-in patio. Guests often try one of the nearby restaurants one night, then stay at the farm and barbecue dinner the next. A dinner at the City Hotel in Columbia is a big attraction, and there are also the popular Italian restaurants in Jackson.

The Carriage Farm breakfast is extended continental (all-you-can-eat), with fruits and a variety of nut breads and croissants.

How to get there: Take Highway 49 north out of Sonora to Parrotts Ferry Road; follow to the inn on the right. Fly-in: Columbia Airport. Pickup available.

olive Metcalf

Gunn House
Sonora, California
95370

Innkeeper: Peggy Schoell
Address/Telephone: 286 South Washington Street; (209) 532–3421.
Rooms: 27, all with private bath, telephone, TV, air conditioning.
Rates: $37.80 to $61.56, tax included, with continental breakfast, bar snacks. Children and pets welcome.
Open: All year. Full bar.
Facilities and Local Attractions: Swimming pool. Walking tour of town's heritage buildings, Tuolumne County Museum and Jail. Five miles to Columbia State Park, theater; three miles to Sierra Railroad in Jamestown. Fishing, boating, backpacking, antiquing, panning for gold.

Gunn House is one of the relics of Sonora's past when it was "Queen of the Southern Mines." It was the first two-story adobe structure in town, built in 1850 by an enthusiastic newspaper editor, Dr. Lewis C. Gunn.

But Sonora is not a sleepy gold-rush town. It's a hub of commerce and the county seat of Tuolumne County. The busy crossroads lead to the Mother Lode, the recreational wonderlands of Sonora Pass, and Yosemite National Park over Tioga Pass.

The house was restored by owner Margaret Dienelt in the early '60s. This was before antique stores dotted the countryside, and she had to scour the area for the antiques and accessories that now decorate the Victorian rooms. She acquired some handsome period pieces—settees, carved chairs, marble-topped tables—and has combined them with the practical comforts of air conditioning, telephones, TVs, and private baths.

Gunn House is on heavily trafficked Washington Street, but being on a steep hill gives it several levels of ☞ covered verandas and patios in back. It is quieter here. There is no sitting room, but tables and chairs are on these verandas and around the oval swimming pool.

The Josephine Room is a small barroom with marble-topped tables. In the morning you'll find a continental breakfast here—coffee, fruit, and rolls. When full bar service opens in the afternoon, the public, as well as inn guests, drop by.

Up and down Washington Street are a variety of restaurants, but making the biggest noise currently is ☞ Hemingway's, just a block east of the inn. It has an intimate, attractive décor featuring photographs of the author, and an ambitious San Francisco–style menu. While I attacked an excellent carpaccio, the waiter assured me solemnly that the recipe was directly from Harry's Bar in Venice, "one of Papa's favorite hangouts." I felt more literary with every swallow.

How to get there: Take Highway 120 from Manteca east to join Highway 49, the Gold Rush Highway. Follow into the center of town. Turn right at stoplight (Washington Street). Inn is two blocks down on the right.

Olive Metcalf

Jameson's
Sonora, California
95370

Innkeepers: Virg and Jean Birdsall
Address/Telephone: 22157 Feather River Drive; (209) 532–1248.
Rooms: 4, each sharing 2 adjoining baths.
Rates: $40 to $60; extended continental breakfast included. No
    credit cards; smoking on outside decks only; no pets; no chil-
    dren under 17.
Open: All year.
Facilities and Local Attractions: Extensive in-house library, games,
    pool table. Close to boating, fishing, skiing, riding. Gold pan-
    ning; Mother Lode exploring; colorful local events.

Although Sonora is Jameson's mailing address, the inn
is actually located ten miles east of town and a hundred miles
away in atmosphere. Jameson's is a beautiful contemporary
house that nestles into its 🐦 wilderness setting so perfectly
that it almost disappears.

It was built over a creek among enormous granite boulders, waterfalls, and centuries-old oak trees. Large expanses
of glass and deck give every room the effect of being outdoors. Bedrooms open to decks where the 🐦 sound of the

284

waterfalls, both front and rear, can be enjoyed in the tranquil environment.

The atmosphere inside is relaxing, too. This is a smoothly run operation by innkeepers who aim to please; your wishes, rather than the inn's schedule, come first. Jean or Virg will drive into town to pick you up if you prefer not worrying about navigating back roads. They'll provide a quiet haven, if that's what you seek, and they're brimming with ideas if you'd rather explore the Mother Lode. Jean puts a note in your room so that you can specify when and where you will take breakfast. The back deck looking at the waterfalls is a lovely spot, but when the trees are touched with snow, you'll welcome a spot by the fireside indoors.

Each of the guest rooms is beautifully appointed but completely different from one another. One is decorated in sunny yellow and greens for an Irish flavor; Charmaine has French touches; Maria Elena, in bold reds and beige, overlooks the deck and creek. Scheherazade is the 🖝 enchanting bridal suite decorated in an exotic paisley print with canopied bed, beaded screen, brass, and even a few peacock feathers. Robes that match the décor are in each room.

The entire house is so inviting and conducive to nestling in, it's perfect for an anniversary or occasion when you don't have to leave first thing in the morning. Besides, Jean's home-baked breakfast muffins, coffee cakes, and breads ("I've never had to fall back on a bakery yet!") are reason enough to linger.

How to get there: Leave Sonora on Highway 108 south. At Phoenix Lake Road (opposite Rube's), turn left; follow about 6 miles to Creekside Road. Turn right onto Crystal Falls Drive and then left onto Feather River Drive. Inn is on the left. Fly-in: Columbia Airport; inn will pick up.

olive Metcalf

Lavender Hill
Sonora, California
95370

Innkeeper: Alice Byrnes
Address/Telephone: 683 South Barretta; (209) 532–9024.
Rooms: 3, 1 with private bath, others share large bathroom.
Rates: $50 to $60, including full breakfast. No credit cards.
Open: All year.
Facilities and Local Attractions: Walking distance to downtown
 Sonora restaurants, shops. Explore surrounding historic gold-
 rush towns; Columbia State Park. Dodge Ridge ski area; good
 stop for Yosemite trip.

The gold country has long lured California history buffs
to explore its beautiful countryside and colorful towns. You
could always find lodgings rich with authentic ambience and
history—qualities less sentimental travelers call dusty,
musty, and old. But something new is happening on the
scene. Inns are now opening that are often still in charming
old buildings, but they're being architecturally restored and
freshly decorated for comfort.
 The Lavender Hill is a premier example of the new
trend. It sits on one of Sonora's quiet streets above the
town, as pretty and appealing as a sedate Victorian lady. A

soft shade of lavender covers its turn-of-the-century lines, and an immaculate newly planted yard, flowers, and trees surround it.

Inside is period charm with polished wood floors, spacious rooms, and tall ceilings, but all newly restored and clean. The attractive entryway has a captivating ☛ working, white iron stove. Opening from here are two elegant parlors and a sunny dining room, all furnished comfortably rather than in prim, hard Victorian. Guests are invited to make themselves at home.

A handsome stairway leads up to the bedrooms. At present, Alice uses only three of them for guests. The largest is the ☛ Lavender Room, named for its luscious carpet color. A few judiciously chosen antiques and colorful linens make an appealing room.

Breakfast is generous here—fresh fruit, perhaps scrambled eggs, and always, says Alice, something fresh from the oven like whole-wheat bread or cinnamon rolls. For other meals, Sonora has a range of restaurants from hearty Italian to the continental Hemingway's. You can walk to many of them.

The house is a lovely setting for a wedding. When I visited, Alice was looking forward to hosting members of the Northern California Inn Association. When they see this quiet, elegant inn above the bustle of Sonora, they'll be glad they came.

How to get there: From downtown Sonora, take Highway 108 east out of town. At Safeway Store on right, get in center lane; make first left onto South Barretta. Inn is on the right.

olive Metcalf

The Foxes
Sutter Creek, California
95685

Innkeepers: Pete and Min Fox
Address/Telephone: 77 Main Street (mailing address: Box 159);
(209) 267–5882.
Rooms: 6 large suites, all with private bath.
Rates: $70 to $115, with bountiful breakfast. Singles deduct $5. No
children or pets. Smoking outside only.
Open: All year.
Facilities and Local Attractions: Walking tour of Sutter Creek his-
toric buildings; restaurants, antiques, specialty stores, art gal-
leries.

The three elegantly decorated suites at The Foxes, and
the three just completed, are the ☞ zenith of Mother Lode
luxury. When they bought this historic house, Realtor Pete
Fox, and Min, an antique dealer, thought they would simply
combine their businesses under one roof. But Min's flair for
creating beautiful settings meant "goodby antique store,
hello innkeeping." Pete keeps his office on the first floor, but
Min spends all her time pampering guests and making every
room a picture.

Their name was an easy handle for a symbol. You'll see

☛ foxes—fluffy, stuffed, patched, toy, ceramic, funny, and artistic—throughout the house. But Min's lavish decorating goes far beyond a cute theme. Her handsome house is the background for ☛ outstanding antiques and her knack for putting things together with great taste.

The Honeymoon Suite is an opulent setting, with a large brick fireplace, a latticed-front Austrian armoire, marble-topped sidetables, and a demi-canopied bed with a Victorian burled walnut headboard. Fabrics are sumptuous in a creamy blue and camel. In the sitting area of each large room is a beautifully appointed table arranged to receive breakfast. A crystal chandelier sparkles in the adjoining bathroom with matching wallpaper and balloon window draperies.

Upstairs are Victorian and Anniversary suites. A Louis XIV tapestry in rich burgundy and cream sets the color scheme for the first suite. There's also a ☛ 9-foot Victorian headboard and matching dresser, and a separate adjoining room as your breakfast chamber. The Anniversary Room has a ☛ massive Viennese walnut armoire—deeply carved in a rose motif against a French blue and amber wall covering—and is crowned with a vaulted ceiling.

Breakfast includes a variety of juices, hot beverages, and muffins. Min also prepares coddled eggs, sourdough French toast, or eggs Benedict. Whatever the menu, it will arrive on an ☛ impressive silver service. She likes to know if guests are celebrating a special occasion and will plan a little surprise for them.

How to get there: Sutter Creek is on Highway 49, which becomes Main Street in the center of town. The inn is on the west side of the street.

J: *Don't rush it. The longer you're here, the more elegant touches you'll see.*

Olive Metcalf

The Hanford House
Sutter Creek, California
95685

Innkeepers: Lucille and Jim Jacobus
Address/Telephone: 3 Hanford Street (mailing address: Box 847);
(209) 267–0747.
Rooms: 9, all with private bath, queen-sized beds, air conditioning.
Access for the handicapped and special facilities in one room.
Rates: $55 to $100, including extended continental breakfast. Some
designated no-smoking rooms. No pets; children over 12 wel-
come.
Open: All year.
Facilities and Local Attractions: Take walking tour of Sutter Creek,
historic houses, antique shops, art galleries, restaurants. Golfing, skiing nearby. Many local wineries.

Modern comfort in California country ambience is the
atmosphere at the Hanford House. A 1930 cottage is at the
core of a handsome two-story brick building with ample off-
street parking in front. Jim Jacobus calls it "old ☞ San Francisco warehouse style," but you must understand that there
are some very chic warehouses in that city.

The interior of the cottage at the nucleus of the inn has
a Spanish feeling, with soaring whitewashed beams. It con-

sists of a delightful parlor, with brightly slip-covered sofas, antique pine tables, magazines and plants, and a cozy bedroom filled with some of the bears that hibernate at the inn.

The new brick wing has guest rooms with luxurious baths, and they are furnished in a captivating mélange of California country, early American, and nineteenth century pieces. Jacobus bought the inn from antique dealer Ron Van Anda (who also designed and constructed Hanford House)—collection and all. Still, the rooms are tastefully "uncluttered," a term Lucille and Jim use to describe their décor.

On the top floor is a large suite with a fireplace. A ☛ common deck up here overlooks the rooftops of Sutter Creek and the foothills. It's a choice spot to take your morning coffee—ready at 7:30 A.M. along with a newspaper.

Breakfast is a relaxed affair. You wander down to the dining room when you're ready, or Lucille will take an attractively set tray to your room. Juice, fresh fruit, and a selection of cheeses, muffins, or sweet rolls make up the continental fare, with your choice of hot beverage.

Jim's past experience as a Bay Area stockbroker and Lucille's former position in a mental-health agency seem remote from life in the Sierra foothills, but now they're both enthusiastic converts to country life. They're eager for guests to know about points of interest and good restaurants around Sutter Creek. Right next door is the ☛ Pelargonium Restaurant and Gallery, which serves elegant California cuisine.

How to get there: Highway 49 runs through the center of Sutter Creek. At the north end of town where the Highway divides, turn left. Immediately on your left is the inn.

Olive Metcalf

Sutter Creek Inn
Sutter Creek, California
95685

Innkeeper: Jane Way
Address/Telephone: 75 Main Street (mailing address: Box 385);
  (209) 267–5606.
Rooms: 18, all with private bath, electric blankets, and air condi-
  tioner.
Rates: $58 to $95, full breakfast included. Children discouraged.
  Two-day minimum on weekends. No credit cards; no pets.
Open: Closed Thanksgiving and the day before, Christmas Eve, and
  Christmas Day.
Facilities and Local Attractions: Enjoy inn's gardens, hammocks,
  library, and games. A good town for walking: art galleries, an-
  tiques, historic houses, restaurants.

When the subject is California inns, the talk invariably
goes to the Sutter Creek Inn and Jane Way. ☞ Jane started
the phenomenon of country inns in this state twenty years
ago. In fact, she's become a legend in her own time. Former
guests like to swap stories about what she did while *they*
were there: Jane captivating her guests with tales of the
house ghost; Jane doing handwriting analysis; Jane ladling
brandy into your before-breakfast coffee; Jane and the fa-

292

mous swinging beds. Her boundless energy and flair have made the Sutter Creek a prototype for country inns.

On a busy street of shops, restaurants, and overhanging balconies, the Sutter Creek Inn is a charming New England–style residence surrounded by a green lawn, trees, and flower beds. Some bedrooms are in the main house, others in outbuildings in back that Jane has extensively re-modeled and decorated with great ingenuity. Their names recall Sutter Creek's gold-rush history—Wood Shed, Lower Wash House, Tool Shed, Miner's Cabin.

Each room is completely different. Some have fire-places, some Franklin stoves, some private patios; others open onto the garden. And there are the 🖝 swinging beds— an idea Jane discovered in Mexico—but not to worry, they can be stabilized if you wish. Room appointments are cozy and comfortable, right down to the selection of magazines and a decanter of sherry.

Gathering in the beautiful living room for coffee before breakfast is the quintessential inn experience. Jane holds court, introducing guests, pouring brandy, and overseeing breakfast. When the breakfast bell rings, you move to four polished oak tables in the large cheerful kitchen.

The meal might include eggs à la Sutter Creek (baked in cream cheese sauce and served on an English muffin) or pancakes full of chopped apples and nuts, served with black-berry syrup and ham. Hot biscuits or muffins and fresh fruit and juice puts you in a benign glow for the day. Or is it Jane's coffee?

How to get there: Sutter Creek is 4 miles north of Jackson on High-way 49, which runs through the center of town. The inn is on the west side of the street.

🪣

J: *Pick up a copy of the* Stroller's Guide to Sutter Creek *at any store along Main Street. It will lead you to the back streets of older buildings and interesting stores.*

Olive Metcalf

Mayfield House
Tahoe City, California
95730

Innkeeper: Janie Kay
Address/Telephone: 236 Grove Street (mailing address: Box 5999);
    (916) 583–1001.
Rooms: 6 rooms sharing 3 baths.
Rates: $60 to $82, including 1 suite. Continental breakfast and
    complimentary wine. No children; no pets. Wheelchair access.
Open: All year.
Facilities and Local Attractions: Walking distance to shops, restau-
    rants, tennis courts. Free buses to Squaw Valley and Alpine
    Meadows skiing 10 miles away. Hiking, bicycling, boating; all
    the attractions of Lake Tahoe.

    Mayfield House is an agreeable alternative to motel or
condo digs while you enjoy the mountain air of Lake Tahoe.
The house is a fine example of ☞ old Tahoe architecture. It
was built in 1932 by Norman Mayfield, one of Lake Tahoe's
pioneer contractors. Refurbished in 1979, it is comfortable
and traditional in atmosphere, serene rather than chic. It's
the kind of place to read and relax in.
    All the bedrooms have down pillows, down comforters,
and robes. They each have a sitting area, very cozy if you like

breakfast served in your room. In the '30s, one room, now called ☛ Julia's Room, was always reserved for Julia Morgan, the architect of San Simeon and a personal friend of the owners'. It's a surprisingly feminine, simple room. I imagined her there happily escaping from her ponderous Hearst project.

The Study is another inviting bedroom upstairs, with an arched window area and built-in bookshelves. One of the bathrooms up here features a ☛ 6-foot-long tub installed by the tall owner who evidently liked to stretch out while he soaked.

A bedroom on the main floor, the wood-paneled former den of Norman Mayfield, is decorated in brown, beige, and rust plaid. With its outside door, it offers easy access for a wheelchair.

The Margaret Carpenter prints on the walls and fresh flowers lend a pleasant feeling to the large living room. With its fireplaces and snuggly sofas, it's a cozy place to read and enjoy your complimentary wine in the afternoon.

Continental breakfast is served in the dining room, if you haven't chosen the quiet of your bedroom or the patio. There are juice, seasonal fresh fruit, cheeses, and homemade breads along with coffee and teas.

How to get there: From San Francisco, take Highway 80 to Truckee; turn south on Highway 89 to Tahoe City. Turn north on Highway 28 to Grove Street; turn left.

J: For all its beauty, Tahoe can either lift your heart or squash your spirits. Mayfield House is an oasis of quiet sanity.

Olive Metcalf

Alpenhaus
Tahoma, California
95733

Innkeepers: April and Roger Taylor, summer; Pat and Vern Lucas, winter.

Address / Telephone: 6945 West Lake Boulevard (mailing address: Box 262); (916) 525–5000.

Rooms: 7 rooms, 5 with private bath; 6 housekeeping cottages.

Rates: $49 to $61. $6 per extra person. Winter ski package. Full breakfast included. Children welcome.

Open: All year.

Facilities and Local Attractions: Swimming, hiking, biking, tennis, ping-pong, horse shoes. Nearby Lake Tahoe attractions. Two miles from downhill skiing at Homewood; one-quarter mile from Sugar Pine Point State Park for cross-country. Basque nights (accordion music) Wednesdays and Thursdays.

"I come up here and always quit smoking—the air is just so *healthy!*" April Taylor shares the feelings a lot of people have about the fresh, beautiful Lake Tahoe area. Tahoma, situated on the west shore, is known for a little more quiet beauty than other parts of the lake. You can quickly get to the nightspots and gambling if the fever strikes, but Alpen-

296

haus seems to lure skiers and hikers to its more country-like atmosphere in the trees.

Most guests were enjoying the pool the hot day I visited, but the inn's Swiss Alpine look is especially appropriate with snow on the roof—and they get plenty of it. Skiers are only minutes away from both ☛ Alpine and Nordic skiing.

The cheerful dining room has a rich green carpet, and pictures and objects reveal a European touch. It's the scene of three meals a day—big breakfasts, light lunches, and robust dinners. Swiss and German specialties are featured—hearty soups, sauerbraten with spätzli and jagerschnitzel. Skiers and locals also request fondue, especially raclette, cooked and served the way it is around the Alps.

But it's ☛ Basque night that really brings people in. In fact, the popular event is now held two nights, Wednesday and Thursday. Typical, authentic Basque food is served family style, in big bowls, accompanied with much toasting, accordion music, and—before you know it—singing. You don't leave Basque night a stranger.

The entire inn was refurbished three years ago. Now a small lounge area with a stone fireplace and a bar provides a place for guests to get acquainted. It's casual, with a friendly atmosphere you'll feel the minute you walk in. Upstairs, the bedrooms are plain and neat, with hand-painted wood furniture and thick comforters for cold mountain nights.

How to get there: From Sacramento, take Highway 80 to Truckee and Highway 89; continue south to Tahoma. Inn is on the right of the highway.

Olive Metcalf

Oak Hill Ranch
Tuolumne, California
95379

Innkeepers: Sanford and Jane Grover
Address/Telephone: 18550 Connally Lane (mailing address: Box 307); (209) 928–4717.
Rooms: 4, sharing 2 bathrooms; 1 cottage (sleeps 5), with private bath, kitchen, fireplace.
Rates: $50 to $73, double or single; $15 per extra adult. Full breakfast included. No children; no pets; no smoking. No credit cards; personal checks okay.
Open: All year.
Facilities and Local Attractions: Walk beautiful countryside. Explore southern Mother Lode. Near Dodge Ridge skiing; 63 miles to Yosemite. Sonora restaurants.

Discovering Tuolumne is a delightful experience, but the capper is to follow a country back road another mile past town, then up the lane to this gracious ranch home. The Grovers say their ☞ Ranch Victorian was completed in 1980, but it's actually 110 years old. Since they began collecting Victorian building materials and furniture more than twenty-five years ago, the house has been their dream.

It was designed by their architect son in the '70s, but

years of stripping old wood (and an understanding contractor) were required before the dream came to life. The result is the period ambience of tall ceilings, wide hallways, and authentic wood detailings in an immaculate background of modern kitchen, plumbing, and heating. If you're from condo-land, the generous size of the house alone is a pleasure.

The 🖝 setting is spectacular, on a wooded hill overlooking miles of rolling terrain with the Sierra range in the distance. On a crisp October morning, the Grovers, 🖝 in period costume, welcomed me into an inviting living room with a fire burning in the fireplace, fresh flowers, and refreshment. It was downright pastoral ensnarement.

A wonderful floral carpet sets the tone of stylish, uncluttered, Victorian charm. The upstairs bedrooms have fetching décors, one with a canopied bed, another opening to a balcony that overlooks pastures and ponds.

Your hosts (retired educators) are naturally hospitable, and they're adamant about always putting their best foot forward. They'll help you choose restaurants in the area and point out some beautiful drives to take.

Many innkeepers endeavor to make breakfast a special treat, but the Grovers know that it's not just a lot of food that makes the occasion special, it's serving it with style. When guests gather for an Oak Hill breakfast in the impressive dining room (it must be more than twenty feet long), Jane, in long skirt and ruffled cap, and Sandy in crisp shirt and arm bands, make the morning memorable. The menu may feature quiche, baked eggs, or French toast, always freshly made in their large farm kitchen and engagingly served.

How to get there: From Sonora, take Highway 108 to Tuolumne Road; follow to center of Tuolumne. Turn south on Carter Street to the schoolyard, left onto Elm Street, and right on Madrone Street, which turns into Apple Colony Road. Follow to Oak Hill sign on left. Fly-in: Columbia Airport; inn pickup.

olive Metcalf

Twain Harte's Bed and Breakfast
Twain Harte, California
95383

Innkeepers: El and Pat Pantaleoni
Address/Telephone: 18864 Manzanita Drive (mailing address: Box 1718); (209) 586–3311.
Rooms: 6, 2 with private bath; sinks in 4 rooms sharing 2 bathrooms.
Rates: $35 to $65 double occupancy, includes full breakfast. Ask about ski and theater packages. No smoking. Children welcome.
Open: All year.
Facilities and Local Attractions: Pool table, TV in game room. Walk to downtown Twain Harte. Hike surrounding woods; fishing, hunting, boating, water skiing. Close to Yosemite; Dodge Ridge Ski Resort (cross-country and downhill).

Mark Twain lived and wrote around this area, and Bret Harte lived here for a time. It's beautiful country just to walk in and enjoy quietly, but the variety of recreational activities in the area make Twain Harte an ☛ exceptional headquarters for family vacations.

This rambling inn welcomes children and makes it convenient for parents to bring them. An unpretentious living room with a fireplace opens to a spacious recreation room complete with a pool table, games, and TV. A family suite upstairs can sleep six. It has a large living room and kitchen with a microwave oven for fixing your own snacks.

A big sun porch upstairs is a sunny place to play. El says several people have had winter weddings up here. In summer, the outdoor decks are perfect places for a mountain wedding.

Newly expanded skiing facilities at Dodge Ridge make lodging at Twain Harte all the more interesting. Families who used to ski all day and then face a long drive home will enjoy coming back to Twain Harte for dinner at one of the good restaurants nearby, then a cozy evening at the inn. After a comfortable sleep and a hearty breakfast, you can be off to ski again.

A long glassed-in front porch is the breakfast room. The entire house is heated with wood, and a huge farmer's boiler in here serves as a unique and efficient stove. The morning menu is usuallly a fruit combination, eggs poached or scrambled, and muffins.

The gold-rush town of Columbia is only fifteen miles away with many attractions, including a theater company. One of the inn's promotions is a package that includes dinner at Twain Harte's Villa D'Oro Restaurant, theater tickets to the Columbia Actors Repertory, an after-dinner drink, and a night and breakfast at the Twain Harte, all for $77 per couple.

How to get there: From Sonora, take Highway 108 to Twain Harte. Just past the town center, look for Manzanita Drive; turn right. Inn is on the left, across from schoolyard. Guest parking behind.

Olive Metcalf

Saint George Hotel
Volcano, California
95689

Innkeepers: Marlene and Charles Inman
Address/Telephone: 2 Main Street (mailing address: Box A); (209)
   296–4458.
Rooms: 20; 14 on two floors in hotel sharing a bath and a half on
   each floor; 6 separate motel units with private bath.
Rates: $75 for two, MAP on weekends; $31 to $48.50, weekdays,
   EP.
Open: Closed first six weeks of year. Dinner Saturday and Sunday
   by reservation; breakfast weekdays if requested. Full bar.
Facilities and Local Attractions: Walk every square inch of Vol-
   cano; visit original jail, stone ruins of Wells Fargo, "Old Abe."
   Close to other historic gold towns, shopping, antiques, restau-
   rants. Indian Grinding Rock State Park.

   Volcano is a ☞ highlight of any Mother Lode tour, the
most picturesque of all the gold-rush towns. Its enduring
charm is that it doesn't change. Located a few miles off
Highway 49, it has somehow remained aloof from gentrifica-
tion, beautification, supermarkets, gas stations, neon, and
boutiques!
   During its heyday, more than ninety million dollars in

gold was taken from the hills and gulches around Volcano and poured into the United States Treasury. It was during the Civil War, and the issue of whether the gold would go to the north or the south was decided by virtue of the abolitionists in town having "Old Abe." The ancient cannon (which would have been more of a threat had there been any cannonballs to go with it) was never tested. The abolitionists prepared by gathering stones from the riverbed for ammunition, but the outnumbered southern sympathizers retired from the fray.

The Saint George Hotel is *the* can't-miss landmark on Main Street. It is a modest three-story structure, but vine-covered balconies give it an Old West appeal. From them, you can look out over the quiet town (population eighty-five) and the rolling hills of the beautiful countryside.

The two upstairs floors contain simple bedrooms, some of them quite large, with shared baths at the end of the hall. Each is decorated with antiques and crocheted bedspreads. A modern annex is available with private baths, but only the hotel has the old-time flavor. On the main floor are the dining room and the lounge, notable for a floor-to-ceiling mirror cracked by what everyone chooses to believe is a bullet hole.

Dinners on weekends offer a single entrée: prime ribs of beef on Saturday and spring chicken on Sunday. Hearty soups, breads, and desserts are made at the hotel.

Marlene says that one winter specialty is tutti frutti. As fresh fruit ripens through the summer it is put into a crock with brandy and sugar. Months later, nicely marinated, it is ladled over ice cream or pound cake.

How to get there: Five county roads lead into Volcano, each a winding route through the foothills. Try the road east from Jackson on Highway 88 to Pine Grove, then north on Volcano–Pine Grove Road to Volcano. Beautiful.

J: *Try to catch the spring wildflower display on Daffodill Hill.*

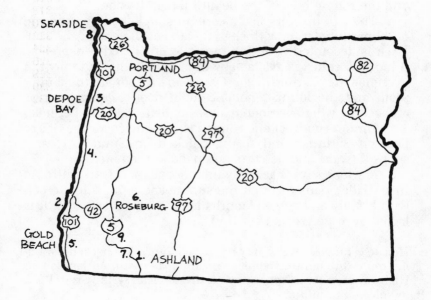

N

SEASIDE
8
26
101
PORTLAND
84
82
5
26
DEPOE 3.
BAY
20
84
20
97
4.
20
6.
2.
42
ROSEBURG
97
GOLD
101
5
BEACH 5.
9.
7. 1. ASHLAND

Oregon

Numbers on map refer to towns numbered below.

Olive Metcalf

Chanticleer Bed and Breakfast Inn
Ashland, Oregon
97520

Innkeepers: Jim and Nancy Beaver
Address/Telephone: 120 Gresham Street; (503) 482–1919.
Rooms: 7, all with private bath, including a suite with kitchen.
Rates: $64 to $69, double occupancy; singles $5 less; includes full
   breakfast. No credit cards, personal checks preferred.
Open: All year.
Facilities and Local Attractions: Walk to Ashland theaters, restau-
   rants, Lithia Park, shops. Convenient to Rogue River white-
   water rafting, Mt. Ashland skiing.

With the success of its Shakespearean festival, Ashland
has become a mecca for bed and breakfast inns. In the past
year I've collected a file of clippings about them, mostly letters written to travel editors from past visitors singing the
praises of one particular inn—the Chanticleer. Now that I've
been there too, I can appreciate the enthusiastic chorus. It's
undoubtedly one of the most attractive, romantic inns in
Ashland.

The name comes from Chaucer's tale of Chanticleer
and the fox, a European barnyard fable. That's the feeling

here—cozy and European. The country living room has a warm appeal with its blue rug, rock fireplace and hearth. Comfortable, cushy furniture, books, and an ever-welcome tray of sherry complete the picture. I'm always favorably predisposed toward *any* room that includes these amenities.

Everything about you looks freshly painted and is immaculate. If you're not off to a matinee, it's a pleasure to spend your day at this inn. Some of the rooms overlook Bear Creek Valley and Cascade foothills; others open onto a ☞ brick patio and a perfectly lovely rock garden.

The seven cheerful bedrooms are engagingly decorated with crisp linens, cotton slipcovers on puffy goose-down comforters, wallpapers, and fresh flowers. Complimentary toiletries, robes, and thick towels appoint your private bath. Several of these rooms accommodate a family of four nicely.

Jim and Nancy think of many ways to be obliging. They're endlessly helpful in choosing where to have dinner, and what to see in the area. But most thoughtful, I think, is having in your room ☞ copies of all the current plays running in Ashland's three theaters. Wonderful for resolving after-the-play discussions.

Everyone who stays here raves about the breakfasts, and with good cause. Even the orange juice and fresh fruit seem tastier than when you prepare them at home. Maybe it's Jim and Nancy's solicitude for everyone's comfort, or perhaps it's the lively conversation with other guests that accounts for this. Of course, the baked pears with orange sauce, blintzes, quiche, or shirred eggs with cream, the hot breads and blueberry muffins, the superb coffee and teas have something to do with it, too.

How to get there: Driving north to Ashland on I-5, take exit 11; proceed along Siskiyou to Iowa Street, and turn left. At Gresham Street, turn right. Inn is on your right.

Olive Metcalf

Hersey House
Ashland, Oregon
97520

Innkeepers: Gail E. Orell and K. Lynn Savage
Address/Telephone: 451 North Main Street; (503) 482–4563.
Rooms: 4, each with private bath; air conditioning.
Rates: $62 single to $75 for three persons; full breakfast included.
 No credit cards; children over 12 welcome. Smoking on the
 porches.
Open: All year except October to mid-April.
Facilities and Local Attractions: Walk to Ashland theaters, shops,
 restaurants, Lithia Park. Explore nearby historical mining
 town of Jacksonville. Biking, golf, tennis, fishing, water sports
 available locally.

No car; no hassle. Those are two great advantages of
Hersey House. It is open almost exclusively for the Ashland
theater season, and you couldn't choose a more comfortable
or convenient place to nestle in while you see it all.
 Ashland's beautiful theaters—including the experi-
mental and conventional as well as the outdoor Elizabethan
Stagehouse—are as highly regarded as the talent they draw.
But what makes Ashland pure pleasure for theater lovers is
the 👉 low-key atmosphere and the easy way you can take it

all in. A few days of first-rate theater in the beautiful setting of the Rogue Valley can easily diminish the allure of more high-powered, metropolitan theater seasons.

At graceful Hersey House, you can have afternoon wine or tea while the innkeepers tell you about the enticing range of restaurants you might try for dinner, and all of them are just a stroll from your inn and the theaters.

The house was built in 1906, and five generations of the Hersey family lived there. When the present owners converted it into an inn, they were careful to keep the Victorian charm while they entirely updated and refurbished it. They evidently succeeded, even in the eyes of Hersey family members, who have lent the inn some grand family portraits of the first Herseys to live in the house. The portraits now hang in the stairway.

There are only four guest rooms, but each one is a beauty, tastefully decorated in airy floral prints, several with matching wallpaper, a queen-sized bed and tiled bath. The Sunshine Terrace Room has a private balcony and a view overlooking the Cascade foothills; the Eastlake Room has a view of Mt. Ashland.

Breakfast in a theater town inn is especially congenial because the conversation has an immediate hook: What did you see? . . . What did you think of it? . . . Where did you have dinner? The innkeepers stoke the talk with freshly brewed coffee and herbal teas, fresh juice and fruit, and home-cooked delights that change daily, like orange nut bread and Eggs Hersey.

How to get there: From I-5, take exit 11 into Ashland. Proceed north along Siskiyou, which becomes Lithia Way, then North Main Street. Inn is on the left.

olive Metcalf

McCall House
Ashland, Oregon
97520

Innkeeper: Phyllis Courtney
Address/Telephone: 153 Oak Street; (503) 482–9296.
Rooms: 6, 2 with private bath, 4 sharing 2 baths.
Rates: $53 to $63, single or double occupancy; $10 for extra person.
  No credit cards; no young children.
Open: All year.
Facilities and Local Attractions: One block to Ashland theaters, Oregon Shakespearean Festival, restaurants, shops. Lithia Park. Winter skiing, Mt. Ashland; rafting, Rogue River.

One of the best reasons to choose an inn called McCall House in this mad-for-theater town is that ☛ your innkeeper is an actress. Phyllis Courtney not only runs an elegant inn, but she also often appears in Ashland productions. For theater lovers, this means the added fun of conversations over breakfast with someone knowledgeable about the plays, casts, and productions. And who doesn't love inside stuff!

The whole house is handsome enough to be a stage setting—a stately Italianate Victorian built by Ashland pioneer John McCall in 1883. Twelve-foot ceilings and spacious rooms are the perfect foil for ☛ outstanding antiques.

Courtney's appreciation for the dramatic is apparent in her decorating. When I admired the chic dining room with its dark brown walls and round tables draped with long, white cloths, she said, "Food looks good in a setting with a dark background."

But breakfast lovers can relax; this is not a case of décor triumphing over food. A full breakfast is served, and it is an elegant one. The day I visited, it consisted of fresh juice, blueberries and yogurt, hot croissants, and scalloped eggs.

This fine house has seen notable guests in its history: Rutherford B. Hayes, General Sherman (though Phyllis says she'd just as soon forget *him*), and William Jennings Bryan. The famous orator was a guest when he lectured at the Ashland Chatauqua. Ironically, it was during a production of *Inherit the Wind* in which Phyllis played the part of the Mrs. Bryan character that she discovered that Bryan had once stayed in her house.

You will be comfortable in any of these large bedrooms with queen-sized beds, sitting areas, and some with a fireplace. In addition, guests have a parlor and a combination library and music room to enjoy.

How to get there: In the center of Ashland, one block west of Main Street on Oak Street.

J: *A production of the seldom-seen* King John *that night was particularly enjoyable because of the lowdown Phyllis gave me on who was who. I'd have been lost without it.*

olive Metcalf

The Morical House
Ashland, Oregon
97520

Innkeepers: Joe and Phyllis Morical
Address/Telephone: 668 North Main Street; (503) 482–2254.
Rooms: 5, all with private bath. Air conditioning.
Rates: $62, double occupancy, $5 less for single. Weekday discount
    in non–theater season. Winter rates, $45. All rates include full
    breakfast.
Open: All year.
Facilities and Local Attractions: Walk to Ashland theaters, restau-
    rants, shops. Skiing at Mt. Ashland.

Theater is the main reason people from all over the world flock to Ashland. The Oregon Shakespearean Festival performs a three-play repertory from June through September in the outdoor Elizabethan Stagehouse, as well as in two other theaters.

But gorgeous scenery has always been Oregon's primary attraction for travelers, and Morical House offers some of the best. The 1880s house is surrounded by an acre of lawns, rocks, shrubs, and more than a hundred varieties of trees, and it looks out on a panoramic view of Bear Creek Valley and the Cascade Mountains.

312

When the Moricals decided to quit their California government jobs and become innkeepers, they visited a number of cities before choosing Ashland and this house. It is only a ☛ fifteen-minute walk to the theaters and a wide range of restaurants, but all of Ashland is a delightful walking town.

They have restored the house as a comfortable country inn with tasteful attention to its period charms such as stained-glass windows and detailed woodwork. The traditional nineteenth-century house has undergone many additions during the years in a way that makes the downstairs floor plan unconventional but entirely pleasing. Several light-filled sitting rooms, with comfortable sofas and chairs and well-stocked bookshelves, call you in to enjoy them. A kitchen you're invited to use for a quick snack, an ice machine, and a ready tea kettle all make this an inviting house to nestle in.

To fully take advantage of the inn's vista, the Moricals added a ☛ glassed-in porch across the back of the house. Eating one of the house breakfast treats, like Dutch pancakes, here, with the sweeping view before you, is a splendid beginning to the day.

Beautifully decorated bedrooms are upstairs, with mountain views and non-Victorian comforts of private baths, air conditioning, and soundproofed walls. The very private third-floor room is a favorite. What bliss to soak in a grand old claw-footed tub and read a play you'll see performed that night.

How to get there: Driving north on Highway 5, take exit 19 at Ashland. Follow to the inn on the left.

J: Real *Ashland theater buffs go to both matinee and evening performances. But this pleasant inn gives you a ticket to such a scene-stealing panorama of sky and land that it could easily become your matinee performance choice.*

olive Metcalf

The Winchester Inn
Ashland, Oregon
97520

Innkeepers: The Gibbs Family: Pat and Colleen, Michael and Laurie
Address/Telephone: 35 South Second Street; (503) 488–1113.
Rooms: 6, all with private bath.
Rates: $48 to $72, depending on the season, double occupancy; breakfast included. Winter packages available. No pets.
Open: All year. Lunch, dinner, Sunday brunch.
Facilities and Local Attractions: Two blocks from Ashland theaters, Lithia Park; one block from shops, restaurants.

West Coast inns that offer all meals are few and far between. The Winchester Inn is the ☛ only one in Ashland that serves lunch and dinner to the public as well as to inn guests.

It's a graceful Queen Anne Victorian in Ashland's downtown historic district. It was first a private home; then it was Oregon's first hospital. White and stately, with a broad front porch, it looks engaging from the outside, and once you enter the handsome double doors, you'll not be disappointed inside, either. Pale blue carpeting runs from the entry, through the impressive parlor with leaded-glass windows, and up the stairs to the bedrooms.

I was there for Sunday brunch and thoroughly enjoyed the atmosphere in the glassed-in dining room. A Vivaldi tape was being played in the background, and my view of the colorful terraced gardens provided a delightful setting. Warm-weather breakfasts and lunches are served on an inviting patio decorated with clusters of potted flowers, where you can sit at umbrella tables under the trees.

Champagne, orange juice, and a coffee cup kept refilled soothe you while studying the menu. As you sip away enjoying the music and flowers, you're served ☛ hot scones with the house nut-butter and marmalade.

Entrée choices that morning were eggs Benedict, sausage omelet, or stir-fried fresh vegetables and chicken. Attacks of desire for California-style cuisine grip me periodically when I get out of state, and this fresh stir-fry filled the bill.

Upstairs are the fresh, attractive bedrooms with high ceilings, antique beds, and green plants. Each one is decorated in a different pastel color—pale raspberry, lavender, blue—with comforters to match.

For theatergoers—and almost every visitor to Ashland is one—the Winchester's location is a great convenience. From the patio, you can hear the trumpets summoning players and audience to the outdoor Shakespearean theater. Forsooth . . . take thine umbrella.

How to get there: On I-5 driving north, take the first Ashland exit; it becomes Main Street. Continue to center of town; turn left at Second Street, and go two blocks. The inn is on the right corner of Hargadine Street.

Olive Metcalf

The Woods House
Ashland, Oregon
97520

Innkeepers: Janice and Allan Pinkul
Address/Telephone: 333 North Main Street; (503) 488–1598.
Rooms: 4 in main house, all with private bath; 1 suite, accommodating 6 people, in the carriage house.
Rates: $48 to $68, single or double; $10 each extra person. Includes full breakfast. No pets; children over 12 welcome.
Open: All year.
Facilities and Local Attractions: Walk to Shakespearean festival theaters, Ashland restaurants, shops. Twenty miles to Mt. Ashland skiing. Fifteen miles to historic Jacksonville.

Don't be deceived into thinking that Woods House is merely another charming old home where someone has decided to put extra bedrooms to use as a B&B. It *is* an ☞ architecturally interesting house, but there's nothing amateur about the way guests are accommodated. Janice is a pro, bringing years of hotel experience to the inn she and her husband now own.

When the Pinkuls bought the 1908 Craftsman-style house, Janice wanted to add a second story and restore the carriage house, all as authentically as possible. But first, she searched for a female architect—("The men didn't seem to understand what I was talking about")—and found Joyce Ward in Ashland. They gave painstaking attention to every detail, particularly in designing a fir staircase that goes to the new top-floor guest rooms and baths. A separate, restored carriage house sleeps six people.

☛ Attention to details is also the way guests are cared for. Janice has hired and trained a staff to look for what needs doing, even before she or a guest notices it. And she is a fanatic about cleanliness. "I don't mind clutter—people have to relax and enjoy themselves—but I want things clean." (Is that music to the ears of you who are not charmed with the casual attitude some inns have toward dust balls?)

The colorful living room is a change from more common inn color schemes. A bold, deep green predominates on velour sofas and woodwork trim. Against the warm wood tones of fir floor and fireplace, the room is both dramatic and inviting.

A family-style full breakfast is served in the dining room or in the garden. Professional touches are apparent here in the artfully arranged fresh fruit platter, freshly baked muffins, and hot egg and cheese casseroles. This day, Janice and her helpers served wearing bright green aprons that matched the interior house color scheme.

Other pleasures are coffee and tea, available all day, and a beautiful yard with a grape arbor. As I left, Janice gave me a ripe bunch of grapes for the road.

How to get there: From Highway 5, take exit 19 to Ashland. Turn left on North Main. The inn is on the right.

♉

J: *The most recent addition to the inn's appointments is fine-quality note paper for each room, with an attractive woodblock print of the house on it.*

Olive Metcalf

Spindrift
Bandon, Oregon
97411

Innkeepers: Don and Robbie Smith
Address/Telephone: 2990 Beach Loop Road; (503) 347–2275.
Rooms: 2, 1 with private bath.
Rates: $45 to $56 for double, deduct $5 for single. Includes breakfast and refreshments. No small children; no pets or smoking.
Open: All year.
Facilities and Local Attractions: Directly on the beach; surf fishing; golf nearby. Shops galleries, restaurants in Bandon.

The bedrooms are delightful, the ambience is comfortable, and your hosts are engaging, but it is Spindrift's location that will stay in your memory forever. The contemporary beach house is perched on a grassy bluff some fifty feet above a spectacular beach. This is the kind of beach that you see in Oregon travel posters: broad, sandy, and dramatically framed with massive, offshore rock formations.

Entire days can simply disappear while you watch the surf, the birds, and migrating whales, wade out to the "stacks" to explore the rocks, and wait for amazing sunsets. If you're lucky, you will be here for the thrill of watching a storm approach.

The inn has a large deck and a common room with floor-to-ceiling windows for an uninterrupted vista. The room is cozy with a vaulted, beamed ceiling, and fireplace. The Seaview Room has a down-quilted queen-sized bed, its own bath, a fireplace, French doors that open onto the deck, and a private entrance with a ramp. The Surfsounds Room doesn't have an ocean view, but it is restful and snug with down-quilted twin beds. Robes are provided for guests in both rooms.

Breakfast menus change daily, and each is a treat. Typical is fresh fruit, homemade breads and jams, a hot egg or cheese entreé, and the inn's specially ground coffee and selected teas. When I arrived, Don and Robbie had been blackberry picking and were making jam.

This is an inn where you can be as solitary as you wish, but if you enjoy good company, you're in luck. Don, a retired university librarian, and Robbie, an accomplished weaver, have raised six sons and enjoy a wide range of interests. They are a friendly couple, happy to share a game of bridge, travel experiences, information about wine making, rock polishing, spinning, weaving, and just good talk. In short, they are the kind of people who *ought* to be innkeepers.

How to get there: Bandon is 25 miles south of Coos Bay on the southern Oregon coast. From Highway 101 at Bandon, continue south 1 mile south of the 11th Street traffic light. Turn west (toward the ocean) on Seabird Drive to Beach Loop Road. Turn right to Spindrift, second house on the left. Fly-in: North Bend airport; pickup available.

♒

J: *Old Town Bandon is being restored and has restaurants, galleries, and unique shops that offer local arts and products, like Oregon cheese and cranberry sweets.*

319

O live Metcalf

Channel House
Depoe Bay, Oregon
97341

Innkeepers: Freda and Greg Glasscock; proprietor, Paul Schwabe
Address/Telephone: Box 56; (503) 765–2140.
Rooms: 7, all with private bath; rooms include 3 suites with kitchens; color TV.
Rates: $35 to $120, double occupancy, full breakfast included. $10 each additional person.
Open: All year. Restaurant serves dinner only, full bar.
Facilities and Local Attractions: Spectacular oceanfront location; watch fishing boats, marine life. Mopeds; VCR. Seasonal whale-watch excursions, fishing, shops, aquarium. September Indian-style salmon bake at Fogarty Creek State Park.

You may actually *wish* for bad weather when you get settled into one of these attractive, cozy rooms on Depoe Bay. The inn is perched on top of a rocky cliff looming over the crashing surf. When the tide is coming in or during a storm it's a ☞ select site to watch spray shooting over the rocks below and sea foam boiling through fascinating crevices.

Whatever the weather, you're blissfully snug inside these exceedingly well-furnished and comfortable rooms with their subdued nautical décor. Navy Levelor shades at the windows and crisp, navy blue cotton covers on puffy comforters stand out smartly against redwood beds, tables and chairs. A radio and a dish of nuts are thoughtful additions, as are the complimentary toiletries in the sharp bathrooms.

Living room furniture is freshly upholstered in warm beige tweeds. You'll find binoculars hanging from a chair for serious viewing as boats maneuver through the narrow channel leading from the ☛ world's smallest harbor into the open ocean.

The streamlined kitchens in three of the units make it especially convenient to nestle in and stay awhile. They're appointed with every need from dishwasher right down to hot pads and wine glasses.

The two oceanfront suites have it all—kitchens, fireplace, and double hideabed sofa in the living room, another fireplace in the bedroom, a whirlpool, and an ocean-front deck. Standing out here is very much like being on the deck of a ship—you feel so close to the ocean. For maximum exposure, one of the suites has a whirlpool out on the deck!

The Channel House Restaurant/Oyster Bar on the main floor has a casually sophisticated look with a deck, brick floor, navy-blue napkins on white tablecloths, and antique nautical appointments. ☛ Fresh oysters on the half shell are a specialty—raw, grilled, or baked. Also on the menu are terrific, tiny steamed clams, a very special fresh pizza, steak, and a selection of Oregon wines. A baked-on-the-spot cheesecake wins the dessert prize.

How to get there: U.S. Highway 101 passes through the small town. The inn is one block off the highway toward the ocean, at the foot of Ellingson Street.

Olive Metcalf

The Johnson House
Florence, Oregon
97439

Innkeepers: Jayne and Ronald Fraese
Address/Telephone: 216 Maple Street (mailing address: Box 1892);
    (503) 997–8000.
Rooms: 5, 1 with private bath.
Rates: $45 to $55, including afternoon refreshment and full break-
    fast.
Open: All year.
Facilities and Local Attractions: Walk to waterfront of Siuslaw
    River; shops, restaurants, antiques in Old Town Florence.
    Lake fishing. Oregon Dunes Recreation Area; clamming, crab-
    bing, beachcombing, bird watching.

The coastal town of Florence could be one of your most
enjoyable discoveries on a driving trip from California to Van-
couver, B.C., for the exposition. It is the halfway point from
San Francisco, just off Highway 101 and situated on the
northern edge of the National Sand Dunes Recreation Area.
This fabulous stretch of coast has beige-colored dunes higher
than those of the Sahara, their contours constantly changing
by sand washed ashore and by the wind. They are wonderful
to drive along or walk. Sometimes the coast lupines, straw-

berries, sand verbenas, and monkey flowers will be in bloom on the fore-dunes or on the open sand.

The historic community nestles at the mouth of the wide Suislaw River. The Johnson House is the oldest house in town, and Jayne and Ronald have restored it with an eye for original structure and details that give every room the atmosphere of warm Oregon coast living a century ago.

From its snow white outside appearance to the beautiful bed linens and puffy comforters, everything here looks fresh, clean, and light. It is a homey, comfortable atmosphere without frills. There are sinks in the rooms that share baths, tall ceilings, antiques, and lace curtains. A living room and a cozy sitting area at the stairway landing are inviting places to curl up in or to browse through the book collection.

Count on a hearty breakfast featuring ham and eggs, fresh juices, homemade muffins or breads, and homemade blackberry jam. For other meals, there is no need to get back in the car.

A walk one block to the waterfront of Old Town Florence will introduce you to a colorful pioneer fishing village with small restaurants and coffee shops. The village is an appealing blend of old and new, with a small fishing fleet, antique shops, and boutiques. Stop in the Siuslaw Pioneer Museum to see the logging and sailing artifacts from the glory days of the sailing schooners.

How to get there: From Highway 101, Florence is one and one-half blocks east. The inn is on the left.

olive Metcalf

Tu Tú Tun Lodge
Gold Beach, Oregon
97444

Innkeepers: Dirk and Laurie Van Zante
Address/Telephone: 96550 North Bank Rogue; (503) 247–6664.
Rooms: 16, all with private bath, including 2 suites each accommodating 6 people.
Rates: $79 to $97, double occupancy, EP. $6 each additional per-
son. Daily rate for two, including breakfast and dinner, $125.
Open: May 1 to November 1. Breakfast, lunch, dinner for guests, or
by reservation only. Full bar.
Facilities and Local Attractions: Swimming pool, four-hole putting
green; jet boat white-water Rogue River trips; salmon and
steelhead fishing, seasoned guides available. Scenic flights
over Siskiyou Mountains. Hiking, beachcombing, scenic
drives. Legalized gambling in Gold Beach.

In case you have the mistaken notion that the Northwest consists of only fir trees and lumberjacks, consider the
motto of Tu Tú Tun Lodge: "Casual elegance in the wilderness on the famous Rogue River."

That's summing it up modestly, for this is a very 🖝

special blend of sophistication and an outdoor-lover's paradise. Top-notch accommodations and superb food are those of a classy resort, but the young owners create a friendly atmosphere that's more like that of a country inn.

Guest rooms are situated in a two-story building adjacent to the lodge. Each has comfortable easy chairs, extra-long beds, a dressing area, and a bath with tub and shower. Special touches that make wilderness life civilized aren't forgotten—fresh flowers, good reading lamps, and up-to-date magazines. No telephone or TV intrudes as you watch the changing colors of the Rogue's waters at sunset from your private balcony or patio.

A bell at 6:30 P.M. calls guests to the lodge for cocktails and hors d'oeuvres. Dirk and Laurie introduce everyone, and by the time they seat you for dinner at round tables set for eight, you'll feel you're dining with friends. The ☞ single-menu dinner they serve is outstanding, and it always features regional specialties. Fresh Chinook salmon, a soup, crisp salad made from locally grown greens, freshly baked bread or rolls, and a raspberry sorbet is a typical dinner.

After dinner, guests usually gather around the two fireplaces on the terrace overlooking the river. There's much to talk about as you share ideas for the next day's plans. If those plans call for an early-morning rising for fishing, a river trip, or hiking, breakfast and lunch baskets are available.

One adventure almost every visitor to the lodge tries is the ☞ exciting 104-mile white-water round trip up (and down) the river. Jet boats stop at the lodge's dock to pick up passengers in the morning.

How to get there: Driving north on Highway 101, pass through Gold Beach, cross bridge, and watch for signs on right to Rogue River Tavern. Turn right and drive 4 miles to tavern; follow signs another 3 miles to lodge on the right.

J: *The name comes from the Tu Tú Tun Indians who lived in a village on the very site of the Lodge. "Tunne" meant "people"; "Tu Tú Tunne" were "people close to the river."*

olive Metcalf

Steamboat Inn
Steamboat, Oregon
97447

Innkeepers: Sharon and Jim Van Loan
Address/Telephone: Toketee Route (mailing address: P.O. Box 36, Idleyld Park); (503) 496–3495.
Rooms: 8 cabins, all with private bath.
Rates: $54, single or double, $14 each additional adult; EP. No smoking in restaurant.
Open: All year. Breakfast, lunch, dinner daily; special Fisherman's Dinner for guests or by reservation. Weekends only during winter season; wine and beer bar.
Facilities and Local Attractions: Steelhead fishing, swimming, nature trails. Drive to downhill and cross-country skiing. Near several vineyards.

After a twisting thirty-eight-mile drive along the North Umpqua River, in a downpour that never slowed, the welcome at Steamboat Inn was underwhelming. I was looking for a cup of coffee and good cheer. Instead, I entered a room pungent with gloom. Seated morosely around a twenty-foot-long pine table were a dozen fishermen, angling fanatics from all over the world who feel very proprietary about this extraordinary 👉 thirty-nine-mile stretch of white water reserved strictly for fly fishing.

They eyed the intruder sourly and went back to staring bleakly out the windows or stomping about the stone floor of the common room, waiting for the storm to slow down to merely a hard rain. Only destiny and the inn's gastronomical reputation had brought us together.

Pat Lee, who doubles as chef and angling guide, rescued me with coffee and a tour that was cheering. This may indeed be "the 👉 greatest stretch of summer steelhead water in the United States," as Jack Hemingway says, but it's also an idyllic spot for readers and loafers.

The rustic main room with a huge rock fireplace opens onto a glass-enclosed sun porch where meals are served. Beyond the flowers and trees are eight cabins sitting right on the river, connected by a long deck. You needn't be a fisherman to have a visceral reponse to the 👉 majestic setting of tall fir trees and white water tumbling past. The cabins are unexpectedly well appointed: paneled and carpeted, furnished comfortably, all with modern baths, good beds, and reading lights. And each room opens onto the deck.

All day, the kitchen serves hearty breakfasts, fast lunches, and early dinners to distracted anglers. But come evening, the restaurant closes, and the inn assumes a different identity. Out come linens, silver, candles, and it's 👉 haute cuisine on the North Umpqua: The Fisherman's Dinner.

In deference to fishermen who can't quit until dark, wine is poured and hors d'oeuvres are set out half an hour *after* sunset. Sharon Van Loan and Pat do the classy cooking that has won compliments from *Fly Fisherman* to *Gourmet* magazines. A typical entrée might be a pork loin in lemon-basil marinade, sauced with a tomato, thyme, and applejack combination; perfectly braised carrots with hints of mustard and mint; then, a watercress salad with hazelnuts, followed by freshly ground coffee and perhaps a Bavarian chocolate torte.

Do real fishermen deserve less?

How to get there: From Roseberg, take Highway 138 east for 👉 38 scenic miles along the Umpqua River. Inn is on the right.

Olive Metcalf

McCully House Inn
Jacksonville, Oregon
97530

Innkeeper: Fran Dennett
Address/Telephone: 240 East California Street (mailing address:
P.O. Box 387); (503) 899–1942.
Rooms: 4, each with private bath.
Rates: $55 to $65, double occupancy, according to season; $10
extra person. Mid-week rates available. Full gourmet breakfast
included. No smoking.
Open: All year; closed Christmas Day.
Facilities and Local Attractions: Explore historic town; thirty-min-
ute drive to Ashland theaters; nearby cross-country skiing.

Jacksonville is a wonderful discovery—the oldest town
in southern Oregon. It began in 1851 with the discovery of
gold in Rich Gulch, but it didn't become a ghost town when
the gold ran out; quartz mining was to follow.

Exploring an old mining town is always a history of
tragedies, and Jacksonville has survived its share. A smallpox
epidemic in 1868 killed many of the original settlers; a flood
in 1869 swept tons of mud and rock through the center of
town; and fires destroyed most of the town's original frame
buildings.

The McCully House is ☞ one of six original dwellings to survive. It was the town's most expensive and palatial residence when Doctor J. W. McCully built it in 1861. But the good doctor got himself deeply in debt and took off, leaving Mrs. McCully to cope with the family. She started a children's school at the house before public schools were established, and then turned it into a boarding house. The mansion is on the National Register of Historic Places and, after ten years of restoration, is now receiving guests as an inn.

The downstairs rooms are quite grand, with polished hardwood floors, Oriental rugs, and antiques, in particular, a ☞ square grand piano the doctor had shipped around the Horn. The living-room fireplace with comfortable furniture around it makes an inviting room for relaxing while Fran tells you about local restaurants and points of interest.

Each of the bedrooms has a special attraction—The McCully Room has the original massive bedroom furniture and a claw-footed tub; The Doll Suite has a king-sized bed (or it can be two singles) and an adjoining sitting room with a double hide-a-bed, making it convenient for families.

Fran is one of those innkeepers committed to fresh flowers, fresh coffee beans, freshly baked breads, and pretty table settings. You know what that means—wonderfully tasty and attractive breakfasts. She says she tries to serve things you don't ordinarily get for breakfast, like fresh figs and cantaloupe, or baked pears with raisins and almonds, mini-loaves of her own whole-wheat bread, and innovative egg casseroles.

How to get there: From Ashland, you enter Jacksonville on California Street. The inn is on the left at number 240. From Medford, you enter town on Fifth Street. Proceed to California; turn right. Inn is on the left.

olive Metcalf

The Boarding House
Seaside, Oregon
97138

Innkeepers: Dick and Carole Rees
Address/Telephone: 208 North Holladay Drive; (503) 738–9055.
Rooms: 6, all with private bath, color TV.
Rates: $42 to $46 for two, including breakfast. Deduct $5 for single;
    add $5 for each additional person. Children under 4 are free.
Open: All year.
Facilities and Local Attractions: Beach walks, clam digging, swim-
    ming; fishing on Necanicum River. Stroll to downtown shops,
    restaurants.

"This old house serves comfort" is the motto posted at
the door. The rustic, 1898 Victorian boarding house keeps
that promise, and at a refreshingly modest price. Built entirely of fir tongue-and-groove lumber, with beamed ceilings
and paneling throughout, the house has recently been completely restored. New comforts include private baths, color
TVs, and a private side entrance. Brass and white iron beds,
down quilts, antiques, and wicker add a country touch.

For relaxing, there is a delightful paneled parlor with an
antique organ and with lovely, soft, blue and rose fabric coverings on Victorian sofas, chairs, and a window seat. The

330

same colors are repeated in the rugs on polished wood floors.

Breakfast is served in a sunny, paneled dining room with beamed ceilings, a built-in buffet, touches of stained glass, and another big window seat. Tables are covered to the floor with blue and white cloths. You can also take your breakfast outside to a wrap-around porch.

Carole's weekday breakfast is a continental plus. There's always a cereal bar, including granola, fresh fruit, juice, and a hot roll, like a sticky bun. The weekend fare is more lavish, perhaps a baked egg and sausage casserole, or—a big favorite—a fancy French toast with cream cheese between slices, topped with a hot apricot sauce.

The town of Seaside is in the extreme northwest corner of Oregon in an area called the North Coast. This marks the end of the Lewis and Clark Trail and encompasses the oldest settlement in the West: Astoria.

One of the joys of being in a quaint seaside town is to forget the car and walk to all the attractions. From the Boarding House, you are four blocks from the ocean and two blocks from downtown. The nearly two-mile beach promenade is lined with charming old houses. You can rent horses, or dig for clams, or surf fish. The resort-atmosphere town has small shops and a variety of restaurants. Carole and Dick will point you in the direction of your interest.

How to get there: Exit Highway 101 at Seaside and follow signs to City Center; the street becomes Holladay Drive. Inn is on the right.

J: *In February, Seaside hosts the highly regarded Trail's End Marathon—one of the country's top road runs.*

olive Metcalf

Wolf Creek Tavern
Wolf Creek, Oregon
97497

Innkeepers: Joy and Sam Angelos
Address/Telephone: P.O. Box 97; (503) 866–2474.
Rooms: 8, all with private bath.
Rates: $22 single, $37 double; EP.
Open: All year. Breakfast, lunch, dinner, Sunday brunch; wine and
   beer bar.
Facilities and Local Attractions: Historic waystop; no town. Twenty
   miles to Grants Pass headquarters for Rogue River fishing and
   boating guides; U.S. Forest Service Office for maps, informa-
   tion about 40-mile Rogue hiking trail.

Looking for all the world just like a stagecoach stop
ought to look, the Wolf Creek Tavern looms up unexpectedly
among dense trees along Highway Five. The imposing two-
story white building was once 🖙 a way station for stages that
stopped on the six-day trip between Portland and Sacramento.

Wolf Creek Tavern's history is surrounded by legendary
romantic—and largely unauthenticated—events, but
records indicate that it was built around 1857. The State

Parks and Recreation Division acquired it in 1975, and it leases it to the Angeloses to operate as an inn.

Today the tavern is providing good food and beverage, comfortable beds, and old-fashioned hospitality for the traveling public, but with some modern conveniences, including heating, air conditioning, and a bath for every room. These are unpretentious rooms, clean, plain, and simple. Furnishings in the first floor rooms represent pieces from the early 1900s to the 1930s, but one of the rooms upstairs has been furnished as an 1870s chamber.

On the first floor, a central stair and hallway divide the ladies' parlor from the men's sitting room—the tap room. Original paint colors were researched and have been reproduced on walls, woodwork, and chimneys. The tavern and dining room have pine floors and rustic tables with red cloths. ☛ Waitresses dress in period costume with long black skirts, white blouses, and ruffled white caps.

At dinner, as I listened to the banter between the staff and familiar locals who had stopped in for the innkeeper's good cooking, I wondered where they had come from. Driving in a few hours earlier, it seemed as though this was practically a wilderness, and now the sounds of friendly travelers having a good time filled the tavern.

Entrée choices included fresh salmon, pepper steak, or pork loin, and a twice-baked potato involved in a winning combination of spinach, cream, and cheese. I planned ahead for the night's special dessert: fresh peach-and-apple crisp . . . à la mode. Good thinking. Homey old dishes like this made with fresh fruit from the garden are so soul-satisfying.

How to get there: Exit I–5 about 20 miles north of Grants Pass at signs to Wolf Creek. The inn sits right in front of you.

J: *This remote stop gives you a feeling for what it must have meant to earlier travelers to find good cheer and hospitality after hours of bouncing in a stagecoach.*

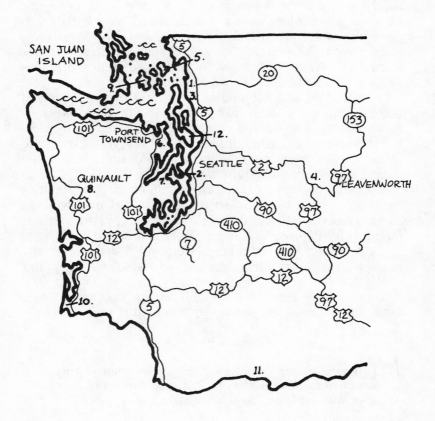

Washington

Numbers on map refer to towns numbered below.

Olive Metcalf

The Channel House
Anacortes, Washington
98221

Innkeepers: Kathy and Sam Salzinger
Address/Telephone: 2902 Oakes Avenue; (206) 293–9382.
Rooms: 4, sharing 2 large bathrooms.
Rates: $43 to $55, breakfast included. Cannot accommodate children or pets; no smoking, no credit cards.
Open: All year.
Facilities and Local Attractions: Hot tub. Minutes from ferry docks leading to San Juan Islands, British Columbia. Explore Deception Pass, Washington Park, Mt. Erie.

   A bedroom off the library was mine when I stayed in this 1902 Victorian. It's a pretty room with a white iron bed, a hilarious "one of a kind" gilded floor lamp, and other antique appointments. But what won my heart was the view from a wicker rocker in front of a ☞ window looking out at the Guemes Channel and the San Juan Islands. Kathy Salzinger sweetened the scene with a tray of tea and cookies while I rocked away in absolute contentment.
   The library itself is a fine place to spend time—a good stereo, comfortable furniture, and interesting books and magazines. Making yourself at home for an evening among

another person's books is almost as personal as moving into his or her bedroom. In the case of the Salzingers, I could see that they love theater (I learned that they met in a little-theater group), travel, the northwest, and good living. My kind of people.

Kathy's decorating is fun—not an all-Victorian theme or mood, but rather a collection of interesting pieces: an elegant antique here, a romantic chaise there, enlivened with a zany item like the purple and green satin turtle lurking by the stereo.

Two bedrooms upstairs have the best view in the house—from the claw-footed tub in the common bathroom. An elegant dining room with French doors going out to the garden is downstairs from the living room. Breakfast here consists of especially fine coffee (made from a blend of fresh beans), fresh fruit, boiled eggs, and homemade muffins with several spreads.

"Doing" the islands is one of the main reasons one comes to Anacortes, but trying to figure out the least expensive route while stopping at all the towns you want to see can loom as a complex undertaking. My ferry schedule was marked beyond the point of making any sense when Sam came to my rescue. He showed me how to plan my travels, and Kathy volunteered "breakfast whenever you want it," depending on what ferry I wanted to catch. This is the kind of ☛ treatment that gives innkeeping a good name.

How to get there: From Seattle, take I-5 north to junction with State 20 past Mt. Vernon. Follow 20 west to Anacortes. Remain on 20 through town. The name changes to Commercial, then Oakes. Inn is on the right. Fly-in: Anacortes airport.

J: *Sam's ☛ suggestion for touring the islands makes sense: Buy cheap walk-on tickets for the ferry, returning at night to Channel House as home base. The savings when you don't take a car are significant, and you can always rent bikes or mopeds for exploring during the day.*

Olive Metcalf

The Bombay House
Bainbridge Island, Washington
98110

Innkeepers: Bob Scott and Georgene Hagen
Address/Telephone: 8490 N.E. Beck Road; (206) 842–3926.
Rooms: 5, 2 on first floor sharing a bath, 3 on second floor sharing
   bath. Air conditioning.
Rates: $45 to $68, continental breakfast included. Children week-
   days only; no pets. American Express or checks preferred.
Open: All year.
Facilities and Local Attractions: An island to bicycle. Visit Fort
   Worden State Park, Eagle Harbor Waterfront Park, Indian
   battlegrounds. Picnic areas, tennis courts, golf nearby. Shop-
   ping, restaurants in Winslow.

   At Bombay House, you can sit at the breakfast table enjoying muffins and croissants and ☞ watch the big white
ferries gliding through Rich Passage. All the ships bound for
the Bremerton Navy Yards go through, too. In the daytime, it
is endlessly fascinating; at night, the lighted ferries look like
ocean liners in the dark waters.
   "Unlikely" is the way the big house strikes me. Part Victorian, part nautical, and part just independent builder, it sits
on a slight hill surveying a marine view. Unexpected sights

are inside, too: a full-sized rabbit named James Brown snoozing on the hearth, for instance. But Bob and Georgene's being there together is unlikely also. They were friends in high school thirty-five years ago but married other people, raised families, and never saw each other again—until recently, that is, when Georgene was sitting in the Bombay Airport and Bob appeared out of nowhere with a cup of coffee and asked, "What took you so long?"

They're having a great time as innkeepers. (They also own the *Krestine,* a floating B&B anchored a few minutes away.) At Bombay House, they've filled the big rooms with unusual art objects from Peru and fine antiques from frequent buying trips in Maine—an eighteenth-century loom, massive armoires, tables, and chests, mostly in pine. So many pieces have been sold to enthusiastic guests that Georgene plans another buying trip soon.

The five bedrooms are all roomy, but a master room upstairs with a sitting area is extra large. A wooden cradle is filled with books (books are all over the house), and there is a beauty of an iron stove. The best view is from a small yellow bedroom, but you have to be in bed to see it.

How to get there: From Seattle, take Winslow Ferry to Bainbridge. Proceed straight ahead to second traffic light (High School Road), and turn left. Continue until road ends; turn right. Continue past Lynwood Center to Beck Road, first road on left. Turn left to the inn at the end of road. From the north, come down Highway 305 over Hood Canal Bridge to second traffic light (High School Road), and turn right; proceed as above.

☀

J: *The thirty-minute ferry ride from Seattle Harbor to Bainbridge Island rates a ten: a glorious panorama of that city's skyline and the romantic fun of heading for an island!*

Olive Metcalf

Krestine, *Bed & Breakfast on a Boat*
Bainbridge Island, Washington
98110

Innkeepers: Jim Hagen and Susan Burch
Address/Telephone: Eagle Harbor (mailing address: Box 11338);
     (206) 842–5100 or (206) 842–3926 (Bombay House).
Rooms: 2 cabins, 1 stateroom, 1 head.
Rates: $45, cabins; $55, stateroom, all with breakfast included. No
     children.
Open: All year.
Facilities and Local Attractions: Ferry terminal to Seattle. Marina
     adjacent to shopping area, restaurants. Picnics, tennis, and golf
     in Winslow city parks.

Among the sleek, modern boats docked in the colorful
Eagle Harbor Marina on Bainbridge Island is a unique sail-
ing vessel—a ☛ floating inn. The *Krestine* is a 100-foot Bal-
tic trading ketch more than eighty years old. She was built in
Germany as a cargo-hauling sailboat in 1904, but until Bob
Scott and Georgene Hagen bought her (they also own the
Bombay House), she had been home to another couple for
seventeen years.

What makes the *Krestine* especially adaptable as an inn is her unusual width—her beam is over 20 feet wide. This allows space for a 🖝 comfortable saloon, as roomy as many a traditional inn's common room.

And what an inviting place it is. Huge oak beams are overhead; the main one is 23 feet long and 3 feet high. There's a thick oak table that comfortably seats eight, a wood stove, bookshelves, chart table, and plenty of room. Openings overhead, through which cargo was once lowered, are now skylights.

Although breakfast is the only meal served on board, the galley would not restrict any cook's ambitions. It has a four-burner propane stove, oven, deep, stainless-steel sinks, and lots of cupboards. Jim Hagen (Georgene's son) or Susan serves juice and fresh fruit, freshly baked muffins and croissants, cereal, coffee, and tea.

Don't bring your matched luggage set—remember, this is a *boat*. The two cabins are compact and have no extra space, but there are all kinds of nooks and crannies in which to stow things away. The stateroom is the larger of the two and even has a small sitting area. The beds are comfortable, have attractive navy-blue cotton-covered comforters, and are equipped with reading lights.

The colorful marina provides great people-watching opportunities. You can walk into Winslow for shopping and restaurant dining, but the best ticket is for sunning on the broad deck and watching the urban sailors.

How to get there: Depart Seattle Ferry at Winslow; go straight ahead to Winslow Way, and turn left. Proceed to Madison, and turn right; go to Wyatt Way, and turn left. Follow to fork in road; bear left on Eagle Harbor Drive to Ward Street. Follow to marina. Boat is at D-Dock.

🍺

J: *The vagaries of insurance prevent Jim from setting sail with guests on the* Krestine. *But you can sit on deck with a glass of wine and wait for a ferry to go by. The gentle rocking it stirs may provide all the at-sea feeling many of us want.*

olive Metcalf

La Conner Country Inn
La Conner, Washington
98257

Innkeepers: Rick and Reinhild Thompson
Address/Telephone: Old Town; (206) 466–3101.
Rooms: 28, all with private bath, fireplace, TV.
Rates: $49 single to $69 double, including continental breakfast. ☛
    Children 12 and under share room with parents at no charge.
Open: All year. Lunch, dinner, Sunday brunch, full bar.
Facilities and Local Attractions: Conference facilities. Walk, ex-
    plore La Conner Historic District, galleries, shops, restaurants,
    waterfront; biking, boating, fishing; Swinomish Indian Village.

La Conner just has to face the music—it's too ☛ picturesque to escape its destiny of becoming the perfect getaway
weekend place, and only an hour and a half from Seattle. One
citizen, unhappy with his town's increasing popularity, sug-
gested in the local paper that signs on I-5 be swapped with
those of another town. I could have told him that that is an
old ploy that merely adds a maverick appeal to the town. Bo-
linas, California, has become famous, not for swapping, but
removing signs to that town.

342

One main street of unique shops, restaurants, and commercial buildings dating from the late 1800s runs along the Swinomish Channel. This protected waterway is lively with commercial and pleasure crafts, and tugboats with rafts of chained-together logs in tow. The bustle of lumbering and fishing and the ☛ pastoral beauty of the surrounding countryside are both part of daily life here. Artists Mark Tobey and Morris Graves, among others, have been attracted to this little fishing community in the fertile Skagit Valley, with nearby mountains visible on the horizon.

The La Conner Inn is the only game in town for lodging, and happily, it can only enhance your stay. It is a new inn with attractive, weathered cedar-wood rooms and fireplaces. Some antique appointments like brass beds are used, but modern comfort is the tone, with private baths, and with TVs hidden in pine armoires. A large common room called the library is where continental breakfast is served—juice, coffee, tea, and hot chocolate, and large cinnamon rolls.

The restaurant adjacent to the inn is good news. Its specialty is local seafood, of course. But it also takes advantage of the ☛ fresh local fruits and vegetables—and prepares them beautifully. Try the tortellini primavera, and the fresh raspberry tart. Another dessert specialty that guests come back for is called Queen Mother's Cake. It's a dense chocolate cake made with pulverized almonds instead of flour.

How to get there: Driving north from Seattle, leave I-5 at Conway; follow signs west to La Conner. From Whidbey Island, go east on Highway 20 to signs for La Conner.

J: *Check out a shop across the street called Chez La Zoom. It has some extraordinary handmade clothing.*

Olive Metcalf

Haus Rohrbach Pension
Leavenworth, Washington
98826

Innkeepers: Kathryn and Bob Harrild
Address/Telephone: 12882 Ranger Road; (509) 548–7024.
Rooms: 12, 3 with private bath; 9 others share 3 baths. Air conditioning. Separate Chalet has kitchen, bath; sleeps 6.
Rates: $45 for single to $88 for Chalet; $10 each additional person; rates include full breakfast. No smoking; children welcome.
Open: All year.
Facilities and Local Attractions: Heated pool, hot tub, sledding, snowshoeing in front meadow. Explore Bavarian-style village of Leavenworth; spring Mai Fest, white-water rafting, winter skiing, tobogganing, year-round fishing, hiking.

Forget about the high price of getting to Europe and take yourself to the country byways of central Washington's Eastern Cascade Mountains. In the Swiss-looking Tumwater Valley, you'll discover an entire town that has adopted the image of a ☞ Bavarian village. Believe it or not, it works.

Similar gimmicks imposed on a town by the local merchants can sometimes have grotesque results, but in this instance, the natural setting is so perfect that the effect is quite pleasing. There are several streets of Alpine-decorated shops and restaurants, with hanging baskets of brilliant flowers in every doorway.

Haus Rohrbach is a country inn nestled among the foothills overlooking the entire valley. The three-story chalet has wide balconies adjoining almost every room, overflowing flower boxes, and views of meadow and mountains, cows, geese, and gardens.

A comfortably furnished common room and an adjoining deck overlooking the valley are where guests gather. After a day of outdoor fun, it's inviting to relax around the fire for conversation.

The Harrilds are always improving their deservedly popular inn. A few years ago, they added the pool and hot tub; most recently, Bob has redone several of the bedrooms and baths. The feeling is rustic, or at least as rustic as you can feel with down comforters, good reading lights, and modern baths. These are appealing rooms with redwood details and colorful cotton fabrics. Families will appreciate the several rooms with daybeds and trundles.

Kathryn serves breakfast on the balcony in good weather—sourdough pancakes, cinnamon rolls, and other delights she bakes while you watch. She'll pack you a picnic, too, for a day of exploring the beautiful countryside.

How to get there: Going east on Highway 2 after Stevens Pass, turn left on Ski Hill Drive at entrance to Leavenworth. Go 1 mile; turn left on Ranger Rd. You'll see the inn on the hillside.

J: *If you can look at valley and mountains from the balcony here without attempting to sing an exuberant chorus of "The hills are alive with the sound of music . . . ," you've more restraint than I. The cows didn't seem to mind.*

olive Metcalf

Mountain Home Lodge
Leavenworth, Washington
98826

Innkeepers: Greg Parrish, Chris Clark, Charlie Brooks
Address/Telephone: Mountain Home Road (mailing address: Box
    687); (509) 548–7077.
Rooms: 8, all with private bath.
Rates: $58 to $78 per couple, summer rates, meals not included;
    $118 to $138 per couple, winter, all meals, complimentary
    wine included. No children under 13.
Open: All year. Breakfast, lunch, dinner.
Facilities and Local Attractions: Pool, hot tub, hiking trails; winter
    snowmobiling, sledding, cross-country ski trails; nearby fish-
    ing, golf, horseback riding.

Mountain Home Lodge was an unexpected discovery
while traveling through central Washington—and one of the
most memorable. This outstanding full-service country inn
in the Wanatchee Valley (apple country) combines the luxury facilities of a resort with the intimate atmosphere of an
inn.

Although it's only three miles above Leavenworth, getting there is an adventure. As the innkeeper warns you over
the phone, it is on a "primitive gravel road" that winds up the

346

mountain. When you emerge into the meadow surrounding the inn, you'll feel intrepidly off the beaten track. During winter, the inn's heated snowcat picks you up at the bottom of the road.

The contemporary cedar and redwood house with a broad deck surveys a ☛ spectacular Cascade Mountain setting. The greeting is a warm one. These innkeepers spare nothing in seeing that you feel at home and have any service that you require. One of them—usually Greg—is always there.

The common-room décor suits the spacious mountain feeling, like the massive ☛ Attila the Hun–style sofas in sheepskin and burled redwood. Not the thing for your condo, but they look terrific flanking the stone fireplace. Carpeted bedrooms have fine tiled bathrooms (with an abundance of thick towels), colorful bed linens, and good reading lights.

The outdoor pool and hot tub (with fabulous views) are always available. There is a 1700-foot toboggan run and ☛ miles of cross-country ski trails, right from the back door. Since this is not a designated ski area, you can enjoy the quiet beauty in rare solitude.

In the late afternoon, I sat on the deck with other guests, sipping wine and watching the sun set over the Cascades. Hunger finally brought us inside to an Italian feast beginning with melon and finger-size pizza for hors d'oeuvres, then on to homemade ravioli *and* lasagna. We sat in one end of the living room looking out at the panorama of sunset and mountains. Soft music played, and deer grazed in the meadow below. The only flaw was the thought of having to leave.

How to get there: From Highway 2 just east of Leavenworth, turn south on Duncan Road (by the Duncan Orchard); it becomes Mountain Home Road. Follow to the inn.

J: Greg walked *from Michigan to the West Coast to make his dream of living in the mountains come true.*

Olive Metcalf

Kangaroo House
Orcas Island, Washington
98245

Innkeepers: Polly and Ken Nisbet
Address/Telephone: North Beach Road (mailing address: Box 334),
    Eastsound; (206) 376–2175.
Rooms: 5, with 2 large shared baths, sinks in some rooms.
Rates: $40 to $50 per couple, including full breakfast. No children
    under 6; no pets; no smoking. Checks preferred.
Open: Closes several weeks in winter; telephone or write for dates.
Facilities and Local Attractions: Walk to beach, Eastsound Village
    for restaurants, shops, historical museum, crafts. Fishing char-
    ter facilities at West Sound, Deer Harbor.

Most proud innkeepers would surrender their dust ruffles rather than show you their inn before the beds are made.
Ken Nisbet regretted my arrival while the morning chores
were in progress, but his friendly welcome was a tip-off to the
atmosphere here— ☞ easy hospitality in irresistible surroundings.

This is a stately, ☞ handsome inn to bear such an odd
name, but considering the origin of the story, there was simply no other choice. It seems the 1907 home on eighty-two
acres was purchased in the '30s by one "Cap" Ferris, an em-

ployee of Matson Steamship Lines. On a voyage to the south Australian coast, he bought a ☞ young kangaroo and named her Josie. The music Cap played aboard ship seemed to tame her, so he brought her home to Orcas Island where she lived with his family for more than thirty years. Old-time islanders still remember how she would bound around the front yard when she heard music coming from the house, how her behavior seemed to predict the weather, and how she loved oatmeal and Mrs. Ferris's geraniums. Josie's home became, irrevocably, Kangaroo House.

But the important thing for Orcas Island visitors to know is that Kangaroo House is a premier inn. The Nisbets have ☞ furnished it with great taste and warmth. The five bedrooms are appointed with fine linens in appealing, restful colors. Common rooms on the first floor have polished wood floors, colorful rugs, and antiques. A huge rock fireplace and comfortable furniture appeal to the nestling urge.

The dining room opens onto a large deck with views of meadows and trees. A full breakfast is served here on beautifully set antique tables: freshly ground coffee, freshly squeezed orange juice, and fresh fruit—the ripe island berries in September were ambrosial. A changing daily special follows, such as baked eggs with herbs, or waffles and smoked ham.

How to get there: From Anacortes, take ferry to Orcas Island landing. Continue on main road following signs to Eastsound. Near the end of the short main street, turn left on North Beach Road. Follow to inn on left.

J: *While you're on Orcas, don't miss one of the northwest's most famous views, from the summit of Mt. Constitution. It's dazzling.*

olive Metcalf

Outlook Inn
Orcas Island, Washington
98245

Innkeeper: John Biethan
Address/Telephone: P. O. Box 210, Eastsound; (206) 376–2581.
Rooms: 29, 11 with private bath, 18 with sink in room, share showers, bathrooms. Some TVs.
Rates: $30 single to $57, double occupancy. No meals included. No pets.
Open: All year. Breakfast, lunch, dinner; wine and beer bar.
Facilities and Local Attractions: Hiking, biking; fishing charters arranged. Small beach across street. Walk to shops, Eastsound Museum.

A glassed-in dining room facing the sound runs across the front of the Outlook Inn. Over hot oatmeal one September morning, I was looking at the mist still hanging over the water and the fir trees beyond, when suddenly a salmon leaped up out of the sound, arched, and returned to the water.

That kind of heart-stopping moment is more than sufficient reason for going to poky, old island towns like Eastsound. There's also a log cabin museum of Orcas Island's history, some shops with handcrafts, a few restaurants, and miles of beach to walk and explore.

The gray-shingled inn built in the 1800s is one of the oldest buildings on the island. You'll find simple, comfortable rooms at reasonable prices that ramble upstairs and down in the original building. They're small but clean and cheerful. A new wing has larger rooms with bay windows and fine views of the sound from upstairs.

Downstairs is a wine bar (the painting of the white cat from the movie *Five Easy Pieces* hangs over it) and a pleasant dining room serving three meals a day. There's no pretense of chic cuisine, but it is good, hearty fare. If you like fresh fish, you're in luck—it's the specialty. The salmon was beautiful during my visit. Homemade soups and the ☞ dark, grainy bread made daily are particularly good.

The Outlook celebrates Christmas in a big way, and the staff spends weeks decorating with a theme, like flowers or teddy bears. Most of the tourists on the island are gone, and old friends, and often performers from Seattle, gather to celebrate the season and entertain one another.

The Outlook is operated by members of a philosophic service group, the Louis Foundation, named for a Western mystic, Louis Gittner, who is usually there. His message seems to be the importance of devotion to others as well as ourselves, and "if you can't share it . . . throw it away, it isn't worth keeping." Nothing terribly threatening there. At any rate, the organization never intrudes itself on guests.

How to get there: From Anacortes, take ferry to Orcas Island. From the landing, continue on main road 8 miles, following signs to Eastsound. Inn is on your left as you enter town.

☼

J: *Eastsound is a wonderful* ☞ *biking town—not too hilly, not much traffic, only an occasional pickup truck to dodge on the main street.*

olive Metcalf

Arcadia Country Inn
Port Townsend, Washington
98368

Innkeeper: James Shrout
Address/Telephone: 1891 South Jacob Miller Road; (206) 385–5245.
Rooms: 8, all with private bath.
Rates: $39.50 winter; $49.50 summer; continental breakfast included.
Open: All year.
Facilities and Local Attractions: Hot tub. On 🖝 route of Port Townsend Marathon and bicycle-racing teams; pasture is site of Jefferson County Air Show ultralight airplane races. Tour town's Victorian homes, antique shops, Fort Worden State Park. Close to clam digging, scuba diving, sailing on Straits of Juan De Fuca and Puget Sound.

What a shame people don't survive a wild youth looking as good as the Arcadia Inn does. Nestled in a pastoral setting of seventy acres of thick forest and meadows, the 1908 red brick house reveals nothing of its rowdy past. Quite the contrary. You have to smile at its wholesome appeal as you wind down the driveway and catch sight of the bright flower beds,

352

the big swing on the front porch, and the flagpole waving Old Glory.

During Prohibition, the city fathers, having vowed to rid the city of prostitution, decided that since Arcadia was already the local "speakeasy," why not make it the centralized location for vice. They made Arcadia an offer it couldn't refuse: In exchange for the public-service gesture of providing a home for the working girls, the city agreed to provide them a two-mile-long private water line from the city water system. What could be neater? The town was made pure, and the inn had all the water it needed.

An occasional federal raid kept business from being completely peaceful, and "The Untouchables" eventually destroyed the still in the biggest law enforcement raid ever held on the Olympic Peninsula. So much for creative politics.

Since its renovation by James Shrout, the big house in its ☞ idyllic country setting is the essence of gentility and comfort. One bedroom is on the first floor, and a stairway leads upstairs to the others. They're spacious, antique-filled rooms with views from all of them—rolling meadows, forests, and the Olympic Mountains.

A large lobby room has a beamed ceiling, a burled-wood grand piano, and a fireplace. Adjoining it is a dining room with round tables and an oak bar where the continental breakfast (croissants, sweet rolls, fresh fruit, coffee, and teas) is set out. In the afternoon Jim serves complimentary wine. You are only three miles from Port Townsend's restaurants.

How to get there: From downtown Port Townsend, follow the main street (Highway 20) south out of town to South Jacob Miller Road, 100 feet north of Johnson's Rentals. Turn right; continue to inn on the right.

☐

J: *This is a place to watch a dying skill—some of the last wooden boat building in the country.*

Olive Metcalf

The Hastings House Inn
Port Townsend, Washington
98368

Innkeepers: Grace and Bruce Pierson
Address/Telephone: 313 Walker Street; (206) 385–3553.
Rooms: 7, including tower suite with private bath; 2 rooms share
  bath on second floor; 4 rooms on third floor have half-bath,
  share shower.
Rates: $45 to $75, including full breakfast; reduced rate from November to February. No pets; no smoking.
Open: All year.
Facilities and Local Attractions: TV available. Walk to town, ferry,
  marina, restaurants. Tennis courts across street; tour Victorian
  homes of Port Townsend.

In a town of fine Victorians, this one is a premier survivor. Like all the really big houses in Port Townsend, it sits on
a bluff high above the town with 🖝 commanding views of
water and mountains. Frank Hastings, the son of the town's
founder, built it in 1889. The Piersons believe that this was
the first house in Port Townsend to have electricity.

Grace Pierson proudly showed me some of the mansion's outstanding features. There's a front parlor with its
original chandelier, formed in the shape of big, green

bunches of grapes, and a fireplace framed with Italian tile that was ordered in a kit. It must have been one of the first. Off the middle parlor (the old-time family room) is a tiny sewing room where the lady of the house could look out at the harbor and watch her children at play in the yard.

☛ Newel posts on the stairway are quite remarkable: an iron nymph on the main floor, and upstairs a Tiffany design. Even the hinges on some of the doors are intricate pieces of art.

Every bedroom is decorated with fresh, light fabrics and colors that contrast with the Piersons' antique furniture collection. Unless you make reservations well ahead, you'll miss the ☛ Ivory Tower, but do take a look, at least. There's a padded, circular window seat in the tower, and, of course, the view of the harbor is splendid.

Guests gather in the ornate dining room for breakfast, family style. Grace serves juice and fresh fruit, cereal, and her own special dishes liked baked egg casseroles and bread pudding. For other meals, Port Townsend has an abundance of interesting restaurants that the Piersons will tell you about.

How to get there: Driving into Port Townsend on Highway 20, take Washington Street exit off to the left, just past signs for Worden State Park. Inn is at top of hill on the left corner.

olive Metcalf

James House
Port Townsend, Washington
98368

Innkeepers: Deborah and Rod LaMontagne
Address/Telephone: 1238 Washington Street; (206) 385–1238.
Rooms: 12, 4 with private bath, 8 sharing 4 bathrooms.
Rates: $38 single, to $80 for Garden Suite sleeping four. Continental breakfast included. No pets; no children under twelve.
Open: All year.
Facilities and Local Attractions: Walk to downtown Port Townsend shopping, restaurants; tour Victorian homes. Convenient base for touring Olympic Peninsula.

Francis Wilcox James was a man who evidently believed in thinking big. During the 1890s, when a fine, large house could easily be built for $4,000, he spent $10,000 building James House for his retirement. The parquet floors are made of oak, walnut, and cherry woods. The newel posts, spindles, and banisters are fashioned from native wild cherry from Virginia. James had the logs brought around Cape Horn, and the carving was done in the house.

Well, why not? He was probably the richest man in Port Townsend. In an 1890 *City Directory*, he lists himself simply as "Capitalist." What a solid, reliable ring it has. Why didn't I major in that at college?

His splendid Queen Anne extravaganza sits on a bluff above the town's waterfront and business district. It's now on the National Register of Historic Places and is one of the town's premier inns—the first bed and breakfast in the northwest.

The twelve spacious guest rooms are furnished with massive antique furniture—the kinds of pieces that look right only in huge, high-ceilinged rooms like these.

☞ The Bridal Suite is the most luxurious of the accommodations. It has parquet flooring, a small, elaborate, mirrored fireplace, a balcony, and an anteroom with a long, cranberry-red fainting couch. The enormous antique bed is perfectly at home here. A Victorian rocker and armchair sit in a four-window bay looking out at Port Townsend's waterfront and the mountains, snow-capped most of the year.

On the main floor are two elegant parlors with fireplaces and a formal dining room. A continental breakfast, featuring Deborah's ☞ homemade scones and muffins, is served here.

How to get there: Three ferries serve the area: from Mukilteo to Clinton; from Seattle to Winslow; from Edmonds to Kingston. The latter two both lead to Hood Canal Bridge. Proceed to junction with Highway 20; follow to Port Townsend. As you enter town, take Washington Street off to the left, past signs to Worden State Park. Inn is at top of the hill on the left.

☒

J: *Summer visitors to the peninsula are often frustrated by the complexities of the ferries and the long lines to get on them. Summer travelers are well advised to take the ferry routes that allow* advance *reservations rather than just line up. Washington State Ferry information (within Washington only): 1–800–542–6400 (outside Washington, 206–464–6400).*

olive Metcalf

Manresa Castle
Port Townsend, Washington
98368

Innkeepers: Ron and Carol Smith, Steve Smith.
Address/Telephone: Seventh and Sheridan (mailing address: Box 564); (206) 385–5750.
Rooms: 36, 27 with private bath; TV, telephones.
Rates: $36 single, to $65 double occupancy; no meals included. Small pets permitted; children welcome.
Open: All year. Restaurants; full bar.
Facilities and Local Attractions: Walk a neighborhood of Victorian houses, fine views of sound. Close to downtown restaurants and shops.

If you visit Port Townsend, you are sure to see the big white castle on a hill above the waterfront. It was the dream castle one man built for his bride and lost when his fortunes declined. It languished as a religious school, then declined to the ignoble status of "white elephant." That is a capsule history of Manresa Castle, up to the point of its rescue in 1973 by the Smiths.

They saw possibilities in the landmark mansion for an inn and set about restoring some of its earlier flamboyance. They have filled rooms and hallways with antiques, overstuffed furniture, swagged curtains, carved sideboards, and scrolly headboards and chests. Some bedrooms have settees and wicker desks, and lace comforters and pillow shams. Period pieces sitting on a modern mixed-color carpet testify to the fact that the renovation is an in-progress project.

"We restored the Castle because it was fun, and we are still doing it," say the Smiths. Most of the blending of old and new is aimed at comfort. There are still turrets, but inside there are also modern baths, TVs, and telephones.

The Castle has two restaurants, one on each end of the hallway from the main lobby. The Heritage Room is a Victorian dining room featuring moderately priced family meals in an atmosphere of old oak tables and high-backed chairs. Country-style dinners feature pasta and seafood. The special breakfast (at a discounted price for house guests) includes two eggs, two blueberry hot cakes, two link sausages, and two crispy bacon slices.

The more sophisticated Le Restaurant Manresa has a full bar. The mood here is of an Old English dining room. It appropriately serves prime rib and steaks, along with fresh local seafood.

Whether you can stay at the Castle or not, the Smiths hope you will come to see it and enjoy the most commanding views in Port Townsend. You can see not only the entire town and Puget Sound, but also both the Olympic and Cascade mountain ranges.

How to get there: Take either Highway 101 or Highway 104 to Route 20, which leads to Port Townsend. As you enter town, turn north on Sheridan to Seventh Street, one block north of Route 20.

❧

J: *Ask for a room on the sound side.*

Olive Metcalf

Palace Hotel
Port Townsend, Washington
98368

Innkeepers: Liz and Bill Svensson
Address / Telephone. 1004 Water Street; (206) 385–0773.
Rooms. 11, 8 with private bath; 3 with sink in room share large
   bathroom, separate shower. Four suites with kitchenettes accommodate 4 people. TV.
Rates $25 single, to $58 double occupancy. EP. Coffee, tea in
   rooms.
Open: All year.
Facilities and Local Attractions: Explore Victorian seaport town,
   restored mansions, historical museum; walk to restaurants, art
   galleries, shops; Fort Worden State Park, picnics, fishing, boat
   launch.

Lodging at the 1889 Palace puts you in the ☞ center of
Port Townsend's thriving historical district. You can park the
car in the off-street area and walk along the waterfront to the
restaurants and shops of Water Street.

The Svenssons—Bill is an architect, Liz an artist—have
restored the building, which is now on the National Historic
Register. Liz runs a shop with crafts and paintings on the
street floor. The tall ceilings, broad stairway, antique furni-

ture, and general spaciousness all reflect the Victorian era, but Bill and Liz have added comforts that travelers welcome. Chairs and a table for working or snacking, coffee and tea makings, and a TV are in every room. Some of them have excellent views of the Bay and the activity on Water Street.

My favorite is Marie's Suite, a large corner room with a fireplace and Victorian sofa. Marie, a famous Port Townsend madam, held court here until 1936. Her color scheme, red plush and green woodwork (and I always thought bordello red was a cliché), can still be appreciated in a wall display featuring a sample of each that some true historian saved.

The most choice item of décor is a large portrait over the fireplace of a smiling lady of "mature years," head poised at an impudent angle, wearing a flamboyant plumed hat. I assumed that it was the infamous Marie, but a brass plate beneath says, "Port Townsend's Marie—but not the original."

My admiration for small-town humor took a giant leap when I learned that it is a portrait of the mayor's mother! During the popular Port Townsend Victorian house tours, when thousands of visitors come to town, she dresses in costume, complete with feather boa and flask, and reclines on the bed greeting startled visitors to the room.

How to get there: From Seattle, drive north to Edmonds; take Kingston Ferry, and follow signs to Hood Canal Bridge. Continue on Highway 104 to Highway 20. Follow Highway 20 north to center of town where it becomes Water Street. Hotel is on the left.

J: *During Prohibition, the hotel was known as the "Palace of Sweets," until the sheriff, who obviously lacked an appreciation for metaphor, intervened.*

Olive Metcalf

Quimper Inn
Port Townsend, Washington
98368

Innkeepers: Mariii and Paul
Address/Telephone: 1306 Franklin; (206) 385–1086.
Rooms: 6, 2 with private bath.
Rates: $47 to $65, including continental breakfast. No smoking; no
　　credit cards; children by arrangement.
Open: All year.
Facilities and Local Attractions: Walk Port Townsend; tour Victo-
　　rian houses. Bike; explore beaches.

Don't worry about driving by Quimper Inn and missing
it; that is not likely to happen. It is a three-storied Georgian
Victorian with a wide front porch and a veranda on the second level—and the whole thing is painted three shades of
green with tomato-red trim around the windows! The innkeepers describe the house as embellished "in an artist's pal-
ette of panache *cum esprit.*" But that is merely an
introduction to the colorful scene inside.

Is the most apt word *mélange,* or *potpourri,* or *conglomeration,* or *pastiche?* All will do to describe the magpie as-
semblage of imaginative, whimsical things that fill the
interesting house. Mariii is an energetic artist, with creativity

running from her fingertips. Her special interest is creating stuffed objects. She has them arranged in wall collections, on beds and chairs, tucked into drawers, piled in baskets—even in an antique bed pan.

It is her good fortune that she has a large house and six big guest rooms to hold it all. The rooms are furnished comfortably with brass beds, cozy comforters, and country antiques like old school desks, and each room boasts a fine view.

But it is the ☞ witty collections of *things* that you will remember after you leave. Do you know of another inn with a display of *bathrobes* in the upstairs hall? This collection runs from a lovely Oriental kimono to the quintessential pink chenille robe. And outside of a museum, you're not likely to see more antique hats, fans, gloves, umbrellas, dolls, roller skates, circus posters, and decoys than are here.

The common room on the main floor has green plants and comfortable sitting places among the objects. Guests are invited to enjoy a ☞ fine library of art books here.

A stuffed chanticleer on the large breakfast table greets you for Mariii's *"petit déjeuner"* every morning. Freshly ground coffee and baskets of boulangerie delights are served. Some are quite unusual, like whole-wheat croissants, stuffed with pears and walnuts. For other meals, Port Townsend has a good choice of restaurants, many within walking distance.

How to get there: Take either Highway 101 or Highway 104 to Route 20, which leads to Port Townsend. Franklin Street is three blocks north of Water Street, the main street along the water front.

J: *If someone gives you a hard time about collecting things, take them here. They'll leave realizing what an amateur you are.*

olive Metcalf

Manor Farm Inn
Poulsbo, Washington
98370

Innkeepers: Jill and Robin Hughes
Address/Telephone: 26069 Big Valley Road N.E.; (206) 779–4628.
Rooms: 6, all with private bath.
Rates: $55 to $85 (subject to change), including full breakfast, afternoon aperitifs. Not convenient for children or pets; no smoking.
Open: All year. Dinner by reservation.
Facilities and Local Attractions: Hot tub, fishing pond; walking the countryside.

Track down Poulsbo, Washington, on a map and you might well wonder, "Why would I ever go to the interior of the Kitsap Peninsula?" Don't say I didn't alert you. Here is merely everything a country inn ought to be: a ☛ tranquil, pastoral atmosphere, completely insulated with fine décor and superior food and drink.

Jill and Robin Hughes are the young couple who have shaped a clapboard turn-of-the-century farmhouse into a French-style country inn. Robin is English and has skills as an architect, horticulturist, environmentalist, farmer, veterinarian, and gourmet chef. He and Jill exude enthusiasm for their 🖝 individual outlook on innkeeping—a "hands-on environment" where people can touch and experience country life while enjoying all the civilized comforts. Dairy cows and sheep graze in the soft rolling countryside; there is Jacques the yak, exotic fowl, and even a pond stocked with clever trout to test your fishing skill.

The six luxurious bedrooms are painted white, with high, peaked ceilings and exposed supporting timbers. 🖝 French country antiques—massive pine armoires, mellow pine writing desks—inviting beds with puffy eiderdowns, and a feeling of clean space are first impressions. Each room's welcoming extras include instant hot water for coffee or tea, homemade chocolates, fruit breads, and 🖝 huge baskets of fresh flowers.

A morning knock on your door delivers fresh juice, hot scones, and jam, all to fuel you for the walk down the covered veranda to the dining room for a full breakfast. 🖝 Dinner is a gourmet event, and Robin is head chef. First you join other guests in the drawing room for hot canapés and imported sherry. (It's a lovely room with raspberry-colored sofas and wingback chairs by a fireplace.) You're escorted to the dining room for a leisurely meal on snow-white linen with fresh flowers. A typical menu might include hot sole mousse, green salad with fresh fennel, poached oysters, scallops, shrimp in truffle sauce, rosemary roasted chicken, fettuccine with walnuts, a choice of sinful desserts (Jill's specialty), imported cheeses, fruit, port, and coffee in the drawing room.

How to get there: From Seattle, take Winslow Ferry; proceed on Highway 305 (about 10 miles) to Bond Road, and turn right. Go to Big Valley Road; turn left, and continue 4½ miles to inn on the left.

olive Metcalf

Lake Quinault Lodge
Quinault, Washington
98575

Innkeepers: Marge and Larry Lesley
Address/Telephone: South Shore Road (mailing address: Box 7);
(206) 288-2571.
Rooms: 54, including suites and fireplace cabins; 8 lakeside rooms
have private bath, main lodge rooms have 1 bath between 2
units.
Rates: $41 to $62; special mid-week packages; EP. Children wel-
come; pets okay.
Open: All year. Breakfast, lunch, dinner, full bar.
Facilities and Local Attractions: Indoor swimming pool, Jacuzzi,
saunas, exercise room, pool tables. Boating, fishing, hiking.
Gift shop.

The Olympic Peninsula has a powerful attraction for nature lovers— ☛ mysterious rain forests, towering stands of
cedar and firs, rugged shores, peaceful beaches, and deep
blue Lake Quinault.

The Lodge, situated on the lake shore, has spectacular
views and a variety of accommodations. Add a good dining
room (specializing in fresh local fish), a cocktail lounge, and
☛ excellent indoor recreation facilities. You will be snug and

well entertained here, even when the not-infrequent rains (this *is* a rain forest) might dampen your enthusiasm for the outdoors.

The imposing lodge was built in 1926 in the staggeringly short time of ten weeks. Lumber, brick, glass, and plumbing fixtures were hauled over fifty miles of dirt road, and craftsmen from all over the northwest came to work on it. The large, rustic lobby and its fireplace are the heart of the lodge. It's filled with original wicker settees and chairs, Indian objects, and art of the Northwest, such as the stenciled designs on the beamed ceilings. There are cozy corners for reading, chess and checkers, and for electronic game tables.

Downstairs is a swimming pool and a recreation room with pool, Ping-Pong tables, and a veritable health spa facility. Outdoors, all the water sports are available. Some of the ☞ finest steelhead fishing in the world is found between Quinault and the Hoh River.

Bedrooms range from simple and rustic to modern suites with fireplace and kitchen. The décor is not designer league, but the rooms are comfortable and clean.

But the real story here is the ☞ beautiful sight of Lake Quinault surrounded with timbered hills. Everything at the lodge is poised to enjoy the view: The broad deck and lawn behind the lobby, the dining room and lounge, even the downstairs recreation room, all look out at the lake.

How to get there: From Highway 101, 40 miles north of Aberdeen-Hoquiam, take Lake Quinault South Shore Recreation Area exit. Follow road 2 miles to the lodge.

J: *Driving through the Olympic National Forest, not another car in sight, I passed a cluster of six buildings, preceded by a State Highway sign reading,* SLOW, CONGESTED AREA; 45 MPH. *I call that wooded tranquillity.*

olive Metcalf

San Juan Inn
San Juan Island, Washington
98250-0776

Innkeepers: Joan and Norm Schwinge
Address/Telephone: Friday Harbor (mailing address: P.O. Box 776); (206) 378–2070.
Rooms: 10, sharing 3 baths.
Rates: $34.40 single, to $62.35 (tax included) for 4 people, summer rates. Rollaway beds available. Lower winter rates. Continental breakfast included.
Open: All year.
Facilities and Local Attractions: Walk to ferry landing; bike and moped rentals; Friday Harbor shops, restaurants. Explore American Camp, English Camp.

San Juan Island is the second largest in this cluster of 172 islands. Still, it's a rather unlikely place to have once been considered an international tinderbox. The "Pig War" of 1859 is now part of the romantic history of the islands, but at the time it was a full-fledged confrontation between Great Britain and the United States. It started when an American potato farmer shot a pig running through his potato patch. The unfortunate pig belonged to an Englishman, and the incident was the spark that ignited the long-simmering dispute between the two nations. The United States actually had cannons poised, and the British had five warships ready for action when an agreement was reached that eventually made San Juan an American possession.

Historic buildings of both the American and English camps survive, with exhibits and picnic areas. Both historic sites are within easy bicycling distance from the San Juan Inn, which also offers the more contemporary diversions of Friday Harbor's unique shops and restaurants.

The inn has been around since 1873, but the Schwinges have wisely rewired, replumbed, and restored it for comfort. (Mindful that a pig almost started a war, who knows what damage an obstreperous toilet might cause?)

As the inn is only a block from the waterfront, breakfast in the parlor is especially entertaining, with a view of the big white ferries pulling in and out of the harbor and dislodging hikers, bikers, and cars. Rigors of the morning watch are sustained with coffee and tea, juice, and hot blueberry and honey-bran muffins. This room is pleasant at night, too, with its old iron stove and big chairs from which to watch the harbor lights reflected in the water.

Bedrooms are named after local islands and ferries. They are small and clean, with a Victorian feeling in flowered wallpaper, and wicker headboards and chairs. Some rooms have brass beds and pine washstands. A few rooms have harbor or garden views.

A tiny brick patio garden—a cozy spot to sun and watch the ferries or perhaps read up on the Pig War—is adjacent to some interesting craft shops.

How to get there: From Anacortes, take the ferry to Friday Harbor. Inn is one-half block from landing on your right. Fly-in: Friday Harbor and Roche Harbor airstrips. Marine facilities.

ᵈ

J: *This is not major information, but the calico cats used as door-stops are awfully cute.*

Olive Metcalf

Hotel de Haro
San Juan Island, Washington
98250

Innkeeper: Neil Tarte
Address/Telephone: Roche Harbor Road (mailing address: P.O.
  Box 1, Roche Harbor); (206) 378–2155.
Rooms: 20; 4 suites with private bath, 16 rooms with sink, share 4
  baths. Cottages, condo rentals available.
Rates: $47 to $80, summer rates; $30 to $65, winter; weekend
  packages. No meals included.
Open: Closes some weekdays in winter; call for dates. Breakfast,
  lunch, dinner every day in season; full bar, coffee shop.
Facilities and Local Attractions: Swimming pool, tennis, boat an-
  chorage, bicycling, fishing, horseback riding, walking beaches.
  Nearby Friday Harbor restaurants, shops. Weekend entertainment.

This is one of those grand old places you ought to know
about in your quest for rational alternatives to homogenized
lodgings. First, there is 🖝 the adventure of getting there.
Unless you fly or sail your own boat, you journey several
hours by ferry through the San Juan Archipelago, a beautiful
cluster of 172 timbered islands. Landing at the cheerful little
village of Friday Harbor, you drive nine miles out back roads

to the north end of San Juan Island and the hotel at Roche Harbor.

It's a fine old white frame three-story building that exudes the same kind of charm it did when President Theodore Roosevelt visited in 1906. Undoubtedly it's more creaky now, but it's still comfortable and immaculately maintained. Most of the rooms are small and simply furnished with rockers and washstands, and they share bathrooms. The Presidential Suite has a fireplace and a sitting room with a veranda overlooking the harbor.

The original owner, John McMillan, owned the largest limeworks west of the Mississippi when he built the hotel and his own house nearby. His house, perched right on the water's edge, is now the Roche Harbor Restaurant. You can walk to it from the hotel through the wonderful gardens. In September they still displayed a gorgeous array of colors.

Fresh seafood is a specialty, and the menu offers an excellent variety. Dining, live music, and dancing all seem quite glamerous as you look out at the colorful marina or watch the lights at night. I almost saw Gatsby's light twinkling out there.

How to get there: From Anacortes, take ferry to Friday Harbor (two hours). From the ferry, drive two blocks to Second Street, turn right. Go ³/₁₀ mile; turn right on Tucker Avenue (becomes Roche Harbor Road); follow 9 miles to Roche Harbor. Proceed through arches; follow signs left to hotel. Fly-in: Roche Harbor airstrip.

❋

J: *Summer crowds are fierce on ferries around the islands, but on a mid-September morning, it was pure pleasure—clean, quiet, and plenty of room.*

Olive Metcalf

The Shelburne Inn
Seaview, Washington
98644

Innkeepers: David Campiche and Laurie Anderson
Address/Telephone: Pacific Highway (mailing address: Box 250);
(206) 642–2442.
Rooms: 13, 3 with private bath, 2 with private half-bath, 8 sharing 3
bathrooms.
Rates: $56 to $72, double occupancy, including full breakfast. No
pets.
Open: All year. Lunch, dinner, Sunday brunch, full bar.
Facilities and Local Attractions: Gift shop; beach walks, walk to
North Head Lighthouse, charter fishing, clamming. Visit his-
toric Oysterville; drive "World's Longest Beach Drive."

Around the Shelburne breakfast table one recent morning, a poll of home towns revealed that all the guests except
one were within seventy-five miles of home. Even people living close by come to stay here because the Shelburne is a rar-
ity in southwest Washington—a Victorian inn with authentic
period atmosphere *and* an excellent restaurant.

It was built in 1896 as a boarding house, and later joined
to another building with a covered passageway. The present
owners kept the original design in mind as they expanded

372

and refurbished. Their most outstanding addition is a treasure from Morcambe, England. Art Nouveau stained-glass windows dating from the late 1800s were rescued from an old church that was being demolished there. These floral-patterned beauties are now in the restaurant wing, looking as though they've been there for the past one hundred years.

The wood-paneled common room is a cozy setting, with a stone fireplace, and with coffee, current magazines, and newspapers at hand. A sun deck and gift shop were added recently.

The creaky-floored bedrooms are cheerful with fresh flowers, antique furniture, and bright quilts that set the color scheme. My fancy for "extras" was well satisfied when I was welcomed with a basket of Crabtree and Evelyn toiletries and a generous sampling of designer chocolates in my room.

The restaurant has many fresh fish specialties prepared with skill and sophistication. No batter-fried fish plates here. Salmon in season always head the list of favorites, but the availability of fresh local oysters and mussels provides wonderful eating. My filet of rockfish was moist and sauced with capers, olives, and fresh tomatoes and accompanied by wild rice with raisins and nuts. The "house salad dressing" is a standout. It involves a sour cream base with Dijon mustard. Homemade desserts, an extensive wine list, and thoughtful service made for a thoroughly pleasant meal.

How to get there: From Seattle, take I-5 through Olympia to Highway 8, then to 101 South. Avoid major detours in Aberdeen by taking Highway 107 or Montesano cutoff before Aberdeen to meet Highway 101. Follow south to Seaview and flashing yellow light. Turn right; the inn is five blocks ahead on the left.

ℨ

J: *Don't* think *of leaving without a walk to the beach. It's a particularly secluded stretch.*

olive Metcalf

Inn of the White Salmon
White Salmon, Washington
98672

Innkeepers: Bill and Loretta Hopper
Address/Telephone: 172 Jewett (mailing address: Box 1446); (509) 493–2335.
Rooms: 20, all with private bath, TV, telephone.
Rates: $60 to $84, including enormous full breakfast. No children under 10.
Open: All year.
Facilities and Local Attractions: Hot tub. Columbia Gorge fishing, hiking, rafting. Maryhill Museum; skiing at Mount Hood.

About Loretta's now-famous country breakfast, my heartfelt advice is to pace yourself. One guest, rationalizing his third trip to the sweet-laden buffet table, kept insisting that it was very European: "Why it's common practice there to have desserts before a meal and afterwards too!" I simply faced the fact squarely that I was taking ten years off the useful life of my arteries and took comfort in dispatching them happily.

European or just good Ohio cook, Loretta's ☛ display of *forty or more* freshly baked pastries is stunning. It is heavenly fare like Pears Frangipane (wine-poached pears in an almond crust with custard), strudels, fruit tarts, tortes, breads, and buttery morsels like Hungarian "Love Letters." I assumed I was looking at breakfast when I saw the astonishing table that morning along with its array of fresh fruit, but *noooooo.*

Loretta or one of her helpers, in lace blouse and long skirt, pours coffee from silver pots into china cups and recites an extraordinary choice of hot dishes. Many have an ethnic flair: Chili Rellenos, Hungarian sausages, several quiches, artichoke frittata, and more. I saw no other sensible course but to spend the morning there eating and chatting with Loretta and Bill. After all, it *was* raining outside.

Although their building's exterior is undistinguished, once inside the beveled-glass doorway to the attractive lobby, you will find the atmosphere warmly inviting. All the rooms have a Victorian look, with particularly handsome wall coverings and brass beds. Some of the second-floor rooms have good views of the Columbia River and Mount Hood.

Bill is a former airline pilot. He sometimes tells Loretta that the work involved in her breakfast "experience" is getting out of hand. But she compares it to his landing a plane and putting the center wheel down on the line precisely. "That breakfast," she says "is my center line. I want it to be perfect."

How to get there: Follow I-84 east from Portland to Hood River; exit to 64 North. Cross Columbia River; follow 141 to White Salmon; continue through town. Inn is last large building on the right.

J: Don't miss a little-known museum a few miles away at Maryhill. Can you believe that it houses Queen Marie of Romania's throne and coronation robes and a collection of Rodin, and that there is a replica of Stonehenge nearby? It's all here, above the mighty Columbia.

Olive Metcalf

The Captain Whidbey Inn
Whidbey Island, Washington
98239

Innkeeper: John Stone
Address/Telephone: 2072 West Captain Whidbey Road, Coupeville, (206) 678–4097.
Rooms: 29, including waterfront cottages and duplex. 9 rooms in main building share 2 bathrooms; newer lagoon rooms have private bath.
Rates: $44.75 to $69.75, no meals included. Children okay; pets in cottages only.
Open: All year. Breakfast, lunch, dinner, full bar.
Facilities and Local Attractions: Explore Coupeville, Victorian homes, museum, waterfront shops, restaurants. Fort Casey State Park; Deception Pass. Near Keystone Ferry to Port Townsend.

A funny thing happened to me at The Captain Whidbey. I blame it on the gray, drizzling weather the day I discovered it. I momentarily forgot that I'm a sunshine-loving, white wine–quaffing, nouvelle cuisine–eating Californian, and I had an overwhelming urge to have double Old Fashioneds from the bar, toast my toes at the stone fireplace, and order steak—rare—with fries! It's that kind of place.

The 🖝 ambience at this funky, offbeat inn has been marinating since 1907. Then it was an ideal hideaway for guests from Seattle. They would come up the sound on a steamer and dock at the inn's private pier. On this dreary day, the wood-smoke smell from the fire, the creaky floors, and the warmth of the madrona log interior were cheering. The sense of being very remote, but in friendly hands, adds to its charm.

The first floor of the inn is as it's always been: a comfortable sitting room and fireplace, with a cozy bar and dining room overlooking Penn Cove. The food is uncomplicated and good: whole baby salmon, oysters, crab, and 🖝 fresh Penn Cove mussels, as well as steaks and roast beef.

Up the stairway at the large landing is a 🖝 library with such appealingly jammed shelves it almost forces you to browse. There are well-worn upholstered sofas and chairs to sink into, and funny old floor lamps. Continuing down the hall to the bedrooms will take some time. The walls are covered with family mementos—everything from John's father's grammar school diploma to his grandfather's naval uniform from the 1800s.

The nine bedrooms are small (or cozy, depending on how you look at these things), with low log ceilings and furnished with antiques. Some have sinks in the room, but everybody in this original building goes down the hall to use the bathrooms and showers. You can have private baths, fireplaces, and kitchenettes in the waterfront cottages. Newest accommodations are the twelve lagoon rooms with verandas and lovely views.

How to get there: From the Mukilteo Ferry landing at the south end of Whidbey Island, take Highway 525, to Highway 20, and go 3 miles past Coupeville. Look for sign on right for the inn; take next right (Madrona), and go approximately ¾ mile. Inn is on the left.

🍸

J: *confess a fervent bias for Coupeville. One of the oldest towns in the state . . . a waterfront setting . . . Victorian homes—it's enchanting.*

olive Metcalf

Saratoga Inn
Whidbey Island, Washington
98260

Innkeepers: Debbie and Ted Jones
Address/Telephone: 4850 South Coles Road, Langley; (206) 221–7526.
Rooms: 5, all with private bath.
Rates: $65 to $75, double occupancy, including generous continental breakfast. No children; no smoking; no pets.
Open: All year, except for 2 weeks over Christmas.
Facilities and Local Attractions: Bicycles, croquet. Walk to Langley shops, restaurants, theater.

An inn has already won me over if it's a shingled, rambling Cape Cod on an island, if it sits on a hill overlooking a sound, and if it has a romantic English garden. Everything about the appearance of the Saratoga Inn, including the 🖝 views of meadows, forests, the Saratoga Passage, and the Cascades, is captivating.

Debbie and Ted Jones bought twenty-five acres on the southern portion of Whidbey Island and built this beauty of an inn on the property in 1982. They made it traditional in style, but spacious and open. Light floods in through the beveled-glass windows onto gleaming woods and an enviable collection of English antiques and beautiful objects.

The ☞ common rooms are decorated in understated good taste, and invitingly warm. There's a large fireplace, books, taped music, and a fine view past the patio and garden to the sound. Some of the ☞ Chippendale and Queen Anne pieces are outstanding, but there is also cushy comfortable furniture.

Each of the five bedrooms is distinct and is decorated so engagingly that I couldn't choose one over another. One has a cozy Franklin fireplace and a good spot for watching storms and ships; another has a white linen chaise, and another a bent-willow bed and rocker. Linens, pillow shams, comforters, and wallpapers are all of fine quality. Each room has a sitting area, ☞ good reading lights, and those extras so pleasant to find—English toiletries and freshly cut flowers.

Breakfast is as first-class as the surroundings. There are freshly ground coffee, teas, freshly squeezed orange juice, seasonal fresh fruit, and then homemade muffins or coffee cake and jams.

The integration of setting and gardens, house and décor gives a feeling of serenity—everything seems so right. You don't build and decorate a home as beautiful as this one without the skills of a lot of people, and the Joneses remember them in a graceful way. Framed and hanging in the entryway are the names of all those who contributed their work and talents.

How to get there: From Seattle, drive north to Whidbey Island-Mukilteo Ferry exit 189. Take 15-minute ferry ride to Clinton, Whidbey Island. Proceed on 525 south to Langley. Inn signs are on the right as you enter Langley city limits. Fly-in: South Whidbey's Porter Field

J: ☞ *Langley's restaurants and shops are a delight to explore. Think of a mini-Sausalito . . . with elbow room.*

Olive Metcalf

Whidbey House
Whidbey Island, Washington
98260

Innkeeper: Priscilla Golas
Address/Telephone: 106 First Street (mailing address: Box 156),
    Langley; (206) 221–7115.
Rooms: 3, each with private bath; continental breakfast included.
Rates: $60 double occupancy.
Open: All year.
Facilities and Local Attractions: Beachcombing, bicycling, hiking
    the island. Langley's shops and restaurants. Ferry to Seattle.

Here's a romantic, intimate waterfront inn on Whidbey
Island. There are only three bedrooms, but they are irresistible. Open a picket gate, walk down a few steps, and you
come to a freshly painted ☞ white deck hanging right over
Puget Sound. All three rooms open to the deck, which is furnished with lounge chairs and decorated with colorful
planter boxes spilling over with flowers.

Quaint lodgings tucked into vine-covered small places
are terribly appealing, but once you're in them, it's especially
winning when they open up to give you elbow room. That's
the case at Whidbey House—cozy but not cramped, and ☞
very private. ☞ Dramatic views from the deck are a major

attraction here: the Saratoga Passage, Camano Island, and the North Cascade Mountains beyond.

I fell in love with Langley, the largest town on the island. It's an enchanting "village by the sea," as it bills itself. There are no traffic lights, but plenty of historic charm and good restaurants, and the inn is tucked into the very heart of the town. The village motif is somewhat turn-of-the-century Western. Antique shops, crafts, and homemade clothing were notches above the usual. The treasures in Silk Road, an attractive shop beside the inn, for a time easily managed to divert my attention away from the scenic beauty of the sound.

Back at the inn after walking Langley, your room is a tranquil retreat. Priscilla says she's furnished them with just the kinds of antiques, fabrics, and wall coverings that she'd choose for her own home. Provincial pastel linens, puffy comforters, clean, polished wood floors, and lots of fresh flowers give them a country French feeling.

A continental breakfast is brought to your room in a basket to enjoy there or out on the deck: freshly ground coffee or tea, fresh orange juice, and homemade muffins.

How to get there: From Seattle, go north to Whidbey Island-Mukilteo Ferry exit 189. Take 15-minute ferry ride to Clinton, Whidbey Island. Proceed on Highway 25 south to Langley. Inn is on the water side at the town's center.

J: *A quiet, romantic spot to stay.*

Indexes

Alphabetical Index to Inns

Inns with Restaurants or That Serve Dinner by Special Arrangement

Romantic Inns and Wedding Sites

Especially Elegant Inns

Rustic and Rural Inns

Architectural Treasures

Inns with Historic or Colorful Pasts

Inns with Fabulous Views

Ocean Sites or Views

Inns Near Water

Inns with Swimming Pools

Inns with Skiing Nearby

Outstanding Inns for Fishing

Mountain Retreats

Lively Inns

Peaceful, Quiet Inns

City Inns

Children Welcome

Inns with Small Conference Facilities

About Reservation Services

Most innkeepers in an area network with one another. If their inn is full, they're usually happy to refer prospective guests to other available accommodations. In addition, the following non-fee agencies give referrals and will make reservations for you.

Bed and Breakfast International
151 Ardmore Road
Kensington, CA 94707
(415) 525–8836 or 525–4569

Bed and Breakfast Reservation
1834 First Street
Napa, CA 94599
(707) 257–1051

Northwest Bed and Breakfast
7707 S.W. Locust Street
Portland, OR 97223
(503) 246–8366

Seattle Bed and Breakfast Inn
  Association
Box 95835
Seattle, WA 98145
(206) 547–1020